McGILVRAY

THE GAME IS NOT THE SAME...

ALAN McGILVRAY

As Australia's premier cricket broadcaster, Alan McGilvray is best known for his authoritative commentaries on ABC Radio over fifty years.

McGilvray was also a player. He played cricket at school – the Sydney Grammar School – where the late, great MA Noble noticed him and called the attention of the school coach to his potential bowling skills. He went on to play for and captain New South Wales before he embarked on a career in radio.

McGilvray lives in a Sydney harbour-side suburb and is very much a family man. He has two children, Ross, a grazier in north-western New South Wales, who has played polo for Australia, and a daughter, Carolyn (Mrs Blair), his research officer for the past few years.

McGilvray has been much honoured for his participation in Australia's sporting life. In 1974 he was awarded the MBE, in 1980 he received the AM and in 1985 he received the Advance Australia award for his outstanding contributions to sports broadcasting.

He has been a keen golfer and fisherman for many years and keeps fit by swimming every morning.

NORMAN TASKER, Sports Editor of the Sydney newspaper *The Sun*, is a well-known Australian journalist. He was *The Sun's* Cricket and Rugby correspondent for fifteen years until 1982 and toured many times with Australian sporting teams including tours to England and New Zealand with Australian cricket sides.

McGILVRAY

THE GAME IS NOT THE SAME...

AS TOLD TO NORMAN TASKER

Published by ABC Enterprises for the
AUSTRALIAN BROADCASTING CORPORATION
Box 9994 GPO Sydney NSW, 2001
150 William Street Sydney NSW

First published September 1985 in hardback
Reprinted January 1986
Reprinted February 1986
This paperback edition first published October 1986
Reprinted January 1987

National Library of Australia
Cataloguing-in-Publication entry
McGilvray, Alan, 1910-
McGilvray, the game is not the same.

ISBN 0 642 52738 5

I. McGilvray, Alan, 1910- , 2. Cricket players—
Australia-Biography. I. Tasker, Norman. II.
Australian Broadcasting Corporation. III. Title.

796.35'8'0922

Edited by Nina Riemer
Designed by Howard Binns-McDonald
Set in 11/12 English by Midland Typesetters, Victoria
Printed by Globe Press, Victoria
0104191-18-1495

The ABC gratefully acknowledges the sources of photography in this book: John Fairfax and Sons Ltd, Patrick Eager, The Adelaide *Advertiser*, The Pollard Publishing Co., Sport and General (London), Central Press (London) and Alan McGilvray's private collection.

CONTENTS

ACKNOWLEDGMENT

It was my good fortune to work with three great men at the ABC and I would like to pay tribute to them.

First to Sir Charles Moses for all the opportunities he gave me and for his thoughtful, direct advice; then to the ABC's former Assistant General Manager, A N 'Huck' Finlay, a member of the famous Rugby Waratahs of 1927; and especially to Sir Talbot Duckmanton, who followed Sir Charles as General Manager of the ABC, for his continued advice and support. I will never forget his action in coming out to the Sydney Cricket Ground when he knew my wife was seriously ill in hospital. He told me I should not be there when my mind was obviously elsewhere and in fact he ordered me off the ground. I told him I was visiting my wife before the game each day, that I would dash out during the lunch interval and that she was listening to the broadcast. It was therapy for her. If I were not broadcasting she would worry. All he said was, 'I am sorry. I should mind my own business'.

I have said in this book that cricket brings friends and goodwill and I am privileged to enjoy the friendship of Norman Tasker, the Sporting Editor of the Sydney *Sun*, to whom I extend my deep gratitude for all the help he has provided in the compilation of *The Game is not the Same*. Not only has he embellished it richly—it could not have been done without him—but because we travelled together on several tours he has supplemented my memories with his own. My very sincere thanks go to him.

PREFACE

Cricket has been my life and my joy. From my earliest schoolboy days, when I often sat entranced with my head uncomfortably settled between the pickets that surrounded the Sydney Cricket Ground, it has been my passion and my comfort. It has been a source of character, spirit and emotion that has transcended the bounds of sport alone.

To many of my generation, cricket has been a way of life, a gentle, humble, almost spiritual thing that aroused us and entertained us, and captured so faithfully the spirit of a genteel age. It was grace and splendour; it inspired, almost demanded, attitudes of courtesy and camaraderie that set it apart from almost any other pursuit in life.

The years, of necessity, have wrought much change. In some ways the gentle game has been tainted by the money and commercialism that have followed its popularity. They have brought their attendant greed and selfishness. My generation perhaps will always lament the shift in attitudes. The game we knew as one of pure sport and pleasant conversation has inevitably become immersed in the quagmire of modern commercial life in which corporate high finance and individual avarice have become the supreme motivations.

Some of the old appeals, for sure, have been lost. But the game endures. Its character is not easily eroded. Its people remain embroiled, for the most part anyway, in the ethic of the noble game in which skill and subtlety will always be pre-requisite qualities.

For all the razzamatazz, for all the mind-boggling player contracts, the wild one-day games, the beer-swilling crowds on the Hill at the SCG, the 'sledgers' who rant and rave and demean the old standards, cricket remains essentially an art form. It will always encourage the artists. It will always bring them reward. Cricket will always be cricket.

As I look back over more than half a century of cricket, first as a humble player who was privileged to play in one of cricket's greatest eras, and later as a broadcaster, I can only marvel at how it has enriched my life.

This is not a book to evaluate cricket in statistical terms. Nor is it a chronicle of deeds and events. It is a book about people. Cricket is a game of people. People provide its soul and its heart, its humour and its pathos and I have endeavoured to remember the people, cricketers and cricket lovers, of many countries and many persuasions, who have given me so much joy and so much friendship.

From the days when men like Monty Noble and Alan Kippax, Victor Richardson and Arthur Gilligan first set me on my course in the world of cricket and cricket broadcasting, I have gathered many wonderful memories.

I only hope that, in this book, I have been able to do them justice.

THE CAPTAIN's ART

In the spring of 1983 Australia's Royal Perth Yacht Club was a focal point of national attention when a syndicate from the club turned 12-metre yachting history on its ear to win the America's Cup. Television viewers all over Australia who had delayed their breakfast to watch Australia II's triumph at Newport, Rhode Island, were treated to the club's revelry, including a champagne shower for the Australian Prime Minister, Bob Hawke. It was a splendid, happy occasion, in which Australian sporting success once again inspired considerable national pride.

A few months later, another face of Australian sport was less happily reflected in that same club. It was a day or two before the first cricket Test against Pakistan, and the captain of the Australian XI, Kim Hughes, was standing toe to toe with his deputy Rod Marsh, the man whom many had assumed might have had his job.

Greg Chappell had only recently announced his unavailability for further duty as Australia's cricket captain. Hughes had filled in for Chappell on and off for more than three years. But now the appointment had a permanent ring to it. Many had thought Marsh might have won the day. He was the popular choice of the hard core of players to survive from the Chappell era of the 'seventies and the matter was one of great public debate. When Hughes finally was given the job, it meant the end of the road for Rodney as far as his captaincy ambitions were concerned.

It all came to a head that day in the Royal Perth Yacht club. I was there with a friend, and the only other people in the room at the time were Marsh and Hughes. They became embroiled in the most terrible argument. In a lifetime of travelling with sportsmen, I have seen some pretty solid disagreements. But never have I seen a confrontation like this between two members of the same team. It was a violent crossfire of abuse and counter abuse in which both parties made it abundantly clear they had no time for each other. I tried to break it up, and after about three minutes they cooled down. I don't know what started it. But I do know a representative of the Australian Cricket Board had been detailed to heal the rift that everybody seemed to know had developed between the two players. The Board member was crestfallen about the confrontation.

As I look back over more than fifty years' involvement in cricket, I cannot help but reflect on that unhappy scene as symptomatic of a host of difficulties that have beset the modern game. I think back to men like Bill Woodfull and Vic Richardson, to Don Bradman and Richie Benaud, and consider their stature. They were the epitomes of strength and dignity in their era. But in many ways they had it so much easier than players have it today. They played much less cricket for a start. There was none of the pressure cooker atmosphere of today, where Test series run into Test series, and one-day games have proliferated to the extent that there is hardly a week off for an international player. Nor was there the intense commercial pressure that there is now. The pace was easier, public scrutiny less intense.

Kim Hughes is perhaps the most obvious casualty of the modern attitude to commercial cricket. Both he and Rod Marsh came to me at a function the day after that Yacht Club row, very contrite and full of apology. On the surface they appeared the best of mates. 'The only reason you fellows have come to me is that you are worried what I might say on the air tomorrow', I volunteered. I told them they had better listen in. I did not mention the matter again, of course, despite several entreaties from Pressmen who knew I had been privy to something rather colourful, and the matter died a natural death. But it was enough to convince me at the time that Kim Hughes, as a captain, had no real chance.

Captaincy, as an art form, has been the preserve of very few of the world's top cricketers. In Australia it is no accident that three great eras in our cricket have coincided with the careers of three truly great captains. To me these men have stood above all others in my experience of Australian skippers.

First came Don Bradman. His consummate batting skill apart, Bradman had a shrewdly analytical mind and a cold ruthlessness about him that pursued victory with resolute dedication.

Later came Richie Benaud and Ian Chappell. They did not enjoy the same quality in their teams as Bradman enjoyed. For a start, they did not have Bradman, and that meant a difference on the score of statistics alone of about 200 runs per Test. But each of them had an enormous attacking flair; a bubbling bent for winning that infected their team-mates and inspired some wonderfully exciting cricket.

The great Bradman, of course, was a man apart. As a batsman he has never had an equal. Sir Robert Menzies, the long-serving Australian Prime Minister and celebrated cricket buff, explained it as well as I have ever heard it explained when I interviewed him at Lord's on the occasion of the 200th Test between Australia and England.

'I saw Bradman bat the first time he batted on the Melbourne ground' Sir Robert recalled, 'and some of his strokes were what you might call agricultural. Some people sitting around me were saying "Rather agricultural don't you think, old boy". And I said "We'll be watching this fellow for the next twenty years, because he's got it".

'There was an inevitability about Bradman's batting. With others there was always a chance, but with Bradman there was an inevitability. One of the reasons for that was that Don Bradman was not only a superb producer of batsman's strokes, a magnificent captain and a first class field, he happens to have been a highly intelligent man in anybody's language. He didn't often discuss cricket with me but he would often discuss international finance or the economic movements in a country, and I often used to say to myself that I was convinced I knew more of these matters than Don I would be very satisfied.'

Sir Robert highlighted the intellectual tone of Bradman's batting. Every ball was computed, its worth analysed, its dangers identified and its despatch programmed with mathematical certainty. He backed up his faith in Don's skills off the cricket field by one time canvassing with him the question of whether he might like to consider being Australian High Commissioner in London. The matter was not pursued, but the very fact of Sir Robert's inquiry reflected his respect for Bradman.

I was privileged to bat with Bradman in my first game for New South Wales in the summer of 1933-34. We were playing Victoria at the Melbourne Cricket Ground and were something like three down for 199 on the third morning when the new ball became due.

'You open for your club, don't you young man?' our skipper Alan Kippax inquired of me before play. I told him I did. 'Well, you can go in with Bradman,' he ordered. 'And I don't want to see you before lunch.'

Bradman had about twenty runs at the time, and with five seasons as an established Australian batsman already under his belt, he was then very much the No 1 commodity of Australian cricket. It is difficult to describe how I felt that morning, making my way to the wicket with Bradman for my first class debut in front of 40 000 spectators. Kippax had asked Bradman to look after me. Victoria had some fairly useful bowlers in Ironmonger, Blackie and Fleetwood-Smith, and it seemed logical that Don should take most of the strike anyway.

Certainly, that was the way the crowd wanted it. My turns at strike were often greeted with roars of 'out of the way, redhead' or words to that effect, so that Bradman's talents could be projected uninterrupted. So much of the Bradman I later came to know so well was evident that day. I remember the Victorian captain Bill Woodfull saying to me as I stood at the non-striker's end: 'Just how do you stop this man?'

Bradman ran to 100 before lunch as I scored about a dozen, and he enthralled everybody with his strokeplay. Nobody was more enthralled than I. I recall getting out to the last ball of the morning when I totally mis-read Fleetwood-Smith's spin. I thought I had done well enough to stay there in the shadow of Bradman's skill, but was not allowed to bask in any glory in the dressing room. 'I thought I told you to stay there until lunch' was Kippax's greeting. Bradman went on to be 187 not out.

I batted with Bradman again in Sydney years later in a testimonial match. We put on 177 runs in a partnership in which Bradman's contribution was 135. I was reduced pretty much to the role of a spectator, standing there and watching as the matchless talents carved up bowler after bowler.

Bradman scored a masterful double century that day, but the one bowler he did not treat with contempt was the bowler he respected above all others—Bill O'Reilly. O'Reilly and Bradman had first locked horns way back in 1926, when Bradman was a seventeen-year-old Bowral boy and O'Reilly a twenty-year-old schoolteacher who played cricket for neighbouring Wingello. Prior to this obscure country match nobody had really heard of either of them in cricketing terms. Nobody, that is, except Don's team mates, who knew O'Reilly to be the scourge of the Southern Highlands.

Don's team watched in awe as the young Bradman, after some early trouble, hit 234 runs in the afternoon. O'Reilly had him first ball on the next Saturday, but that innings was the first real sign that Don was a batsman out of the ordinary. In later years he coupled O'Reilly with the Englishman Sydney Barnes as the two greatest bowlers who ever lived.

That afternoon at the SCG years later Bradman treated O'Reilly with the utmost caution. He did not face him until he was well past 50, and was dropped off O'Reilly's bowling immediately he came on. From there, Bradman cut loose, yet 22 overs from O'Reilly brought him a creditable 4-96. They were marvellous figures from anybody who bowled through a Bradman innings in full cry.

'Tiger' Bill O'Reilly was perhaps the only bowler who ever drew total respect from Bradman. Most of the others were either psyched out or hammered out. To bowl to Bradman set up a negative thought pattern that had the average bowler in a state of fear. Through my early playing days I suppose Bradman would have taken 1000 runs off my bowling, without my ever getting his wicket. Through all of that I recall the feeling of terrible inferiority I had.

In my case I was not a particularly accomplished bowler, but I know a lot of highly accomplished bowlers who felt exactly the same way. I often have wondered whether the psychological impact of bowling to Bradman so affected the quality of much of the bowling he received that he had things a lot easier than some of his contemporaries.

The way he faced up to a bowler beamed confidence and self-assurance. The quickness of his eye, the early backlift, the nimble way in which he moved those dainty feet of his . . . there was, as Sir Robert put it so eloquently, an inevitability about the whole process that had a bowler beaten before he started.

Against a Stan McCabe or a Lindsay Hassett you always knew you had a chance. You could deliberately over pitch a ball to tempt an error, or toss one in short to draw something rash. In Bradman's case you were simply not game to try things like that. He very quickly set up in the minds of those who bowled to him the feeling that the only way you were going to get him out was to wait until he saw fit to make a mistake.

Bowlers found themselves bowling to contain him. Experimentation was stifled. In many ways he had a whole era of bowlers so psyched out that their bowling became terribly predictable. Bradman, in that light, even dictated how the bowlers would bowl to him. I spoke to many fine bowlers who agreed they were simply frightened to try things against Bradman that brought them wickets against other players. They were psychologically restrained to the point that they bowled below their full potential.

From the very start, Bradman was different. He even held the bat in a unique way. His bottom hand was a lot further round than was considered technically sound at the time. Many tried to change it. The theory was that he would not be able to play a range of shots on the off-side because his grip, developed on concrete wickets, was geared mainly for on-side play. Bradman listened to all the criticism and advice, then did it his way.

It is interesting to imagine how some of those well-meaning advisers must have felt in later years as they watched Bradman rewrite cricket's record books. Figures tell a large part of the Bradman story. At twenty years of age, in his very first season in the Australian side, he managed 468 runs in the Tests at an average of 68, despite being dropped after the first Test for being a sloppy fieldsman. He made a point after that to develop into perhaps the best outfielder I have ever seen.

All up he had a first class average of 94 that first season, including in his achievements a score of 340, and by the time he headed off for his first tour of England at twenty-one years of age, he was clearly an emerging genius.

There were those who thought his batting would come unstuck on English pitches, where the ball seams and jags, and where hitting across the line can be fatal. The young Bradman responded to that by hitting 2960 runs on tour. He had a Test average of 139 on that first visit and a tour average of 99. He had one score of 300-plus in a Test, five double centuries and four centuries. He scored 974 runs in seven Test innings. That was more than 300 better than Victor Trumper's record 661 against England in 1910-11.

Records cascaded about Bradman for the next twenty years. His career produced 28 067 first class runs at an average of 95.14. In 52 Tests he hit 6996 runs at 99.94. By 1948, when he was forty, he was still good enough to hit 508 Test runs in England at an average of 72.57. But it was not just sheer weight of runs that made Bradman exceptional. It was the way he got them.

If you averaged out the time he took to score his 117 first class centuries, it boiled down to 128 minutes for each century. That's just eight minutes more than one session of play. A little more than two hours per hundred, for 117 centuries, in a twenty-year career.

What a testimony that is to Bradman's skill, to his placement of the ball, to his timing and his concentration and his stamina! Through those centuries forty-five per cent of his runs came from boundaries. He was simply unconquerable. Statistics do not always paint the complete picture of a cricketer. But in Bradman's case, they are so extraordinary as to be the most eloquent measure of his unique position amongst the cricketers of history.

There was a calculating ruthlessness to Bradman's batting. He would rarely talk to anybody on the field. He always seemed to be in total communion with himself, his concentration maintained at levels which allowed no intrusion whatever from those around him. He knew the value of his own ability. He knew bowlers would devise all manner of schemes and plans to try to dismiss him. The very stature his extraordinary skill gave him demanded he concentrate that much harder than anybody else.

He communicated by means of his bat. If he received a particularly good ball, he would acknowledge it by defending, without a word. If a ball deserved to be hit he would whip it away, again without a word. He was like a machine. But he was an aggressive machine. He had a high regard for the entertainment value of cricket. He saw no percentage in grinding out an innings.

Bradman had an almost perfect co-ordination of eye, brain and body that set him apart. He had powerful, sinewy legs and forearms, and small feet – he took only a size five in footwear – that allowed him to shuffle into position with lightning speed. His reflexes were sharp and true, his eyesight piercing. But above all he had a mind which was quicker than any other I have known to size up where a ball would pitch, its speed, its movement and its worth. He started his backlift earlier than most players, and he never seemed to hurry. Such was his natural co-ordination, he also became one of Adelaide's best golfers, and a fine squash player.

In terms of sheer power, Bradman was never in the mould of men like Walter Hammond, Gary Sobers or Graeme Pollock. But he valued control above power. His placement was uncanny, his range of shots unmatched. He minimised mistakes and timed his shots immaculately. When he unwound into a pull shot or leaned back to cut, he hit with great flourish. In essence, he simply did everything right.

I bowled to him in a club match one afternoon at Trumper Park in Sydney. He had already passed 100 and was in a playful enough mood to relax and offer me a challenge. That he would open his mouth on the field was rare enough. He nominated to me three positions on the

Alan Kippax, *above*, captain of NSW in the early 'thirties when Alan McGilvray first played for NSW, and one of the game's everlasting gentlemen.

The late, great MA Noble . . . an early McGilvray mentor and the man who introduced him to broadcasting.

The young McGilvray, *above*,—plenty of ambition and plenty of hope.

Bill Woodfull, the Australian captain of the Bodyline series, and almost a prized McGilvray scalp.

field to which he would despatch my next three deliveries; I didn't think he could.

I bowled three balls virtually in the same spot, just outside the off stump and moving away. They went away all right. One went just forward of point, one through extra cover and one through mid-wicket, as if to make the point he could hit it anywhere. He grinned. He did that sort of thing to many bowlers of the very best quality. And when it really counted, there was no grin.

Those who watched him through his career are rarely in agreement as to Bradman's best innings. It's a little like picking the nicest painting in the Louvre. It's all a matter of taste.

Bradman himself, as the most critical judge of all, was once asked on an ABC interview what he considered his best innings. 'In terms of sheer technical satisfaction,' Bradman offered, 'perhaps my 254 at Lord's in 1930, simply because with one or two exceptions every ball went exactly where I intended it to go.

'I suppose my scores of 452 at Sydney and 334 at Leeds must rank highly, but I made errors in them, and from a team viewpoint neither was as important as perhaps my 173 at Leeds in 1948, which helped bring a rather historic and unexpected victory. It gave me much satisfaction because of its value to the side, and because of the batting difficulties I had to overcome in that innings.

'And the same applies to my century in Melbourne in the 1932-33 series. But there is not much personal satisfaction in making a hundred and being missed several times', he went on. 'Any artist must surely aim at perfection, and that is why I think Lord's, 1930, is my first choice. It was the nearest I could ever hope to get to such a goal.'

Bradman, of course, was a mere youth of twenty-one when he scored that 254 at Lord's. The 173 not out he referred to as his second best was scored at Leeds eighteen years later, when he was just a week short of his fortieth birthday. That was his second last Test match, and the very time span that those innings encompass is further testimony to the man's unique talent.

The 1932-33 century he nominated was achieved against Douglas Jardine's Bodyline, when Harold Larwood and Bill Voce had Australia's batting nailed to the wall. That season, the most bitter of all Australian seasons, revolved around a device specifically designed to cope with Bradman. It curbed him, but it could not totally destroy him as it destroyed others.

But if Bradman's innings of 254 at Lord's in 1930 was any better than his match-winning 173 at Leeds in 1948, then its quality is simply beyond the imaginings of my mind. I saw that 1948 innings, along with a Headingley full house. It was the centrepiece of a magnificent day's cricket in which Australia achieved the impossible.

Superb batting from both sides already had registered 1319 runs when Australia faced up to the last day needing 404 runs to win. It was generally agreed to be an impossible winning target from the start. But it was made doubly so when the England captain, Norman Yardley batted on for two overs on the final day, having found the heaviest roller in Leeds to break up the pitch as much as he could. He did a pretty good job, too. Australia were left 345 minutes to score their 404 runs. They made it with fifteen minutes to spare and seven wickets still standing, and the feat will remain for all time as one of the most superlative in the annals of cricket.

Bradman was still there at the end on 173. Arthur Morris had contributed 182 and between them the pair had put on 301 for the second wicket. At one stage I could not see Bradman's foot from the broadcasting box because it had disappeared into a hole at the batting crease which I later measured to be nine inches deep. Such was the quality of the pitch on which this extraordinary final day target was achieved! On inspection after play I found a variety of holes in the pitch ranging around two and three inches deep. There was an absolute beauty right on a good length for a leg-spinner.

Unfortunately Yardley did not have a decent leg-spinner in his armoury. The best he could do was Len Hutton, who was very much a part-timer, but who was worth a try when he seemed to have plenty of runs up his sleeve.

Bradman told me later he recognised a real danger in Hutton. Part-time bowler he may have been, but the pitch was so bad all he had to do was land on the right spot and the ball could do anything. Bradman determined he had to go. Four overs from Hutton yielded 30 runs. Yardley had to take him off. Bradman simply did not let him hit the pitch. Jim Laker, bowling off-spinners, represented a similar danger to the left-hander Arthur Morris. Bradman took a hand here, too. He kept Morris away from Laker so expertly the NSW opener hardly saw him.

And through all this scheming and manipulation, Bradman kept the runs coming at a quick enough rate to keep victory within sight. It was a truly magnificent exhibition of batting artistry. His own score of 173 not out was value enough, but Morris owed so many of his 182 to Bradman as well.

For sheer design, thought, purpose and utter craftsmanship, I have not seen an innings to match that one.

The final day of that fourth Test, too, was marked by a commendable piece of sportsmanship by England captain Norman Yardley. The match had drawn huge crowds, and on the previous day when England had built their 400-run lead, the spectators had spilled on to the oval. The boundary line had become the people, rather than the boundary rope, meaning the boundary was a yard or two shorter than it should have been. On the final day when Australia batted and the crowd was somewhat better restrained, Yardley asked that the boundary rope be brought in a yard or so, so that Australia's batsmen might enjoy the same advantage England's had had.

Bradman was to have only one more Test innings. He needed just four runs in that final Test for a Test match aggregate of 7000 runs and a Test average of 100. He went to the wicket at The Oval to a standing ovation. When he reached the pitch the whole England team doffed their caps to him and burst into three cheers. It was an extraordinarily emotional farewell.

Bradman was bowled second ball for a duck. And this was a Test match which Australia won by an innings and 149 runs to put the finishing touch to a triumphant, unbeaten tour.

Perhaps it was a sad farewell. I think not. Bradman's place in cricketing history was by then too well entrenched to be reliant upon anything that happened in his last game. He was beyond statistics.

BRADMAN AT THE HELM

Considering the unarguable weight of figures that stands behind him, and the results his batting achieved, it is extraordinary to look back on Bradman's career and count the critics who continually looked for flaws. Either he didn't hold the bat right, or he hit across the line too much, or he was not so good on bad wickets. There were those who claimed he was not a team man; that he distanced himself from his contemporaries. There always seemed to be somebody having a go at him about something.

The great England opener Herbert Sutcliffe, for instance, once qualified Bradman's greatness by saying he was the best batsman he had seen 'on good wickets'. And so many of Bradman's critics felt compelled to say things like 'he was not as good as Victor Trumper on wet wickets'. If that is so, Trumper must have been absolutely magnificent.

Others would bring up Archie Jackson, who came into the Test side about the same time as Bradman and hit 164 on debut, and claim that, had he lived, he would have been a better player. How they could possibly know that escapes me. But throughout his career, despite the fact he scored so many more runs than anybody else, Bradman had to suffer those who would seek to minimise his greatness.

It has always been a queer trait in the Australian character that we feel compelled to claw at the stature of those who excel. To cut down the tall poppies, as it were. So many, so often, were only too ready to carp at Don Bradman for inconsequentials as diverse as the clothes he wore, or the way he spoke. The constancy of such irritating criticism took its toll.

He tended to build a wall around himself. He developed an aloofness and distance in his bearing that made him hard to know. There were other factors responsible for this intensely private side to his nature. He had much personal tragedy, including the loss in infancy of his first-born son, and a difficult period of family illness. He found it hard to live under the intense spotlight that his cricketing deeds brought upon him. To a large extent, he simply withdrew into a private world of his own.

Through the early 'thirties, I played in the same team as Don Bradman and played against him. I had plenty of opportunity to know him and to understand him. Yet I didn't really know him at all. There is a depth to his personality that is hard to penetrate. In later years, when my career in broadcasting started to establish itself, I got to know him better. But still, there was always that force field around him. Even in recent times, it is hard to feel completely at ease when talking to him. There is a fastidious side to his nature that picks up the slightest error in anything you might say. He can be very direct in picking you up. In all my dealings with Don Bradman I have been careful to be more of a listener than a talker.

That is not to say that I have not enjoyed his company. I find him extremely interesting. His knowledge of cricket and cricketers is vast and compelling. But he has learned to so discipline himself that relaxation is reserved for very private moments.

Bradman was never a great mixer in accepted cricketing terms. You would rarely find him at the bar, drinking with the boys. Keeping to himself was a basic requirement of captaincy as he saw it. Before the War, when he captained essentially the men he grew up with, that distance counted against him. They saw it as loftiness, a setting apart that many of them resented. I suspect through those times, however, Bradman's success as a batsman, as much as his manner, encouraged the disdain of some of his contemporaries.

Throughout his cricketing life he was the subject of much envy. Some of his team-mates, and those who criticised from a more distant vantage point, were simply jealous of him. Making it worse was a certain untouchable quality Bradman had about him. No matter how much people attacked him, he rarely reacted. Critics found him as difficult to ruffle as bowlers. And his aura remained such that much of the criticism was of the whispering kind. Plenty was said behind his back by people who, face to face with him, would be all sunshine and light.

Nevertheless, that brittle relationship did sometimes exist with the players under him, and of necessity it restricted to an extent the level of performance he could extract from some of them.

Tactically and technically, Bradman was a superb captain. He could sum up the weaknesses and the strengths of players in an instant. He could anticipate how his opponents would think. So often would he astound me by pointing out things which would completely escape my notice. The only player I have known who could touch Bradman for this kind of perception was Keith Miller. He, too, could watch a player perform for just a few moments, then analyse in technical detail all his good points and his bad points. A shoulder would be too high, a foot placed in the wrong spot. Bradman was superbly swift in working players out and taking the necessary action to cope with them. His brain was always in overdrive.

Only once, I think, did I ever find it within myself to risk criticising his captaincy on air. That was an occasion in England in 1948 when he bowled Ray Lindwall and Keith Miller for a long period before a new ball was due. When the new ball became due, he took off the world's leading new ball partnership and threw the ball to Sam Loxton, who was way below their pace. I was astounded, and said so. Loxton then took a couple of quick wickets, England went into minor collapse, and I was left with egg on my face. I asked later whatever had induced Bradman to manipulate his attack in so unorthodox a way.

'Well, they were expecting Lindwall and Miller with the new ball' Bradman replied. 'I thought if we gave them something they weren't expecting, they might just relax a bit and do something silly.' Again his perception was proved spot on.

He made another decision on that tour which I thought strange at the time. Bill Brown had scored a heap of runs as opening batsman on the 1938 tour of England, but Bradman decided to play Arthur Morris ahead of him at the start of the 1948 campaign. Bradman explained that he wanted a left-hander in there early to give the batting balance. Morris went on to score 696 runs in the five Tests.

I quickly learned never to underestimate the Bradman mind. If he did something on the field that I could not fathom, I soon learned that it was probably my inadequacy, not his, that was being shown up. Making critiques of Bradman's on-field captaincy was a very dangerous business. For the three series my commentaries covered in which Bradman was captain, I was always prepared to give him the benefit of the doubt. Rarely was my faith misplaced.

It was a big decision for Bradman to resume at the start of the 1946-47 series when Walter Hammond brought the Englishmen to Australia to resume cricketing relations after the war. It had been eighteen years since he played his first Test for Australia and eight years since he had played his last. He had a lot to lose and, it seemed, not very much to gain.

Bradman had been medically discharged from the army with a bad back, he had set up a new stock-broking business in Adelaide, and he had been elected a member of the Australian Board of Control. There were plenty of reasons why he should, at thirty-eight years of age, be content to confine his cricket interests to administration. But for Bradman the job did not seem quite finished, particularly as Australia would field a very inexperienced side. He lined up for the visit by Walter Hammond's team not knowing quite how he would handle it.

As a selector at the time, Bradman had shrewdly built a new

Australian team. Only Sid Barnes, Lindsay Hassett and he himself had survived from the pre-war team, so much depended on promising newcomers like Keith Miller, Ray Lindwall, Ian Johnson and Arthur Morris. Bradman was far from the lithe youth who had dominated world cricket in the ten years before the war. England had a formidable newcomer in Alec Bedser, who would thoroughly test any dulled reflexes. Bradman was tense and fidgety when he took the crease and played out the early overs in the first game of that series. He took a long time to look comfortable. Then came an incident which probably set the course of post-war cricket.

Bradman had made twenty-eight when he played at a ball from Bill Voce, the veteran fast-bowler who had been so much a part of Bodyline. The ball jammed from the end of Bradman's bat into the turf, and flew to Jack Ikin in the slips. The Englishmen appealed for the catch. Bradman stood his ground. Umpire George Borwick quickly responded 'not out'. The Englishmen were upset, to say the least. I remember discussing the matter with Jack Ikin years later. He remained adamant it was a fair catch. Borwick was equally adamant it was not. So was his square leg umpire Jack Scott, who went on record later to confirm Borwick's assessment.

I was broadcasting at the time and I had not the slightest doubt it was a bump ball. Lindsay Hassett, at the other end, couldn't work out what the fuss was about. He saw it as I saw it. But the Englishmen saw it very differently.

Had that decision gone against Bradman I am almost certain he would have called it quits. He was suffering from gastric illness, he was having some trouble with his legs, and his return to the captaincy of Australia at that stage of his career was a considerable strain.

But as if some divine hand decreed that Bradman should rise again, he suddenly blossomed forth into much of his old glory. He finished with 187 out of a total of 645 and Australia won the Test by an innings and 332 runs. It was some comfort for Bradman, whose previous Test against England in 1938 had brought a somewhat different result. On that occasion England's first innings had realised 7-903 declared, and they had won by an innings and 579 runs. Who knows how much that result influenced his decision to return to the Test match scene?

In the second Test Bradman was again troubled by illness and a painful leg injury. But his indomitable spirit triumphed once more. He and Sid Barnes scored 234 each, sharing a mammoth partnership of 405 runs. Australia won that Test by an innings and 33 runs, and both Bradman the batsman and Bradman the captain were very much back in business. Bradman went from strength to strength on that tour. His health and his fitness seemed to feed on his success, and much of the old sprightliness, so obviously missing when the series started, was there at the end. Australia won the series 3-0, beginning an era of post-war dominance to which England simply had no answer.

That was a very difficult period for England. Walter Hammond's team, on paper, was a particularly strong one. Most of them had been around in pre-war years, and the average age of the side was thirty-three. But while they were strong on paper, they were not the players they had been when last Australia encountered them.

England, of course, had had a very tough time through the war, and most Englishmen were still subject to dreadful privations. Rationing, and the scarcity of substantial food, had taken a significant toll on the strength and the stamina of the visiting side. I can remember Bill Edrich, on arrival in Perth, tucking into a steak with all the trimmings as if he had never seen one before. It was such a shock to his system, he broke out in boils and carbuncles. The skipper Walter Hammond was forty-three when he made the tour. Hammond first toured Australia in 1928-29 and had finished the Test series with 905 runs. Eighteen years later with a very hard war behind him, Hammond was a shadow of his former self. He was ill for much of the tour, could manage only a handful of runs in the four Tests he played, then stood down in favour of Norman Yardley for the last Test. It is difficult for a touring team when a captain so loses his form that he cannot maintain his place in the side. Hammond's difficulties greatly eroded the direction of that England side, and made the going a little easier for Bradman.

Curiously, the war that had so decimated England's strength probably worked the other way for Australia. The men, generally speaking, were younger and fitter and a good deal stronger. Most of them had weathered the war reasonably well. And by virtue of their service, they resumed international cricket as mature men, accustomed to discipline and trained to compete. Mentally, they had everything going for them. Again Bradman was lucky. He had chosen his team carefully, and the men under him were already trained to accept the disciplines necessary to weld a team into a tight combat unit. With Bradman calling the shots it became a very fine unit indeed.

That team stuck together by and large through the next summer's visit by India, then on to England for the historic summer of 1948. If there was any doubt about Bradman leading that 1948 team it was dispelled against India in the 1947-48 season. He took three centuries and a double century from the Indian bowling in five Tests, in which his batting again displayed much of its former glory. The season was notable for Bradman's 100th century in first class cricket.

I recall broadcasting the completion of that century, scored for an Australian XI against the Indian tourists in an early-season match at the SCG. He was batting with Keith Miller, and a big crowd had come to watch history in the making. No other Australian had got within coo-ee of 100 hundreds, and it was an event of some moment in the community.

Bradman was on 99 in the last over before tea, and the crowd was riding every ball. Bradman said later he had never before felt such crowd emotion out in the middle.

The young Bradmans . . . living in the spotlight was not always easy.

The great Bradman was a natural. Potentially a champion golfer, he loved to get out and have a hit while on tour in England.

The Sydney Test, 1946. Don Bradman and Sid Barnes each scored 234, and the Bradman comeback was assured.

Bradman hit his 100th run just after a horse race started in Sydney. The ABC had switched over for the race description. I screamed down the line for them to come back to me so I could get in that fateful run. Thankfully the studio controller had the initiative to cross back. I described the run, caught the crowd's reaction to the history they had seen created, and still got back to the race for the last furlong.

Bradman's stature by the winter of 1948 was as high as it had ever been before the war. He was cricket's elder statesman. Like Al Jolson, a popular American singer of the time, he had come back more mellow, his art refined and seasoned and richer in character. Those who remembered his pre-war heroics could see the change. And a new generation of cricket lovers now had the chance to appreciate his greatness. He was already a legend.

The team Bradman led to England in 1948 was quite simply the finest cricket team the world has ever seen. I hear people today talking about Clive Lloyd's magnificent West Indies side, which has so demoralised England and Australia in recent years, as challengers to the title. Lloyd's team has been a truly great one, brilliantly led and beautifully balanced. But I doubt the likes of Malcolm Marshall and Joel Garner would have dealt so catastrophically with batsmen like Barnes, Morris, Bradman, Hassett and Miller as they have Australia's current crop of players. Likewise, the pressure that Miller and Ray Lindwall would have exerted on men like Richards and Lloyd would be a huge factor. The current West Indies team have been subjected to nothing like that.

It is impossible to make accurate comparisons over a period of nearly forty years. But I have watched them both closely, and I have seen no team to touch Bradman's.

Bradman was a superman among men on that tour. He was thirty-nine when the team set off for England. He was twenty years older than the youngest team member, Neil Harvey. Yet he was still the best batsman in the side. His deeds won him tremendous respect from his team. His courage and his will, as well as his ability, were examples that shone to the men underneath him.

His manner won him a different kind of respect. There was an aura about Bradman. He was simply on a different plane to the rest of the team, and that suited him. He kept them at arm's length. There is not the slightest doubt the team respected him highly, but they also found it difficult to get close to him.

Bradman exuded a quiet, understated discipline over his team. I remember chatting with him very late one evening during a Test. Suddenly it was 1 am and he saw me to the front door of his hotel. At that moment Keith Miller came bounding in, obviously having had a fairly big night on the town.

'Evening Braddles' he said. 'Hullo Keith' said Don. Next morning Miller was quite apprehensive. 'What did he say?' he quizzed me. I told him Bradman had said nothing.

Nor did he say anything to Miller, but the dashing young fast-bowler was clearly judged to be out of order for being out so late during a Test. Next morning Bradman worked him relentlessly, running him from third man to fine leg when he was not bowling. He didn't give him a minute's peace. The message was received.

Bradman's relations with those outside the team were also distant. He played his cards close to his chest. He was extremely wary of the Press. Despite several long talks with him I found him evasive and non-committal. It was hard to get an answer, particularly if there was the slightest hint of controversy on a subject.

Bradman had set himself a definite course and he was sticking to it. He felt captaincy required a particular dignity. He remained a very private person, and he wanted it kept that way. That was his right, and it achieved the result he wanted.

Bradman's shrewdness in building the team he had was quickly borne out in England. The rule had been recently varied to allow a new ball after 55 overs, and this played into his hands. He was magnificently equipped in the pace bowling department with Lindwall, Miller and Bill Johnston, and he used them expertly throughout the tour. England simply had no answer to them. The inroads they made on the Englishmen became habitual. Often I can recall having a cup of tea in the marquees that were set up on various grounds when the new ball came and Miller and Lindwall were thrown into the attack. Suddenly there would be an influx of Englishmen into the tent. They found it hard to watch, so predictable was the result of these uneven contests. Australia won the series 4-0 and the Bradman era was over.

Bradman's contribution to cricket over that twenty-year period is inestimable. As a batsman he had no peer. As a captain he achieved exactly what he set out to achieve. And he did it his way. Don Bradman was very much the master of his own destiny.

The Bradman aura has diminished not a whit in nearly forty years since he retired. He contributed long and mightily as an administrator, and his counsel is still widely sought. He has offered me much constructive suggestion through my broadcasting career. And when the occasion has warranted, we have wheeled the same barrow. One such project was the restriction of leg-side fieldsmen, which Don saw as a prime requisite if cricket were to fulfil its obligations as a public entertainment. While he hammered the point around the conference table, I hammered it on the air. Don was one administrator who firmly recognised broadcasting's role in cricket, and I know he had a high regard for the ABC's long-term contribution in that area.

That soft spot for the ABC once almost induced him to allow us to do his life story as a television documentary. Bradman's life remains a fascination for so many Australians, and as well as capturing huge public interest, such a project would have provided a marvellous contribution to Australia's sporting archives.

I had lunch with Don to canvass the prospect. He nominated he could only spare half an hour, but the lunch went for two hours and the idea had a very favourable reception indeed. Don at no stage committed himself, but he did indicate he would like to do it for the ABC, since they had been so good for cricket. We got to the point of discussing how much time I would have to spend in Adelaide, and where he would have to travel—Cootamundra and Bowral and various places like that to retrace his early days. I told him I would have to check out fees and such like with the ABC management.

'Oh, I wouldn't want any money for it, Mac,' he responded. 'Perhaps some expenses for travel to Bowral and places,' he said, 'but no fees.' I was astounded. Though he had not committed himself, I was more than pleased with the progress of the meeting and felt the project was a real goer. I reported events to a section head at the ABC.

'Oh, I don't know, Mac, I think he's past it' came the reply. I was utterly flabbergasted. I argued, and left with an assurance that the matter would go higher, for further consideration.

Time passed and the matter lapsed. When I next saw Bradman, some months later, I asked him if he was still interested in doing the documentary, and whether he had heard any more from the ABC. I got a sharp 'no' on both counts. Years later the general manager of the ABC, Sir Talbot Duckmanton, brought the matter up again.

'Do you think Don Bradman would agree to us doing his life story?' Sir Talbot asked. I related the events of some years earlier. Sir Talbot was horrified. The section head had merely let the matter die on his desk, with further reference to no-one.

Later entreaties to Bradman got nowhere. Sir Talbot wrote to him, but received a courteous reply in the negative. What a pity! A great document for cricket's archives had been missed, and all because of one bad decision.

I was embarrassed about that. I felt Don was somewhat slighted by the whole affair. He never said so, but I felt he was peeved by the train of events, having indicated his preparedness to do something like that when he had so often rejected similar offers, then heard nothing more. Ever since, in my dealings with Don, I have felt uncomfortable about that matter.

Ironically, some time later I had a request from a television producer in England to see if they could do the same sort of thing. They quoted a fee of £100 000 sterling. I rang Don rather tentatively to pass on the proposal. 'No thanks' came the reply, definite and irrevocable.

One rather poignant occasion on which my wife Gwen and I had a glimpse of the inner Bradman came in the early 'seventies, when Gwen was being treated for a malignancy that later took her life. Don rang me at the hotel in Brisbane on the morning of a Test and asked if he might walk to the ground with me.

He expressed his concern at Gwen's condition, and asked if he could have a chat with her. He feared at the time he may have been suffering from a similar problem. I was naturally taken aback at the request, and the fears he held for himself.

Gwen did have a long chat with him some weeks later at the Sydney Cricket Ground. As it turned out, Don's fears were groundless. But the circumstances of that chat represented life at its most basic. Throughout all humanity there is a constant which defies all the embellishments of glory and achievement, of station and title, and leaves us all the same.

Just a couple of years ago, Sir Donald Bradman did me the honour of asking me to launch his biography, *Bradman*, which is an expansive volume compiled from his own recollections and his private collection of records, photographs and correspondence. I was very touched by the invitation. Again, I reflected on the record the ABC might have had.

I said at the book launching that Bradman was a legend. There seems always to be a certain mystery surrounding men whose stature is such that they stand above their environment. Bradman has always had that mystery. Sometimes it has been misunderstood.

But his record as a cricketer and his standing as a sportsman of a rare kind have proved impervious to anything that would seek to undermine them.

If anything, time has enhanced his greatness.

THE GOLDEN PAIR

Richie Benaud began his first class career about the time Bradman ended his. He had developed his cricketing skills and attitudes through his youth at the time Bradman's team reigned supreme. He had come to expect Australian success as a matter of course, and his approach to cricket was positive in every sense. Benaud was a different type altogether from Bradman. He was expansive and extroverted, in a sensible and moderate way, and had a bent for public relations that won friends.

Benaud was essentially a cricketing personality. He had a certain film star quality that made him a natural centre of attraction, and cricket had become such a passion with him he simply bubbled enthusiasm whenever he played. He was a natural captain.

Benaud captained Australia through 28 Tests. Of those 12 were won, four were lost, 11 were drawn and one was tied. Bradman had been captain for 24 Tests for 15 wins, three losses and six draws. Ian Chappell's record stood at 30 Tests for 15 wins, five losses and 10 draws. The figures bear remarkable comparison, and stand as a testimony to the inspiration three of its very best captains gave Australian cricket.

The job did not fall easily to Benaud. It took, in fact, a reasonable amount of perseverance from the Australian selectors to keep him in the team through the 'fifties, and when Ian Johnston retired their first choice for captain was the twenty-one-year-old Ian Craig, who led Australia to South Africa in 1957. But a bout of hepatitis and failing form put Craig out of consideration before Peter May's England team arrived at the start of the 1958-59 season. Even then, there was a considerable body of opinion that considered Neil Harvey, by then the batting supremo of Australian cricket, to have a prior claim. But the job went to Benaud, and as events transpired, it was one of the more inspired decisions of modern cricket.

Benaud arrived at a time when Australia had slipped into the doldrums. England had won back the Ashes from Lindsay Hassett's team in 1953, defended them successfully in Australia in 1954-55 and again in England in 1956. Through this period cricket had also hit one of its dull periods. Len Hutton, as captain of England, and Hassett and Ian Johnston, as captains of Australia, had developed a conservative outlook that bogged the game down. There was a feeling that winning was fine, but losing was untenable. The result was timid, lack-lustre and riskless cricket that brought a more than acceptable number of draws.

Benaud's attitude breathed new life into the game. His philosophy was that winning was everything. The game could not possibly be enjoyable if you set about trying not to lose all the time. You had to go for it. Aggression, flair and daring became the name of the game. It was an approach to which players and public responded enthusiastically. Even when he took the Australian team to England in 1961 and was faced with the usual grind of county games, he decided to try to win them all. Declarations that were highly sporting, to say the least, occasionally brought him undone. But he preferred to lose, trying to win, rather than just let things peter out.

Benaud also made a very clear decision that the game should be sold to the public as much as possible. He created a new atmosphere of co-operation with the Press and the media generally. There was a new spirit, a new drive that imbued all levels of the game with a happy, convivial air of enthusiasm and purpose.

This attitude quickly infected the team. Benaud was always applauding and exhorting them on the field, slapping backs and generally whipping up co-operative performance. He had a very keen sense of team effort. His object was to make the side a total unit, in which every man complemented every other man. He succeeded so admirably a new era of success enveloped the game.

Benaud knew cricket, and he was very thoughtful in his plan of attack for any particular situation. But above all he had the courage to give those plans a chance. If he set himself upon a certain course, he was not easily deterred.

When Peter May's team arrived in 1958 they were universally regarded as the best team in the world. Men like May himself, Colin Cowdrey, Tom Graveney, Fred Trueman, Brian Statham, Frank Tyson, Jim Laker and Tony Lock had been terrorising Australian teams for years.

In tandem with the Australian selectors, Benaud decided a heavily concentrated left-arm pace attack was the best means of unnerving the leading English batsmen.

He wanted the ball to run away from their better batsmen, and the selectors gave him the partnership he wanted in Alan Davidson and Ian Meckiff. Davidson finished the series with twenty-four wickets and

Meckiff seventeen. By the time some pace support was added from an ageing Ray Lindwall and a fiery young giant in Gordon Rorke, the England team was placed under very heavy pressure indeed. In the end Australia triumphed by the staggering margin of four Tests to nil. It was very much a victory for Benaud. He had developed a fierce will to win in the team. They were alert and alive in everything they did, hustling through their overs and bustling in the field. They simply did not let England relax.

That first captaincy experience for Benaud was not all beer and skittles, mind you. His determination to provide bright and entertaining cricket did not get a very enthusiastic endorsement from his opponents when the series opened in Brisbane. One day's play in that Test, for instance, brought just 106 runs for the loss of eight English wickets. That averages out at 22 runs per hour. The pre-lunch session of 90 minutes brought just 19 runs.

Trevor Bailey, the 'Captain Stayput' of English cricket, distinguished himself by scoring just 41 runs in four-and-a-half hours. He had been batting 357 minutes when he finally reached 50 which gave him the slowest half century in the history of first class cricket. He finished up with 68 in 458 minutes of pure agony for spectators. He hit only 40 scoring shots from 425 balls he faced—that's 385 balls he either let go or patted back defensively. It was absolutely horrible cricket. Jim Burke responded for Australia with 28 runs in four hours, but in his case runs came at pace at the other end.

The only good feature of it was that Australia managed to win anyway, but it left Benaud with a lot of work to do if he was to rekindle public interest in the tour and the game, as he vowed he would. That he ultimately did was an enormous reflection of his resilience and his determination to accentuate the positive, and eliminate the negative.

With that series gloriously parcelled up, Benaud's role as Australian captain was solidly entrenched. He was seen as something of a saviour for the game. Benaud himself declared it was a new era for Australian cricket, and he was not wrong.

Benaud's attitudes had borne much fruit by the England tour of 1961. In partnership with Frank Worrell's West Indians, Benaud's Australians through the summer of 1960-61 had produced a succession of marvellous matches, and cricket which entertained as no series had before it.

The first day of the first Test produced a West Indies score of 7-359, for instance, which compares rather starkly with that English effort of 8-106 just two years before. That was the tone of the tour throughout. That first game ended in a tie, achieved on the second last ball of the game, and the dynamics of the cricket reflected Benaud's way.

At the start of the 1961 tour of England he announced he was not interested in anything dull. Results would be pursued in all games. True to his word, he became renowned for first day declaration in county games which produced some marvellously exciting cricket for the next two days. It made it more interesting and more fun for the players, and much more appealing for everybody else.

Benaud was responsible on this tour for one of the most brilliant individual pieces of tactical captaincy I have ever seen. It was the fourth Test at Old Trafford, Manchester, and the series was locked at one match each. Australia were in trouble on the last afternoon when England, with nine second innings wickets intact, needed a comfortable 106 runs to win. Benaud was bowling his leg-spinners without a great deal of success against Ted Dexter, who had moved rather impressively to 76 and looked like getting the winning runs himself. Then Neil Harvey and Benaud went into conference.

Harvey had been Benaud's deputy throughout his captaincy career, and was highly supportive of his captain. Disappointed though he might have been at not having the job in the first place, he put all his weight solidly behind Benaud, contributing a great deal to the success of his teams, not only with his immaculate batting, but with some shrewd judgment and some sound advice.

On this occasion Harvey suggested to Benaud he might try to vary his line. There were some rough patches on the pitch he might pick up if he switched to bowling around the wicket. Benaud concurred. He was not averse to a gamble, nor was he prepared to concede defeat, despite the strength of England's position. The move brought immediate and spectacular results.

Dexter was deceived and gave a catch to Grout at the wicket, and with the very next ball Benaud bowled the England captain Peter May around his legs. From there the Englishmen seemed to go into a blind panic. Benaud wrapped things up with an astonishing spell of 5-12 in 25 balls, and England were all out 55 runs short of their winning target. It was one of the great comebacks.

Benaud's aggression and daring had turned seemingly certain defeat into victory. Instead of losing the series 2-1, they won it 2-1.

In 1962-63, when Ted Dexter's team challenged again in Australia, England won the second Test and Australia the third, and the series was tied 1-1. That left the Ashes with Australia, and meant Benaud had led his team successfully through three Ashes series. But it was a rather hollow victory, in the end, for Benaud. A 1-1 series result, with three draws, was simply not his style. He made public his disappointment after the drawn last Test. 'It was a miserable match for all—spectators, administrators and players' he said. 'Players never like to go through five days of inconclusive cricket.'

Benaud's attitude to the game, however, was summed up best in what he said next. 'Players take credit for good cricket matches and I have never been interested in dodging the blame for the bad ones. The twenty-two players in the match were the main culprits.'

Benaud lived by his convictions. He saw a responsibility to make cricket enjoyable and attractive, and he did everything in his power to see that it was. Richie has long continued to provide enjoyment for cricket lovers as a TV commentator and writer, and in that capacity he has excelled. He has done and is still doing a wonderful job for the game.

When the World Series split came in 1977 Richie Benaud was deeply involved with the establishment of the new venture. He earned a sort of 'excommunication' from established official circles over that. The International Cricket Conference even went so far as to declare him *persona non grata* for his involvement. At the time the battle was at its height, and emotions were charged. That episode was a shame. I am sure Richie saw long-term benefits for cricketers and cricket in what he was doing. He has always been one of the game's most faithful servants.

Ian Chappell's accession to the Australian captaincy was something akin to Benaud's. Again there had been a period of rather dull and unenterprising cricket through the 'sixties, where Australian teams under Bob Simpson and Bill Lawry had battled on stoicly, without providing a great deal of excitement.

Simpson had taken the 1964 team to England for one win and four draws. He followed up with a 2-1 series loss to the West Indies, a 1-1 shared series against Mike Smith's Englishmen, and a 3-1 loss to South Africa. Bill Lawry took over for a 1-1 drawn series against England in 1968, a 3-1 series win against West Indies in Australia and a 4-0 drubbing by South Africa in early 1970. Lawry lost his place in the Australian team for the last Test of the 1970-71 series against Ray Illingworth's English side.

It was a tough time for Chappell to take over. Australia were doing it very hard against the relentlessness of John Snow's bowling. And, again, the game had been bogged down in an era in which drive and flair had been lost.

Chappell was a fighter from the start. Even the circumstances of his appointment raised his competitive hackles. He felt the selectors and the Australian Cricket Board had shown gross disloyalty to Lawry. They failed to inform Lawry of his impending dismissal, leaving him to hear it on the radio, and read it in the paper. Chappell saw that as a monstrous discourtesy. He vowed then and there that he would never let it happen to him.

His first game as captain, too, was a rare baptism of fire. That was the Test at the SCG in early 1971 when the crowd turned nasty after a John Snow bouncer had hit the No 9 Australian batsman, Terry Jenner, on the head. Snow and the England captain Ray Illingworth were the targets of a raucously hostile crowd demonstration. As if to flaunt their derision, Illingworth sent Snow to field on the fence in front of the Paddington Hill, where some of the rowdiest elements of the crowd were prone to gather in those days. Snow egged them on and the noise and the hostility continued long after Jenner had recovered.

One of the spectators was sufficiently fortified by the beverages he was consuming, and sufficiently riled by Snow's attitude, to grab the Englishman by the arm and pull him to the fence. Snow quickly pulled himself away, but Illingworth got very hot under the collar indeed, gathered his team about him, and departed. The Englishmen simply walked off, leaving the Australian batsmen Greg Chappell and Dennis Lillee, and the umpires Lou Rowan and Tom Brooks, clustered at the pitch like shags on rocks. The crowd responded with a shower of beer cans and bottles. A right royal battle then raged in the England dressing room as umpires and administrators, with a rather confused mixture of threatening and cajoling, tried to induce Illingworth to get his team back on the field.

Col Egar, who had retired earlier that season as Australia's premier umpire, later told me the umpires would have been well within their rights to call stumps. In fact, Egar said, had he been umpire he would have done so. The law, he explained, specifically stated that a team that abandoned the field without the umpires' permission, as Illingworth's had done, was automatically liable to forfeit.

What a nice old ruckus that would have caused! Chappell, for his part, was not going to let England get away with anything. He reasoned that the best way to make them look petty over the whole affair was merely to stand his ground. The Australian batsmen thus refused to budge until Illingworth relented. The tourists returned to the field once the various missiles had been cleared.

It was a fairly historic entry for Ian Chappell into the world of Australian captaincy. It ended in defeat for him. But the series had introduced some promising new names in Greg Chappell, Rod Marsh and Dennis Lillee, and there was clearly room to build. Chappell attacked that re-building job with a vengeance.

First of all, he made sure he did his bit with the bat. Chappell batted at No 3 for Australia 48 times. On 27 of those occasions he went in when the opening partnership had been broken for less than 20, so he was a virtual opener. Yet from that position he managed seven centuries, and he passed 50 on no fewer than 13 occasions. That is a remarkable success rate for one of the real pressure spots of cricket. And the courage and dedication that Chappell showed in that role was one of the bases on which he built a highly successful period as captain. He led by example. He practised what he preached, fighting for every run, competing aggressively and doggedly for any and every advantage that would help his team. His players respected him mightily for that.

Chappell's prime quality as a captain was the devotion he drew from his players, and his unique ability to drag every last ounce out of their performance. In fact, he drew more than the last ounce. He could get 101 per cent out of every man in the side, to the extent that they regularly played above themselves. Three examples stand out in my experience of Chappell, the captain.

In 1972, the Australian selectors sadly restricted him on the tour of England by the omission of the West Australian pace bowler Graham McKenzie. McKenzie had first toured England with Richie Benaud's side in 1961, then backed up in 1964 and 1968 under Bill Lawry. He also had a vast amount of experience under English conditions as a county bowler with Leicestershire. He was strong, resilient and wily enough to make the most of English wickets. McKenzie had lost his place in the Australian team after the fourth Test largely because of his tiredness after a long stint of continuous cricket. The sensible thing to do was to rest him, then send him off to England where he would have been a tremendous support for Dennis Lillee and Bob Massie.

As it was, the Australian pace contingent was restricted to Lillee, Massie, David Colley and the young South Australian Jeff Hammond, none of whom had ever made a tour of England. Yet Chappell worked that supply of bowlers into such a formidable unit that Lillee finished the series with 31 wickets and Massie with 23 – 16 of them in his debut Test at Lord's. Had McKenzie been there as well, how much easier it might have been for them.

As an example of what players would give for the cause under Chappell, David Colley was called upon to spell Lillee for seven overs as England collapsed in their second innings of the second Test and Australia pressed towards victory. Lillee had absolutely terrorised the Englishmen with his pace in this match and Massie, moving the ball in the air and cutting it sharply off the slope in the Lord's pitch, was cutting a swathe through the innings at the other end. It was essential the pressure be maintained when it became necessary for Lillee to have a spell.

Colley was never a particularly tearaway bowler. He was the work-horse type who would bowl a brisk fast-medium all day, and a solid team man who realised the value of hard work. When Chappell threw Colley the ball he left no doubt about his requirements. They had to keep the pressure on. Colley had to be quick. Very quick.

It is doubtful if Colley has ever bowled more quickly in his life than he did that day. The Englishmen were given absolutely no respite. Seven overs conceded only eight runs, and Massie carried on to pick up his eight wickets at the other end and have England all out for 116. Chappell had dragged out of Colley something he did not realise he had, just as he dragged out of Lillee and Massie and the team as a whole a highly creditable tour that ended with two wins apiece and put Australia back in the winner's circle they were to occupy for quite a few years thereafter.

The other examples of Chappell's ability to inspire performance from his men followed in the next season against Pakistan, and again on tour in the West Indies in early 1973. By the third Test of the 1972-73 series against Pakistan, Lillee was starting to feel the back trouble, later diagnosed as stress fractures, which cost him a year's cricket and almost finished his career. By the third Test in Sydney he was in a great deal of pain. His difficulties were at their worst on the last day, when Pakistan needed just 159 runs in their second innings to win the game.

Lillee and Chappell were kindred spirits. They each had a competitive edge that was almost obsessive. Winning was overwhelmingly important to them, and difficulties or obstacles placed in their path were there only to be overcome. Chappell would occasionally fire up his fast bowlers with comments like 'if I needed a slow bowler I would have put on a spinner'. He rode them hard. In Lillee's case there was never a need. Lillee was the supreme competitor as well.

That afternoon at the SCG Lillee was so obviously affected by his back Chappell considered taking him off. 'You're kidding', Lillee replied. He commandeered the ball and bowled unchanged through the Pakistan innings. He bowled at pace too, forcing the Pakistanis into hard defence and generally maintaining a huge psychological edge that he had gathered through the previous two Tests. They were scared of him, and Lillee knew it. He bowled twenty-three overs straight while Bob Massie and Max Walker shared duty from the other end. Walker finished up taking 6-15 as Pakistan crumbled to be all out for 106 – still 53 runs short of victory. Everybody knew, though, how much Lillee had contributed to those wickets. Lillee won the match that afternoon on sheer courage. He bowled under terrible duress, in pain at every delivery, and goodness knows how much damage he did himself. But he bowled and he bowled well, because his captain and his team needed it. Chappell created that atmosphere. Lillee merely responded to it.

Again in the West Indies Chappell's ability to lift people was portrayed in sharp focus. I remember sharing a cab with him to a television studio shortly after the first Test. 'Mac, we're in a bit of strife', he offered. 'Bob Massie won't play a Test on the tour, and Lillee's back is so bad I don't know whether he'll ever bowl again.' That, of course, meant that his strike force was well and truly shattered. 'What do you think about Max Walker?' he inquired.

Well, both Chappell and I had seen Max demolish Pakistan a few weeks before, but neither of us had really seen a great deal of him. We talked about him for a while, the quality of his inswing and the value his obvious strength might be to the team. 'It looks like he is going to have to do it', Chappell concluded.

From that point Chappell started working on Max Walker. He turned him into an absolute lion of a bowler. He finished the series with twenty-seven wickets, and was the principal factor in Australia's 2-0 triumph. He bowled through one Test with his feet black from bruising. He figured somebody had to do the job.

Chappell turned what looked to be a very ordinary attack without its two best bowlers into a most worthy one. Jeff Hammond supported Walker extraordinarily well. They each bowled above themselves, because they knew he required it of them.

In the area of man management, in his ability to get the best out of a whole team, in the fierce loyalty and respect he earned and held from all his players, Chappell was supreme. Neither Benaud nor

England's skipper Peter May and Richie Benaud inspect the pitch during the 1958–59 tour.

The old campaigner Graham McKenzie introduces the young lion Dennis Lillee to the Duke of Edinburgh.

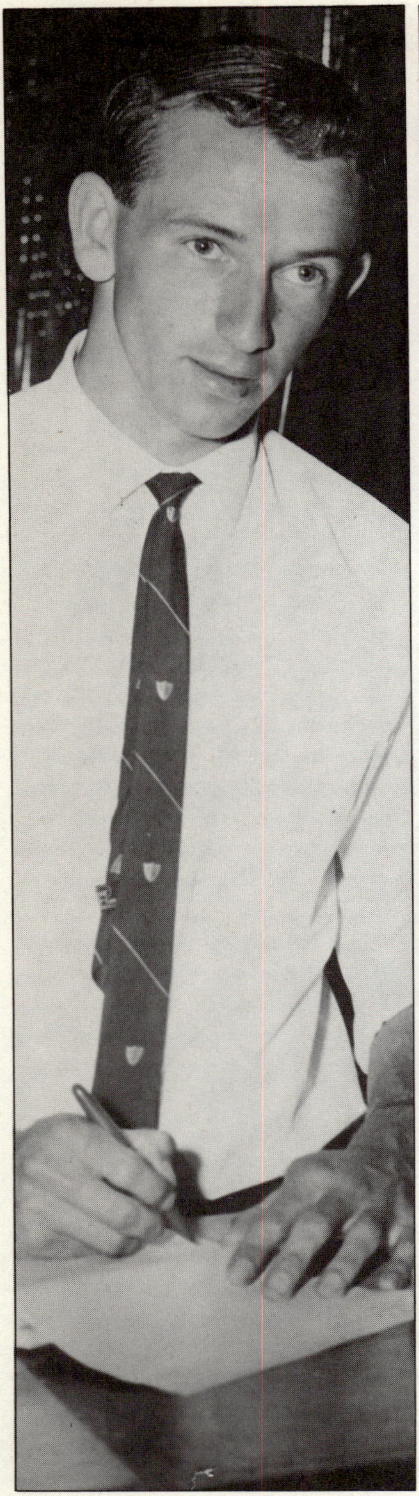

Doug Walters and Ian Chappell, the youthful tyros of the 'sixties who turned into long-term champions of Australian cricket. Chappell, *above*, became perhaps Australia's greatest captain.

Bradman—nor any other captain I have known—could get from his players the ultimate effort that Chappell could extract. Benaud and Bradman had other strengths that Chappell perhaps could not quite match. Maybe he didn't have quite the same tactical mind as Bradman, or the same uncanny judgment as Benaud. But when it came to getting the team to work, he had absolutely no peer.

Chappell was a rather unorthodox appointment as Australian captain in the first place. He was very much a knockabout sort of bloke. He enjoyed a beer, he liked to play up a little, was not averse to the odd practical joke, and was occasionally disrespectful to the staid and conservative traditions of cricket. He was, in fact, a bit of a rebel. He had a little of Vic Richardson's mischief about him. He was also the same sort of straight-shooter as his grandfather, intolerant of fools and unwilling to conform to attitudes and constraints which he felt were pompous and unproductive.

He quickly shook off the grey suit and white shirt image of Australian captaincy. He would present himself in mauve safari suits, or wildly checked shirts. He was a man of his era, and he wasn't going to turn fuddy-duddy simply because that was what Australian captains were supposed to do. He had no time for petty disciplines and old-fashioned ritual. He worked out what he saw as sensible and productive, and acted accordingly. And everything he did was done for the good of his team, and the ultimate goal of winning.

Sometimes he appeared a bit rough. And there is no denying some of the things he did were unnecessary and out of court. He could be rude, he probably swore too much, and he sometimes went overboard in his determination to flout authority if he considered it to be out of touch. Dropping his pants to adjust his protector in the middle of the Adelaide Oval, for instance, and walking into a disciplinary hearing at the South Australian Cricket Association with a cigar and a beer in his hand were hardly proper.

But for all his rebellion against imposed disciplines of that kind, he was in fact a very stern disciplinarian in his captaincy. But it was an encouraged self-discipline, a communal desire to do everything necessary to produce ultimate performance and to win. He couldn't care a fig how much a man played up so long as he did the job on the field, when it counted. Woe betide him if he didn't. He was straight, direct, and as far as his team was concerned, just plain fair dinkum. They knew he would defend them to the death. In turn, they would go with him, all the way.

The result was a bond within the team that was simply impregnable. There was a mutual respect, and a group responsibility, that meant players fed off each other's strengths. For opponents, it was a huge factor to surmount.

One of the difficulties Chappell encountered was the distinction he had to draw between being one of the team, and being in charge of it.

He had developed some very strong friendships through his time in the Australian team. Men like Doug Walters and Brian Taber, then Dennis Lillee and Rod Marsh, were very close to him. I recall a conversation in which he wrestled with the dilemma.

Chappell was lying on his bed in a hotel in Kingston, with the door wide open, when I happened to pass. 'Got a minute, Mac' he called. In I went. He had a golf putter in his hand and as he lay on his back he shut one eye and traced a join in the ceiling.

'It's a fine line, isn't it Mac?' I looked at the putter, then at the ceiling. 'I suppose it is. What are you talking about?' I replied.

'This captaincy business' he continued. 'It's a fine line between being part of it, and being far enough away to do the job as captain. I'm great mates with some of these guys, but it's difficult knowing just when you have to stay away. I can't just go and have a beer with my mates the way I used to. I can't afford to be too close. I've got to keep that fine line. It's a problem,' he said.

'Well, the only fellow who can solve that is you', I offered.

'I know that. I'll get there all right, don't worry about that' he said.

He did too. He maintained his friendships without forming cliques in the team, and he kept just enough distance to have the control he needed and the respect he needed when he wanted it.

One man who was an enormous support for him in this regard was his great friend and ally Doug Walters. Not only could he rely on Doug for a very competent all-round job on the field, but Walters was a magnificent sounding board for him, a reliable tactical contributor and a superb emissary of goodwill and good spirit. On the field Chappell would often call on Walters when things were grim. If he didn't call on Dougie to actually grab the ball and break a partnership, as he did so often, he might send him down to field around mid-off so he could chat to the bowlers as he returned the ball to them. Walters had a marvellous effect in this area. A pat on the back, a word of encouragement. Walters bubbled such good spirit and such hope and optimism the bowlers could hardly remain unaffected. It was another means Chappell employed to get the best out of everybody.

Off the field Walters was his captain's most able lieutenant. For all his happy-go-lucky nature, Walters was a shrewd judge of a cricketer, and he offered quite a bit when the plan of attack had to be worked out for battle.

Once in the West Indies, Walters had paid particular attention to a batsman he considered was very vulnerable when he tried to hook short bowling. He suggested to Ian Chappell he field just a little deeper behind square leg, that they feed the hook shot to this particular character, and see if Dougie couldn't pick up the catch. Plan A went into operation next morning. Walters positioned himself exactly as he thought he should be positioned, only to be called in by Chappell. Walters waved him away. He had the right spot. Chappell again waved him to come in a few paces.

Again Walters objected. Eventually Chappell ordered him in. Next ball was dropped short on schedule, the batsman hooked, and the ball sailed a yard or two over Walters' head, just to the point he had been standing before Chappell intervened. Walters held his arms apart in mock protest, as if to say 'whoever picked you for captain?'. Chappell refused to look at him, lest he had to admit he was wrong. The pair laughed their way through the whole exchange. But it was typical of the relationship they had, and the support that Walters gave his friend.

I imagine one of the hardest things Ian Chappell ever had to do in cricket was to drop Walters from the final Test of the 1972 campaign in England, where he had great trouble getting runs consistently. It was the first time Walters had been dropped since he started off in the Australian team with a first-up century against Mike Smith's team seven years before. But Chappell put the team first, as was his duty, and out went Dougie.

Walters' reaction to that was to deliver an emotional entreaty to the team at the dinner before the Test that this was the game they had to win. He was with them all the way. Chappell believed that little speech to be the turning point, the final motivation for one of the great Australian victories.

Ian Chappell ended his captaincy stint in England in 1975 when he led Australia in the World Cup, and played a short Test series of four matches against England. Australia won the first of these, but the rest were drawn. That was an unsatisfactory result in Chappell's eyes. He was not interested in draws. He played to win.

Even in his retirement, Chappell's consideration for his team was paramount. He said at the end of the 1975 visit to England he wanted to stand down as captain for the following series against the West Indies because he had 'had enough' of the auxiliary roles the job entailed. He was sick of being pursued for statements, appearances, dinners, speeches. He simply wanted to play his cricket and enjoy it. And he knew the captaincy would pass to his brother, Greg, who by this time had been in the Australian team for five years and was very much its premier batsman.

Ian would never admit it, but I am sure he wanted to play under Greg to give his brother as smooth an entry as possible into the testing responsibilities of Test captaincy. Ian knew he could still exert an influence on the field. He knew his presence and his experience would be a considerable assistance to Greg as he settled into the job.

That is very much how things panned out when Clive Lloyd's team began the series in Brisbane. In the first Test Ian scored 41 and 74 not out. For much of that time he batted with Greg. Greg had a century in each innings and the Test was won by eight wickets. In the second Test Ian scored 156. From there Ian slipped into the background and Greg took over, scoring 702 runs for the series at an average of 117 and leading Australia to a whopping 5-1 series win at his first attempt. Ian

Chappell, I am certain, arranged his exit from the captaincy for that series to give his younger brother a flying start. Not only because Greg was his brother, but because a smooth and successful transfer of power was best for the side. He wanted to disrupt it as little as possible. He wanted to see that the drive the team had gathered through the early 'seventies was maintained under Greg's command. He wanted continuity.

To me, that summed up Ian Chappell's attitude to the game and to captaincy. He was utterly selfless, and every bit the team man.

When it came to playing winning cricket, Ian Chappell was the master manipulator. In the fifty-odd years that I have watched Test cricket played around the world, I have seen no better captain.

THE START OF IT ALL

I am often amused to look back on my earliest days in cricket, and to wonder how I ever survived them. Long before I had been privileged to meander through the Long Room at Lord's, or sit before a microphone to relate great deeds and great moments, I had to run the gauntlet of the Sydney Grammar School first XI.

They were a tough bunch in the bustling days of the 1920s. The overhanging influence of the Victorian era and the rigours of the Great War had established a rigid pecking order in school activities. In sport, it was particularly so.

To be a prominent sportsmen in the Great Public Schools (GPS) of those days was to be something special. They were the supreme achievers of school life, the men at the top. Boys stayed on at school until they were nineteen or even twenty in some cases, and the cricket teams of the day often had a maturity about them a little out of place in a schoolboy competition. As such they somewhat resented the introduction of young McGilvray, aged thirteen, into the school first XI.

How I actually achieved such exalted status at such a young age remains something of a mystery to me. But I vividly remember the hard time the senior boys felt obliged to give a young upstart. Their first target of derision was the fact that I wore short pants. I imagine they considered that to imply some sort of embarrassment by association. They were the big timers, and to be lumped in along side a scrawny junior was not conducive to their image. The penalty for wearing short pants became an unceremonious dumping under the shower. I would be hustled under, fully clothed, while the rest of the team rolled about in great merriment.

Despite continued entreaties, I was condemned to this sort of treatment for many weeks before my parents would relent and allow me to wear long pants. Even then, it was only my arrival home for dinner drenched to the skin that provided the final persuasion.

Through those early Grammar days I was very much the brat. I had to change in a different room from the 'senior' boys; I was denied the traditional inducement of a boiled lolly that often came around to sweeten long hours in the field.

Their *coup de grace*, however, was on a bright day in the summer of 1925 when the school was playing its annual practice match against a team from the psychiatric institution at Callan Park. Each year our school first XI would take on a team from the staff at the hospital. It was a diversion to which the boys always looked forward.

On this occasion I had been batting before lunch, and at the adjournment I had been cruising along merrily with about seventy runs to my credit. The seniors suggested a tour of the institution during the luncheon break. I was hardly in a position to refuse.

They took me to a number of buildings, then stopped at a wing which housed the dreaded padded cell. 'In there' they ordered, and firmly slammed the door behind me.

Those were days when psychiatric care was somewhat less enlightened than it is today, and the thought of the padded cell was enough to scare the wits out of the average schoolboy. A half hour or so actually in one was absolutely terrifying. By the time they let me out I was beside myself with fear. Needless to say I lost my wicket straight after lunch. I think the senior boys considered that about the ultimate initiation, and thereafter they left me in relative peace.

At the time, I resented all those hurtful schoolboy pranks. I didn't like them; it was a very uncomfortable time for a young man who was taking his cricket pretty seriously. But in retrospect, I think they shaped a lot of my thinking on cricket and the men who play it. I did not get the chance to captain Grammar, but when I did become a senior player, and in later years when I captained grade and State teams, I always remembered the discomfort of those early days. They may have been good natured pranks and good fun to those who had been through it all themselves in their earlier days. But I was always careful later to recall my own reaction to those days, and to appreciate the feelings of young, new players.

Cricket for so many young men down the generations has been a question of opportunity. Being in the right place at the right time; getting the break that launches or enhances a career. So it was with me.

My first good fortune came with the interest of Dr L O S Poidevin, a leading administrator of the day who was instrumental in establishing a competition in Sydney for under-twenty-one players which is still going strong today. Dr Poidevin had a strong influence in the Waverley club with whom I played straight after leaving school. I had become a moderate all-rounder, having supplemented my batting with some fairly straightforward medium paced bowling that somehow managed to earn me top bowling average of the GPS competition.

It was the age of the all-rounder, and when I began my career in Sydney club cricket Dr Poidevin took an immediate interest. Out of the blue, he invited me to captain the combined Sydney Poidevin-Gray Shield team on a visit to Newcastle. It was my first taste of captaincy.

At the time I was developing a very sharp ambition for cricket, and an invitation to be captain among my peers was an enormous thrill. I don't remember doing anything particularly distinguished on that trip to Newcastle, but at least I was now before the notice of those who counted.

I first made the New South Wales team in the summer of 1933-34. The captain was Alan Kippax, an immaculate person, as artistic in his nature as he was in his batting. He was a small, gentle man with a kindly way about him that immediately made a young man feel at ease. He was meticulous in his dress and his life, a man with a squeaky-clean image who would never raise his voice or allow his emotions to run away with him. In all the years I watched him play cricket or played cricket with him, I don't think I ever saw him ruffled. His shirt would always be buttoned the same way, the crease would always be sharp in his trousers, no hair would ever be out of place. He was an admirable engaging man.

He was also a consummate batsman. I recall going in to bat with him one day near the end of an innings when he had already completed a century. He nominated to me that he would cut each ball from the next over through a different gap in the slips. The first would go between first and second slip, the third between second and third slip and so on. Such artistic control of a batsman's wares was something I could barely imagine. But he did it, and he did it so sweetly and so majestically one could only stand and marvel at him.

During that summer of 1933-34 my first selection was for the southern tour for matches against South Australia and Victoria, and it was a moment of some significance for the McGilvray household. The crowd of relatives to see me off at Sydney's Central railway station would have done credit to Marco Polo as he set out on his trek into the unknown.

Joining that particular team was an awesome thing. It comprised an array of cricketing giants rarely equalled in NSW cricket.

I thought it fitting to present myself to the captain once on the train. I gingerly knocked on his compartment door and was bade enter to find myself in the presence of the greats. Bertie Oldfield, Don Bradman, Bill O'Reilly and Stan McCabe were in earnest discussion with their captain, and the sight of them all together knotted my stomach. I had of course played against these men in club cricket but to actually be there with them, in the one team, was a moment to make me tremble.

'Nice to see you, son,' Kippax offered, with that kindly smile of his. 'Make sure you get an early night.'

His words of gentle conversation were iron-clad orders as far as

I was concerned. I think I was in bed before the train reached Strathfield, in Sydney's western suburbs.

The senior players of that team were institutions in the game. I was very much the brat of the outfit, and they all knew it. They also played to it. My first morning in Adelaide I was getting dressed after practice when Bert Oldfield tugged at my arm with that impish glint in the eye that was so much a part of his nature.

'Hey, Al,' he beckoned. 'You know you have to go into town and pick up the bats don't you!'

Bertie Oldfield, or Mr Oldfield as I then called him according to the upbringing of the day, was something of a national hero, particularly in Adelaide. It was here the previous season that he was cracked on the skull by a ball from Harold Larwood—the one event above all others that triggered the souring of relations between England and Australia over Bodyline. He was not a man with whom a newcomer to such a Sheffield Shield team could argue.

'What bats?' I enquired rather apologetically.

He gave me an address. 'Room 15, up the stairs' he said. 'It's a sports store and they know all about us.' When I got there and dutifully inquired about the bats I was greeted with blank and puzzled looks. 'Bats?' said the girl. 'This is an optician's office.'

My red-faced return to my team-mates was greeted with much hilarity. 'Just a bit of fun, son,' Oldfield consoled me. 'Just a bit of fun.'

Young players were expected to wear such things. I guess it helped make them tough. It certainly steeled one's determination to succeed; to provide the necessary personal success to win total acceptance into the first class cricket fraternity of the day.

Alan Kippax took me to breakfast on the morning of that first match to run through the team and our tactics, to advise me as to the strengths and weaknesses of the men we would face, and generally to encourage me and exhort me to gird my loins for the battle ahead.

It was a breakfast to pump the adrenalin. As I prepared for the match my heart raced and my stomach churned. I took ages to dress, determined that everything should be just right. You can imagine my distress then, when the skipper nonchalantly advised me just as the teams were readying themselves to take the field, 'Hey, Sandy. You're 12th'.

Twelfth man! I couldn't believe it. Why the breakfast? Why the big turn-on? Just another passing moment, I was told later, in the making of a first class cricketer.

It was during that first Adelaide match that I was introduced to the extraordinarily competitive edge of the great Bradman.

The Adelaide Oval is the most picturesque of Australia's cricket grounds and, I would suggest, in the top two or three in the world when it comes to beauty. One of its more pleasant features is the area behind the Members' Stand, where a battery of superb lawn tennis courts is given over on big match days to the luxurious enjoyment of the luncheon break, and a good deal of time either side of it. Marquees go up, rugs are spread about, picnic baskets abound and champagne corks pop. Many a balmy summer afternoon has passed there with a good section of cricket's social set enjoying themselves splendidly, completely oblivious to the cricket battle being waged just a couple of hundred yards away.

As I attended to my 12th man duties, Bradman decided to avail himself of the tennis courts and invited me down for a social game as our team-mates built the NSW innings.

It became fairly obvious fairly quickly that Bradman did not like to come second in such contests. I could handle a tennis racquet reasonably well, and at that stage of my sporting life I was a fairly fit and agile youth. The harder Bradman tried, the more obvious it became to me that I had his measure. I won something like 6-4, 6-3.

When Bradman was serious about something his eyes actually burned at you. I can remember the look in his eyes that day as we left the court. 'You won't do that again,' he told me, not in a nasty way, but with the sort of grim determination that I later came to know to be the very hub of his nature.

If I needed any convincing it came some time later, when we had another game. This time he whipped me. He played as if his life depended on it. He was a born winner, and the determination he mustered even in so inconsequential a contest as that had to be seen to be believed. If I thought it curious and a little petty at the time, I soon came to know it was the supreme quality, perhaps above all others in the man, that made him the unique champion he was. Certainly I left Adelaide after that first taste of Sheffield Shield experience believing in the greatness of Bradman and the men who made up that team with him.

By the Melbourne match against Victoria, I actually got the chance to play with them. Sheffield Shield selection had come to me because I fell into that happy category rather generously termed 'all-rounder'. For that I can thank Monty Noble, the great Australian captain of the early 1900s. He was very much cricket's father figure of the '20s, a big, erect and imposing man of great presence. Noble in bearing, as well as in name.

When I started off with Sydney Grammar School I was purely a batsman. It was Noble's practice in my school days to take an interest in the Grammar teams. He suggested to our coach after a visit to our first XI practice one day that 'the red-headed kid' looked like he could bowl a bit. Our coach virtually scoffed at him.

'Oh no,' he said. 'He doesn't bowl.' 'Well he bloody well ought to,' Noble is alleged to have said, and when the great M A Noble put it like that, that was the way it would be.

I started bowling next match, a sort of hairy fast-medium that was neither one thing nor the other. Noble watched me again at practice, advised me to slow down and try to make the ball work, and settled me into a rhythm that brought me quite a bit of success in those early days.

As I lined up for NSW for the first time on the MCG I was grateful for Monty Noble's interest and advice. Kippax had lost the toss and we were in the field. It was a hot, oppressive day, and as I headed off for a fielding position somewhere about square leg, I reflected on what I considered to be a long, hard job ahead. I looked forward to watching events unfold from the relative obscurity of the field.

'Where do you think you're going?' Kippax inquired. Before I had a chance to reply he thrust the new ball into my hand. 'Take this' he demanded. 'You're opening the bowling.'

If my knees started to wobble then, they were jelly by the time I turned towards the Jolimont end and saw the lordly figures of Bill Ponsford and Bill Woodfull ambling towards the wicket. These men were giants to me, legends in their own time. My mind retreated to those days back at the SCG when my brother and I, with our packed lunches, stuck our heads between the pickets and ogled their excellence. Now here I was, with a ball in my hand, waiting to bowl to them. I felt much as King Louis, last of the Capets, must have felt as he awaited the guillotine.

'Please God,' I prayed. 'Let me land it on the pitch.' I had this mortal fear that I could not possibly control the ball in the presence of such cricketing aristocracy. I still considered myself rather unworthy of my place among these men.

I reasoned that I would bowl an inswinger first up, not because I thought it would provide any better result but because I felt I had better control over it than I did the outswinger. These men had shown much courage against bowlers of the calibre of England's Harold Larwood. Ponsford was tough, battle hardened, and Woodfull, the Australian captain, was an absolutely prolific batsman. Positive though I was determined to be, I knew there was nothing much in the McGilvray armament to strike fear into their hearts. In the end I abandoned thoughts of bowling the inswinger, too. Better to play safe, I thought. Just bowl straight; just let it land on the pitch.

Ponsford took strike to that first ball. It moved a little in the air, then for some reason jagged off the pitch to whip inside his bat. Ponsford had come forward to drive and, as was his habit so often when he was driving, he got to the pitch of the ball and moved with the shot, leaving his crease in the process. As the ball zipped past the bat Bert Oldfield, who was standing up over the wicket, threw his hands into the air, expecting the ball to hit the stumps. It just missed. By the time Bertie retrieved the ball, the stumping chance was gone too. But I had bowled it straight, and my confidence suddenly took a marvellous turn for the better.

If in every life there is one decisive moment in which its direction is changed forever, one cataclysmic event that irreversibly shapes the future, I imagine that moment came for me in that very first over I bowled in Sheffield Shield cricket.

By the third delivery the batsman had scored a single, and the bulky figure of Woodfull was on strike, standing there like the Rock of Gibraltar, defying any intrusion into his domain. By this time, I had gathered enough confidence to have a go at an inswinger. Woodfull hit it, Oldfield caught it, threw it into the air, and joined in the loud appeal that seemed to come from all points of the compass. To me it was an absolute crescendo echoing around the MCG. Woodfull, caught Oldfield, bowled McGilvray, for nought, and in my first over in first class cricket! What a moment!

'Not out' came the judgment from George Hele, the No 1 umpire of the day and as upstanding a gentleman as ever graced the game. Umpires' opinions were generally respected in those days. Certainly the code of behaviour was very different to that of recent times, when it seems an irreverent mouthful is pretty much part of the game.

I felt no particular disappointment about that decision. I was happy enough to have bowled usefully in the eyes of my team-mates.

At the end of the over I approached Woodfull, somewhat gingerly. 'I'm sorry about that appeal, Mr Woodfull,' I offered, much as a schoolboy might have approached his headmaster in confessing a minor misdemeanour.

Woodfull looked straight past me to George Hele. 'Hey George,' he said. 'I hit that hard. I was ready to walk when you called "not out". I stayed there because I didn't want to offend you.'

It was typical of Woodfull to go to such lengths to avoid offence. He didn't throw his wicket away thereafter, mind you, to even things up. But he was very sporting about it, and even if I didn't get the result, I did glean much satisfaction from the knowledge of what might have been. The full significance of that delivery however and umpire Hele's decision, was not really driven home to me until some years afterwards.

Later that summer the rather quiet figure of Arthur Chipperfield was introduced into the NSW team, as much for the absolutely uncanny skill he showed as a slips fieldsman as for his batting. I recall his taking a couple of excellent slips catches off my bowling when we played Queensland in Sydney, catches which, as it turned out later, probably earned him a trip to England with the Australian team of 1934. The Australian team of the time was in dire need of a quality slipper, and in that area Chipperfield had few peers.

Some years later, when my cricket career had run its course and I was increasingly becoming involved as a broadcaster, 'Chappie' Dwyer, a selector of those earlier years and an enormously influential figure in the game, explained to me that much discussion had surrounded Chipperfield's place in that 1934 team. He told me the debate had surrounded the question of whether Chipperfield or McGilvray should have had the spot.

Now, to be honest, I have to concede that I don't really believe I was good enough to make the Australian third XI of that era. There were simply too many good players, players whose stature has not been bettered to this day. Still, Dwyer's insistence that I had got so close gave me a nice feeling.

I might never have thought more of it, except for the fact that Dwyer obviously related the same story to George Hele. The information seemed to pitch George into lifelong remorse about that decision he gave against me, and in favour of Woodfull, in that very first over at the MCG. I can still remember the pained expression on George's face the first time he mentioned it to me in later years.

'Mac,' he said, mournfully. 'I'll never forgive myself. If that catch had been given you'd have been a certainty for the team. I cost you a trip to England.'

Even if there was anything in what Chappie Dwyer told George and me, I've no doubt my life was better for missing that team. Broadcasting has offered me a life in cricket my ability as a cricketer could never have made for me. I would have disappeared from the game I love many moons ago. As it is, I have been privileged as few men have been privileged to have had a deep and involved association with the game, its people and its greatness, for more than half a century.

So if George Hele felt badly about his effect on my life over that one decision, whether that effect was real or imagined, I could always say to him, as I often did: 'George, if you had given Woodfull out and I had gone to England I might never have been a broadcaster. Fate has treated me well. Thank you, George, for that decision.'

I don't think that ever really comforted George Hele, and I suspect he carried his regrets to the grave. But whether he believed it or not, I meant it. Broadcasting gave me a scope that my cricket never could.

Stan McCabe, *top left*, one of the most elegant batsmen ever to grace the international cricket stage.

Australia's premier umpire of the 'thirties, George Hele. He never forgave himself for the McGilvray decision.

Don Bradman, and a black cat for luck—the one commodity of which he had little need.

The 1936 NSW team. Back row (from left): ES White, A Cheetham. Middle row: AE Marks, LJ Fallowfield, WJ O'Reilly, LC Hynes, V Jackson, RH Robinson. Front row: AG Chipperfield, AD McGilvray (captain), CL Gentle (manager), WA Oldfield, H Mudge.

THE CAPTAIN's LOT

By the summer of 1935-36, the great NSW team of the early '30s was starting to break up. Alan Kippax had retired and Don Bradman had accepted an offer to work in Adelaide with a stockbroker and play cricket for South Australia. It was a deal to put him into the superstar class that is now so much a part of modern sport.

The Australian team had taken off for South Africa with a good section of the NSW team in it, among them Stan McCabe, who in the absence of Kippax and Bradman would surely have taken over as NSW captain. With the natural line of succession well and truly broken, the captaincy fell to me, and when McCabe returned, his health under something of a cloud, it stayed with me. It was a tremendous honour. I enjoyed captaincy and felt it was something for which I had a reasonable talent. The experiences of my school days and my early Shield cricket in which I was always a boy amongst the men, had sharpened my appreciation of how young men responded. Unfortunately I was never convinced, and nor I suspect were many others, that my form as a batsman and bowler in those years ever kept pace with my bent for captaincy. Still, it was a rich experience, and the ultimate springboard to my career in radio.

An enormous influence in my days as NSW cricket captain again was the wise counsel of the former Australian skipper M A Noble, who had taken such an interest in my school career. I doubt a match ever passed, certainly never one in Sydney, that I did not go to him and seek his ideas. To me he was a cricketing oracle, a fountain of knowledge at which I often slaked an enormous thirst. He helped me in many ways, but easily the most spectacular and most satisfying success we had was in trying to cope with the marvellous talents of Bradman.

Our first encounter with Bradman as a rival, rather than a team-mate, was in Adelaide, and it finished up very much round one to Bradman. I had injured my back early in the piece, and was confined to bed in the hotel, trussed up like a Christmas turkey. The local doctor had strapped me right around the upper body, with both arms tied to my torso so the only movement I had was from the elbows down. The pain in my back did not quite match the pain in my spirit as I listened to the radio and heard our wickets falling. We had managed 300 or so in pursuit of South Australia's 575. It became obvious we were looking at a follow-on, and the boys needed all the help they could get.

I dressed as best I could. I managed to pull on some trousers and shoes, and tossed an overcoat over my pyjama top. The boys at the ground got me into my playing gear and padded me up, and by the time I was required to bat we were only 24 runs short of the total we needed to stave off the follow-on.

It was a weird experience to bat like that, with my arms strapped to my side, but I could still play a straight defensive bat and, hopefully, my partner could pick up the few runs we needed. The straight bat worked alright against the fast-bowler Tim Wall, but the slow man Frank Ward proved more of a problem. I hadn't been there long when Bradman, who had assumed the captaincy of South Australia, walked over to Ward. I had no way of knowing what he said, of course, but Ward came on to bowl immediately and his first ball was a shoulder-high full toss. Unable to get my bat up to it, I had no way of handling that sort of ball. It fell on my stumps and we had to bat again.

Bradman came under some criticism for that delivery. Some looked upon it as a little bit tough to take advantage of my injury in that way.

I didn't see it like that. It was hardly Bradman's fault that I was injured, and he did nothing more than respond as a captain should, trying to get the best result for his team. After the day's play, I felt obliged to tell him so. He was very gracious about it all, but his switch from NSW to South Australia had obviously sharpened his competitive edge when it came to playing against NSW. It was a bit like those tennis matches of a year or two before, when winning was everything.

'Mac,' he said, with that same determined look in his eye. 'When I get to the Sydney Cricket Ground I'm going to score more runs than I have in any match this season.'

Well, I was well aware he had scored 300-plus in a game earlier that year, and his promise embodied some fairly uncomfortable prospects for us. 'I came up to congratulate you for winning this game,' I retorted, 'but I'll say this. If you're going to score 300 runs on the SCG, you'll be doing a lot of running.'

The exchange certainly inspired in me a new spur for the return game, which I brought up in conversation with Monty Noble. A plan was hatched. Since Bradman's form that season included scores of 117, 233 and 357, we knew it had to be a pretty good plan, to say the least.

Analysing the strengths and weaknesses of cricketers is a captain's job. There is always something to be attacked, some little flaw that offers a glimmer of hope even with the most accomplished players. In Bradman's case, finding a weakness was like finding the lost city of Atlantis. I doubt one really existed.

As Noble and I tried to work out what we might attack, all we could do was analyse his *modus operandi*, and hope that we could in some way take advantage of a pattern.

The best we could come up with was a feeling that Bradman was an uncertain starter. Uncertain, at least, when compared with the majesty of his batting in full flourish. I believed he always liked to get off the mark with a shot around square leg, or slightly behind it, so we reasoned we would feed that shot and try to tighten it a touch for him. But we knew we had to get him before he was ten, or we were gone.

The NSW team of that year had a fairly useful inswing bowler in Bob Hynes. He was the mainspring of our plan. We put a man at fine leg slip, and I parked myself virtually on Bradman's bat, just a yard or so away at short square leg. I knew I had no hope of catching him there, but our object was to force him to play the shot a little more finely than he normally would, and hope that the ball would do enough to give us a chance of a catch at leg slip. In the event, Hynes' first ball was a screamer, which ripped through the Bradman defence that had so thwarted the world's bowlers and caught him on the pads, dead in front.

Up went the appeal. 'Not out' came the response. Hynes was distraught. 'Mac, he was out!' he pleaded as he came back for the next delivery. Inclined as I was to offer enthusiastic agreement, I could do little else but try to keep his mind on the job. 'Remember what we planned' I said. 'Forget the last ball, work on the next.'

Down Hynes came again. Bradman shaped to flick him away as we had thought, the ball kicked on him and flew to the fine leg slip, and the mighty man was gone. It was an eerie feeling. You can make a thousand plans on the cricket field and have none of them work. And here we had Bradman for nought, according to a scenario almost identical to that worked out in Monty Noble's office.

'Well, we can dream about that 300' I said to Bradman as he headed for the pavilion. It was a fairly cheeky thing to say, and it did me no great credit. The eyes burned back at me. At the right moment those Bradman eyes carried as much power as any of his flourishing cover drives.

Not everybody shared our team's joy at Bradman's dismissal. As I left the field I was accosted by a mountain of a man who grabbed me by the shoulders and hoisted me off the ground as though I were a bag of chaff.

'I came 350 miles to see this man bat,' he complained. 'And he's out for a duck. I'll curse you lot with every turn of the wheel on the way home.'

I could offer little more comfort to him than a feeble 'sorry', and headed for the safety of the dressing room as fast as I could get there.

I felt compelled to go to Bradman and ease my conscience over what I had said to him as he left the field.

'I'm not sorry for getting you out,' I began. 'But I am sorry for what I said out there. It was not very gentlemanly, and uncalled for.' I meant it, and I'm sure Bradman knew I meant it. That little smile that says 'You're in trouble, sonny,' creased his face. 'There's always a second innings, you know' came his retort. I never had any doubt that Bradman would have scored a mountain of runs in the second innings. He believed NSW people considered him washed up, a rather curious judgment when you look at his record over the next twelve years, and he had a passionate desire to succeed spectacularly on the SCG to make his point.

Unfortunately, King George V died that day, the match was abandoned, and we escaped his retribution.

All up, I had four seasons in the NSW team, the last two of them as captain. It was, of course, a rich experience to play with and against many players whose names live on today, such was their greatness. It was also immensely gratifying to have held a position of responsibility as NSW captain at a time in the game when Australian cricket was building to one of its finest peaks.

My greatest regret of those years was that I never really achieved the heights in my own performance which my club career suggested I might, and others obviously thought I could. I always thought of myself as an above average grade cricketer, yet never really in the class of those with whom I mixed in the first class arena. Maybe there was some sort of subconscious inferiority complex there, holding me back. Or maybe I was right. Maybe I was simply not good enough.

I always thought at the time one of the reasons my career never flourished as I would have liked was the demand forced upon us by the Great Depression. My father had a footwear business which supplied many of Sydney's leading department stores. It was a good business, and one which allowed us a comfortable life. The Depression changed all that. We didn't actually go broke, but we went awfully close, and to keep afloat in the immediate post-Depression years required an enormous amount of my time, as well as my father's. We would work from 6 am to about 7 pm or 8 pm each day, and there was little scope for attending to non-survival matters like cricket practice. In that area, I was left desperately underdone. For a whole summer I laboured, telling myself that everything would come right with ten minutes' practice 'in the centre'. Unfortunately I was not very often allowed that ten minutes in my final season with the NSW team, and my form, such as it was, fell away badly.

The pressures of the family business and then my marriage had led me to a decision at the start of the 1936-37 season that it was perhaps time to concede the inevitable and retire. I mentioned it to the powers of the time. The side as a unit had done reasonably well under my captaincy the previous year, and with a considerable rebuilding underway, the selectors decided they'd like to rock the boat as little as possible. 'Keep it going for another year,' they asked.

Their encouragement, and the fact that it was the year of an England tour of Australia, were spur enough to set aside thought of retirement. Unfortunately, my cricket refused to keep pace with my ambition. The season became more of a disaster for me the further it went. I simply couldn't get an innings off the ground, and it became perfectly obvious to me, and I suspect to a good many others, that I simply did not deserve my place in the side.

Back I went to the selectors. 'Look,' I offered. 'I'm not getting any runs and it is obvious to me that I really should be dropped. I'm not arguing that, but if you are going to drop me, would you please tell me. I wouldn't like to go out on a bad note, and since you asked me to come back, I'd like the opportunity to retire if you think I should be out of the side.'

'Oh no, Mac,' they responded, with suitably horrified looks on their faces. 'We couldn't do that. We wouldn't want to drop you.'

'Well, I would like to play against England again' I conceded, and left, fairly comfortable in the security of a season ticket and a chance to play the return match against Gubby Allen's MCC side.

Not very long after that ever-so-friendly chat, I jumped on a tram in Sydney, heading for my home in the eastern suburbs. Peering over the shoulder of the man next to me, I caught the newspaper headline that told the world of changes in the NSW team to play the MCC.

'Who's out for him?' I wondered as the new names struck me. Sure enough, McGilvray had been dropped. I spent the rest of the tram ride to Waverley reflecting on a first class cricket career that had seen me on stage with the greats.

My tilts with Ponsford and Woodfull, the thrill of batting with Bradman, the kindly words of Alan Kippax, the fateful finger of George Hele, the gentle urgings of Monty Noble . . . they were all in the past. My first class career, launched just four years before with such high hopes, had come to an abrupt end.

RADIO
A NEW CAREER

The possibilities that broadcasting was offering the game of cricket had become acutely apparent through the early years of the 1930s. It offered a huge range of people, who had been denied such luxury in the past, the chance to live the game while it was actually taking place. It gave cricket and those involved in cricket a new exposure, and added a considerable new dimension to Australia's national game.

The change it was to wreak in my life certainly was beyond my imagination when I first became involved in broadcasting in the summer of 1935-36. My first experience was quite horrific.

Charles Moses, later a knight of the realm and a long term general manager of the Australian Broadcasting Commission, was the first big influence on sports broadcasting in Australia. Moses was a tremendously keen sportsman himself, a first grade Rugby forward with the Eastern Suburbs club in Sydney and long-term president of that club. He loved sport, and as the head of sports broadcasting in the early days of the ABC, he was the first really to perceive what radio offered sport and, more particularly, what sport offered radio and what radio offered the sporting public.

It was a phone call from Moses that started it all for me. The NSW Sheffield Shield team was heading off to Brisbane. It was my first year as captain and we had been doing moderately well, considering the loss of people like Bradman and McCabe, and the necessary influx of young, relatively inexperienced players. Moses had started to gather a small army of former cricket greats to provide authority for the ABC cricket broadcasts. He was not the sort of man to do anything sloppily, and he believed if the ABC was to broadcast cricket credibly, it would have to use commentators who had been through the mill. He wanted people who knew what they were talking about, and whose names and obvious experience would give instant authority to whatever they said. Former Australian captains Vic Richardson and Monty Noble were making their names as cricket broadcasters, and I suspect it was Noble who first suggested me to Moses.

For that first Brisbane trip it was obviously a matter of convenience. I was there, I was the NSW captain, and on Noble's recommendation I knew something about the game and its tactics. An end-of-day summary was a fairly harmless experiment anyway. I didn't know quite how to react to Moses' call. I had a suspicion the rather austere powers of the NSW Cricket Association might look upon the State captain moonlighting as a cricket commentator as being a little avant garde for their conservative tastes. And I certainly did not want to take on anything that would detract from my performance as a NSW player and NSW captain.

But radio was an exciting new field in which to involve oneself, and Moses was a very plausible apostle of its value. 'Why not?' I reasoned. It seemed harmless enough, not terribly time-consuming, and an experience I undoubtedly would find interesting. Besides, I thought, it's only a one-off thing. Little did I realise!

I had to do that first report from a studio in Brisbane. I was asked to sit in front of a microphone and fix my eyes on a light on the wall. When the red light went off and the green came on I was to start my report. When the green went off, and the red came on, I was to wind up, quickly. The first part offered no real problem. The green light came on and away I went. The trouble was there was no way of anticipating when the red light would light up again, and I raced through what I had to say in not very long at all.

It was a very amateurish broadcast, but at least the substance of what I had to say was reasonable, even if the manner of saying it was not. But once I had said it, I had said it, and still the green light beamed down at me. I babbled on about anything that came into my head. Goodness knows how many times I repeated myself, or contradicted myself, but I was determined I would not be caught with my mouth open, speechless and without a thought, like a small boy, stage struck at the school concert.

That broadcast lasted only a few minutes, but to me it was seemingly endless. The green light burned down at me like the work of some sadistic sorcerer, and the babble of words poured from my mouth. By the time the red light released me from my torment, my mouth was dry and I had broken out in a panic-stricken sweat. But I had done it, and it was to prove the most significant few minutes of torment in my life.

Moses obviously thought me worth some perseverance, and I continued to do after-play reports throughout the rest of that season and into the next, when Gubby Allen's MCC tourists were in Australia.

There were those who thought my involvement in broadcasting had proved a little offensive to the moguls of NSW cricket, who thought the role of State captain should be a little more distant from the public. It was hardly fitting, went the theory, to be broadcasting to the mob, while at the same time enjoying the privilege that went with the lofty perch of State captain.

I have often thought it one of the great shames of cricket that the game has encouraged that viewpoint, and in many ways distanced itself from the public. Captains who make statements to the Press are often frowned upon; players have been discouraged from, or legislated against, talking to the Press. Cricket administrators have through the ages adopted a fairly pompous and high-handed attitude to public relations, at the game's cost. The public contributes a great deal to cricket and to those who play it. They pay its way, for a start. They are entitled to consideration. The Press, and the media generally are, after all, only the means by which the game, its officials and its players, can relate to the public and as far as I am concerned, the more relating the better.

That, at any rate, was my feeling at the time. Those who considered I should not have been making those broadcasts, limited though they were, certainly never expressed their feelings to me. Had they done so I imagine I would have had to make a ticklish decision, and probably would have put my cricket first. But they didn't. I therefore never gave much truck to the theory some expounded after my demise as NSW captain that my dabbling in broadcasting had contributed to my exit. If it was a factor, it surely must have been an insignificant one. Lack of runs, I would have thought, carried a lot more weight.

Fifty years on, I look back on that start in broadcasting with some bemusement. It all just came to me, out of the blue. At no stage did I really seek to be a broadcaster. I was helping my father run the family shoe manufacturing business, and the natural order of things dictated that was where my life's work would be. But there was a challenge, an excitement, embodied in broadcasting cricket that I simply could not turn down. Looking back, I don't think it was within me to refuse that first invitation to broadcast while I was NSW captain. Nor did I consider the negatives at any great length when another invitation was forthcoming in the autumn of 1938.

This time Charles Moses' invitation embraced one of the most brilliant conceptions ever attempted in the history of broadcasting. These were the 'synthetic Tests' of 1938. Since those days cricket broadcasting has taken me to many places and offered many magic moments. The Australian team's tour in 1985 was my tenth visit to England. I have been three times to the West Indies, twice to South Africa, once to New Zealand – I have seen every series to unfold in Australia, and broadcast every day of them, since Walter Hammond's team made the first post-war visit in 1946-47. But nothing through those years could match the brilliance, the masterful improvisation and the sheer daring which those synthetic Tests embraced. They were to radio broadcasting what

Kingsford Smith's epic flights were to aviation. They required imagination and co-ordination of extraordinary depth. They demanded the pioneering spirit. They were my highest experience in broadcasting, an historic radio event. In my mind, they fell into the same category as the immortal commentary Neil Armstrong delivered from the Moon in July 1969. A few giant strides, indeed.

The 1938 tour was led by Bradman at the absolute peak of his powers. It was a time in Australian sporting history when cricket was truly the national game. Bradman was a folk hero. Everybody was interested in what he was doing, and what his Australian team was doing. And it was still the time of Empire, when Britain was very much the Motherland. Australian school children started each day with a hearty rendition of 'God Save the King', and nobody grew up without knowing the words of 'Rule Britannia'. The nation looked upon England as a benevolent parent. The brash and independent spirit which has enveloped Australia in recent times had not yet manifested itself to the extent that the populace as a whole could shed the feeling of inferiority that still existed in relations with England.

One important part of life in which that feeling could be set aside, however, was on the cricket field. We had long since established ourselves fairly handy competitors in that area, and with Bradman in charge, the Australian public as a whole was very much behind our team's effort to give England what we all assumed would be a healthy spanking.

Moses well realised all this. The ABC had been established to fill public need and he was determined to feed that public interest in the most spectacular way possible.

Radio of the day was not sufficiently advanced technically to rely on direct broadcast from England. Short wave transmissions were occasionally receivable, but they had not at that stage developed procedures to bounce the signal off the ionosphere with any reliability. Moses decided we had to do something ourselves. His *modus operandi* was to establish a commentary team in the ABC studios in Market Street, Sydney, who would re-create what was going on in England.

Their information would be provided by a cable service specially provided from England. The effect would be the same. The commentators would describe the scene as if they were watching with their own eyes. The only thing that would be different was the fact that the eyes had to be on the other side of the world. Those eyes belonged to Eric Sholl, an ABC employee with an eye for detail who worked in the Sydney office.

He was despatched to send back the cables according to an elaborate code. Outside our studio, a team of five or six decoders would put the cables into readable form from which the commentators would operate. The cables covered everything we would need to paint a word picture of what was happening. Sholl would tell us about the weather, the crowd – even the traffic getting to the ground.

He would keep us totally informed as to where every player was on the field. Any time the field changed, he would fire off a new cable, and each over, he would send a cable with a complete run down on every ball—where it pitched, what the batsman did, where the ball went, who fielded . . . absolutely everything.

In the studio, every possible step was taken to set up an atmosphere for the commentators. A large photograph of the ground, for instance, was suspended in front of us so we had a mental picture of the scene, and the best chance possible for adding some colour into our broadcast. There were four commentators involved, Vic Richardson, Monty Noble, Hal Hooker and myself. Richardson and Noble had been to England, so they could identify with each of the grounds. Hooker was a fine Sheffield Shield player, but never quite made the international arena.

Since Vic and Monty knew the scene best, we left most of the background descriptions to them. Vic knew where all the cathedrals were, what the pavilions were like, where the noisy section of the crowd would congregate. But if we were stuck, there was always that faithful photograph to fall back on.

We had a scorer and a records man, who could keep track of events and turn up whatever figures we needed to kick things along. And there was the all-important sound effects man.

He had a series of recordings which would provide the applause and crowd noises. We had to make a quick judgment as to whether a shot was a good one or not, whether a player would be loudly cheered as he left the field or mildly applauded, whether the crowd would take umbrage at an umpire's decision. Accordingly we would signal the sound effects man for wild cheering, loud applause, booing or gentle clapping, depending on how we thought it would be.

How closely we judged the scene we could never know. But after a time the sound effects man was an artist at what he did, and in all my experience of international cricket I doubt I have ever known a crowd more animated than that which Australians knew through the England tour of 1938.

The most basic sound effect of all we provided ourselves. This was the charismatic crack of leather on willow, the marvellous ring of bat on ball that has so enraptured cricket followers through the generations.

This we provided with a pencil. A spanking drive through the covers, hit with a presumed high back lift and a poultice of flourish, would require a very firm bang on a round piece of wood on the table. Defensive taps and more gentle strokes were handled with appropriately proportional force. This led to occasional difficulty. Sometimes our enthusiasm to describe the shot meant we would have told the world all about it, suddenly remembered the pencil, and had the crack of the stroke arriving somewhat belatedly. Other times the effects man would get in first with the crowd cheering before the shot came. Co-ordinating mind, voice and pencil through some long and arduous innings must have been every bit as hard as coping with Farnes, Verity and Co, as our batsmen were doing.

Sound effects were not the only area in which our enthusiasm initially made it tough for us. The information we were fed came at the end of each over, covering that over in entirety. We would work our way through the six balls, then look for the new cable and the new over.

At first, we were finding an extraordinary delay between the end of an over as we described it and the next cable.

'Where's the telegram?' we would plead as we thrust ourselves into long and arduous fill-in chatter, sometimes to take up several minutes.

Some simple arithmetic eventually forced on me the realisation that I was whipping through in two minutes an over that the bowler in England was taking four minutes to bowl. Since the cables couldn't come any quicker than the balls were being bowled, we soon learned to take more notice of our stop watch and spread each over to more realistic lengths.

But the mistakes and the rough patches were surprisingly few. As we grew accustomed to this rather revolutionary method of describing a cricket match, we became extremely polished at it. We got faster as time went on, and in the end I think it was every bit as colourful and comprehensive as the real thing became in later years.

The key to everything of course, was the information with which we were supplied and the slick work of those who decoded it. The raw cables, sent at the end of each over, were masterpieces of improvisation.

A typical cable would begin: 'BRIGHTENING FLEETWOOD HAMMOND FULL FIRSTLY TWO HASSETT SECONDLY FULL FOUR STRAIGHT UNCHANCE BOWLER THIRDLY NO BALL FULL TWO OFFDRIVEN RUN APPEAL HUTTON FOURTHLY FOUR SWEPT BOWLER KEEPER OFFPUSHED.'

The decoders would get hold of that, and the message would come into us in slightly fuller form.

First of all we would establish that the weather was brightening and Fleetwood-Smith was the bowler. 'HAMMOND FULL FIRSTLY TWO HASSETT' would come back 'Hammond batting, first ball pitched up, driven, Hassett fielded, ran two'.

Then the cable continued, 'SECONDLY FULL FOUR STRAIGHT UNCHANCE BOWLER'. That would be interpreted as the second was full length to Hammond, driven straight but uppishly past the bowler for four. Almost a chance.

So we would work off that information, add a touch of atmosphere, try to imagine the scene, and come up with something like this:

'In comes Fleetwood-Smith, he moves in to bowl to Hammond and Hammond comes down the wicket and takes it on the full and he drives it beautifully past Hassett who moves around behind the ball and fields brilliantly just before it reaches the boundary rope, and meantime they've run through for two.'

The second ball we'd read: 'HAMMOND, FLEETWOOD-SMITH, FULL TOSS, UPPISH STRAIGHT DRIVE, ALMOST CHANCE, FOUR.'

We'd get that out something like this: 'Hammond again moves down the wicket and hits him beautifully past the bowler. My word, that carried. That was almost in the hands of Fleetwood-Smith, but it went just past him and although he put a hand out he didn't get near it and it raced past him for four. But it was certainly past him round about knee high.'

A fair bit of imagination was called for, although we were desperately careful not to be so carried away as to significantly risk the accuracy of the reports.

A cable which read 'HAMMOND SWEPT BARNES FOUR' might end up, 'Hammond sweeps him. He's really got on to that one and Barnes is tearing around the boundary to cut it off, but I don't think he'll get it, and he doesn't, and the ball just beats him over the boundary rope for four.'

Barnes' race around the boundary, of course, would be greeted with some enthusiasm by our sound effects man, who would bring an excited cheer from the crowd, reaching its peak as we nominated the boundary. He really became quite expert at producing a crowd reaction fitting for each event, and timed to perfection.

We could operate with quite remarkable efficiency on fairly skeletal information. We always knew where everybody was in the field, for instance, so with brief information on the rough direction of a shot we could assume a likely scenario as far as the fieldsmen were concerned. And the advantage of having men like Richardson and Noble involved, men who knew their cricket and their cricketers backwards, was that they could read the game with singular clarity.

Their knowledge of how the Australian players, particularly, thought and performed, their habits and their idiosyncracies, allowed them to gauge reactions and assume trends of play with extraordinary accuracy.

There were, however, times when we were confronted with absolute disaster. Occasionally the flow of cables from the Post Office would be interrupted for one reason or another. When the delays were long we would simply announce a loss of communication and cease operations until they resumed.

But when the loss of contact was brief, or while we thought it would be brief, we tried to tough it out. We might slip in a few balls to mark time. We were always careful in such crises, however, never to advance the score beyond what we knew it to be. Any of these 'fill-in' deliveries would of necessity be insignificant, 'back-to-the-bowler' stuff.

And we filled the gaps with some of the most horrendous discussion. We used to get quite animated. We would be locked in heavy discussion and quite lively argument on subjects that were only imagined.

'He really should be moving forward to those deliveries that are pitched up to him and having a bit of a go' Vic might offer. 'Well, I don't know about that Vic' I would reply. 'The bowling's pretty tight and I think the batsmen are quite right in being cautious and taking their time.' The verbal battle would ensue. We would argue the point hammer

COMMONWEALTH OF AUSTRALIA—POSTMASTER-GENERAL'S DEPARTMENT

RECEIVED TELEGRAM

URGENT RATE

TELEPHONED

TO .... No. ....

TIME 10.26½

BY R.Y.

CHIEF TELEGRAPH OFFICE · SYDNEY · 22AU38

... QUICKLY SAFELY AND ... TRANSFERRED BY MONEY ORDER TELEGRAM (PLEASE TURN OVER)

The first line of this telegram contains the following particulars in the order named

... of Origin 46/46 Words. Time Lodged.

Sch. C1672. 11/1936.

ATEST, SYDNEY

... message has been received subject to the Post and Telegraph Act and Regulations.

... received at this Office is shown at the end of the message

... the date both of lodgment and of reception ... shown after the particulars of time lodged.

To

AUSTRALIAN BROADCASTING COMMISSION
SYDNEY

BRIGHTENING FLEETWOOD HAMMOND FIRSTLY FULL 2 HASSETT SECONDLY FULL 4 STRAIGHT UNCHANCE BOWLER THIRDLY NOBALL FULL 2 OFFDRIVEN RUNAPPEAL HUTTON FOURTHLY 4 SWEPT BOWLER KEEPER OFFPUSHED

10-26 PM WB

Message	Over	Bowler
46	34	Fleetwood Smith

Ball	Batsman	Where Hit	Fielded	Score	Comments
1	Hammond	full toss off drive - Hassett		2	Chasing fields brilliantly
2	"	full toss - uppish straight drive		4	Almost a catch to bowler
3	"	full toss - NO BALL - off drive - Hassett		2	appeal for run out against Hutton at bowler's wicket
4	"	Swept past Barnes over fence		4	at deep square leg
5	"	Back to Bowler		—	
6	"	Keeper.			
7		played slowly to cover - McCabe -			

REMARKS: Weather Brightening

The synthetic Tests were a masterpiece of pioneer broadcasting. The cables would come in from England, *top*, be deciphered and interpreted and passed on to the commentary team.

The commentary team had a photograph of the ground for atmosphere and a scoreboard for realism.

and tongs, completely oblivious to the fact that neither of us really knew how the batsmen were approaching it, or whether the bowling was good, bad or indifferent. But we became so involved in the broadcasts we almost convinced ourselves we were there. It is quite amazing how the mind and the imagination can take over completely in such circumstances.

Charles Moses fed this line by brain-washing us as much as possible into feeling like we were there. He insisted, for instance, that we lived the nights as if they were balmy English summer days. We kicked off at 8.30 pm Sydney time each evening, and were required to take morning tea at 9.30 pm.

Moses insisted we had 'lunch' at 10.30 pm. Lunch would be sandwiches, fruit, etc, as if we were schoolboys and our mothers had packed them for us. Moses monitored everything, shaping our attitudes and our approach to the point that, in the end, whether we were in Manchester or Sydney made precious little difference.

Only rarely did it go badly wrong. I recall one occasion when the cable came through identifying one of the Australians simply as 'MC'. There were two 'Macs' in the Australian team, Stan McCabe and Ernie McCormick, and at this particular time both were batting.

The cable came through announcing that 'MC' was out. Which 'MC', of course, we had no way of knowing. I quickly switched off the mike and looked at Vic.

'Who'll I give it to?' I pleaded.

'Oh, give it to Stan' Vic responded. 'He's got his hundred and he'll be throwing the bat at anything.'

In I plunged. 'McCabe steps into the drive. He's lofted it . . . it's in the air and I think he's gone, yes he's out, McCabe is out. And what a glorious innings it was.'

On I trekked into the unknown, rolling along valiantly as the picture unfolded in my mind. I described McCabe's standing ovation. I had him clapped all the way to the pavilion. The sound effects man had a field day.

Then came the next cable. It was McCormick who had gone, not McCabe.

I could do nothing but launch into abject apology. I explained exactly how the error occurred. It was one of the more embarrasing moments of my broadcasting career, but explaining the error quickly and honestly served only to enhance the credibility of the broadcasts.

The ABC, and Moses in particular, were concerned that there should be no dishonesty involved. We were seeking only to inform in as colourful a manner as possible, not to 'con' people into believing the commentaries were the real thing.

That particular error was made infinitely worse by the fact that the innings I so prematurely ended is remembered to this day as one of the finest innings ever played in Test cricket. It was the first Test of that series, when our broadcasting techniques were far from finely tuned. It was played at Trent Bridge, Nottingham, and McCabe's final scoreline read, c Compton, bowled Verity, 232. So stunning was the performance that his skipper, Bradman, still recalls it as the finest innings he ever saw.

Bradman was so enthralled at the time that he went to the dressing room and summoned the whole Australian team to the verandah. 'Come and watch this,' he demanded. 'You will never see anything like this again.'

Of all the innings I could have picked to make a mistake and end prematurely, it had to be this one. It was the only really calamitous error we made through the whole of the synthetic Tests exercise. In many ways it was sheer bad luck, for the whole operation was geared to be scrupulously honest.

We still received plenty of derisive letters, complaining that the ABC should not involve itself in such transparent nonsense.

But Moses was determined the broadcasts be appreciated for what they were and arranged to have a film made, to show the world how it was done through the newsreels of the time. The whole studio was transported to the Movietone News studios where we staged a typical broadcast for the benefit of the cameras. We went through the whole routine, pencil taps and all. In the end our acceptance in the public mind was almost total.

It wasn't hard to prove the point. Vic Richardson was a man who was always one for a bit of a laugh. Occasionally, when we were not on the air, we would wander down to one of the radio shops that operated in the city in those days and mix with the small crowds who would occasionally stop to listen to the broadcasts for a time. Vic and I would join them to gauge reaction as Hal Hooker and Monty Noble carried on the commentary.

On one occasion Vic almost started a riot. 'What a lot of nonsense,' he said, loud enough for everyone to hear. 'They can't really expect us to believe any of this rubbish.'

Australia were doing rather well at the time, and it became obvious to me that the small band of devotees listening was fairly emotionally involved in the Australian progress and the broadcast bringing it to them. The fact that it was emanating from a room a few hundred yards up the road didn't seem to matter.

'Why don't you shut your trap?' came the retort from a rather portly lady, whose love of cricket obviously rode roughshod over minor irritations like manufactured broadcasts. 'Surely you know this is all made up' Vic came back. 'Surely you don't believe it.'

It was only quick action on my part that got Vic out of there ahead of a posse, simultaneously flailing umbrellas and enunciating the marvels of modern cricket commentary.

They were hard nights through the winter of 1938. On the rare occasions reception was good enough to take a direct broadcast from England, we would steal a catnap, in a chair or under the table. When the signal faded, we would be quickly roused to continue. It was a tough, extremely tiring experience. But it was magic. It was broadcasting as an art form. We learned lessons through that experience that have lasted to set the standards of cricket broadcasting ever since.

It was a pioneering adventure that left no doubt in my mind where my future lay.

CHAMPIONS OF THE AIR

Victor York Richardson was one of the finest sportsmen Australia has ever produced. He was captain of South Australia at cricket and Australian Rules football and represented his State at hockey and baseball as well. He was a very handy lacrosse player, very nearly unbeatable at tennis, and dabbled at boxing, where he handled himself pretty well, too. He always reckoned he would even have been OK at polo, but for the fact he never owned a horse!

He was also a consummate cricket broadcaster, perhaps the first of the great ones. He lent knowledge and understanding to his commentaries, tinged with a humour and wit that typified the Australian nature. With the former England captain Arthur Gilligan he formed a commentary team that became immortal. 'Vic and Arthur' became a catchcry of Australian cricket through the 'forties and 'fifties that made surnames totally irrelevant.

'What do you think, Arthur?' was the lead-in to a never-ending torrent of arguments and discussions that seemingly knew no bounds. They captured a nation and held it spell-bound through the glorious days of Bradman and Hammond, Brown and Bedser, Miller and Lindwall and a small army of the game's champions.

It was my privilege to be able to rub shoulders with Vic and Arthur for many years from the time I began cricket commentary on a regular basis in the summer of 1946-47.

World War II had left the world hungry for relief from the pain of six hard, cold years, and for Australians and Englishmen what better vehicle for joy and celebration than a Test cricket series? The combination of Richardson and Gilligan fed that hunger, not only through that series of 1946-47, but for many years thereafter. My life was enriched by tagging along with them, and forging with them and their wives the deep and lasting friendships that life offers only rarely.

Vic's career in Test cricket started in 1924 and finished in 1936. He scored his only century in 1925 against England, and was in and out of the side throughout his career. He was in the thick of Bodyline in 1932-33. From batting in the middle order he was promoted to opener for the fourth Test when the horrors of Bodyline had taken their toll, and contributed a gutsy 83 at a time when there were suggestions the tour should be cancelled.

For any of those involved, Bodyline was a highly emotive subject when it came up for discussion in later years. Vic saw it as a bloody and bitter feud that cut deep across the cricketing ethic on which the game as a whole set its store in those years.

'It ruined the Test series,' he used to say, 'and it completely undermined the goodwill and spirit that had existed between the teams.' For Vic that was only the start of it. 'Bodyline Tests were horrible, but they weren't the real problem' he would say. 'The real problem was that that sort of behaviour became acceptable. Kids started to copy it; it became the thing to do, and that harmed the game terribly.'

Vic had a theory that Douglas Jardine, the England captain of the time, was not Bodyline's prime motivator. He laid a lot of the blame on Herbert Sutcliffe, the long-serving England opening batsman.

'Often Harold Larwood would bowl a couple of orthodox deliveries, and without any recourse to their captain, Sutcliffe and Walter Hammond would simply walk into the leg trap positions,' Richardson recalled.

'That left Harold no option but to bowl Bodyline. They packed the legside field and bowled at your head and body. You had to defend yourself or get hit and in defending yourself, of course, you risked getting out. Actually, I called it Headline. That's where it was aimed.

'There was another occasion in Sydney when it became obvious to me that Sutcliffe was doing a lot of the captaining. I was out for a duck on the last ball of the first over. As I was walking off, the ball was thrown to Gubby Allen, who refused to bowl the Bodyline stuff. Sutcliffe walked straight up to Gubby and pinched the ball off him and threw it to Bill Voce. Bradman was in next, and there was no way they were going to bowl orthodox to him. It was Bodyline straight off. And it was Sutcliffe, not Jardine, who seemed to be calling the shots.'

The Australian captain of the time was Bill Woodfull. He was an immensely strong individual with a very high sense of duty and a keen appreciation of right and wrong. He stood up to Bodyline and he copped it. But he refused point blank to give it back. In his mind, two wrongs did not make a right. He once told the English manager Pelham 'Plum' Warner, who tried to apologise for the manner in which his team played, that 'one team out here is playing cricket and one is not'. Woodfull was determined that his team would play cricket.

Vic, whose competitive profile was as high as any man in the team, subscribed to a rather different view. His was the more urbane ethic which said if a man hits you, you must hit him back. It was a principle he had applied through countless Adelaide football matches, and one which was forged from the purity of the Australian character.

I once asked Vic how he would have handled Bodyline had he been in charge of the team.

'Well, I had enormous respect for Bill Woodfull, and we were very much behind him in the strong and steadfast manner in which he stuck to his convictions,' Vic confided. 'But I would have thrown it right back at them straight away, and I doubt that Bodyline would have lasted five minutes. In fact I know it wouldn't have. Herbert Sutcliffe and Walter Hammond both told me later there is no way they would have played under those conditions. They said they wouldn't have lasted ten minutes.'

Appalled as he was at the concept of Bodyline and the damage it did the noble game, Vic could never bring himself to totally condemn the Englishmen for it.

'They had watched Don Bradman murder them in England in 1930, and they came up with Bodyline as the means of winning' he said. 'They did nothing against the laws of cricket, even if they ignored its spirit.'

The Englishmen, however, well knew the likely result of their tactics. When Richardson went to Perth to meet Jardine's team at the start of the tour he engaged fast-bowler Bill Voce in innocent conversation with a simple inquiry about what sort of team they had.

'Well, if we don't beat you, we'll knock your bloody blocks off' came the reply. Sadly, they managed to do both.

Vic always considered, too, he was within an ace of killing Bodyline before it had really started. It was the first Test in Sydney and, after a 'trial run' against an Australian XI in Melbourne, the first serious workout Jardine's men had given their new strategy. Stan McCabe scored a glorious 187 not out against tremendous odds in that match, and Vic Richardson stuck it out with him for a fifth wicket partnership of 129.

'I got out for 49 at a time when we were getting on top of things.' Vic recalled years later. 'Had I stayed there a while longer, I think we might have cracked Bodyline. We might have killed it stone dead.'

As it was, England won that match by ten wickets, and the die had been cast for Australia's summer of infamy.

Richardson's strength and his leadership qualities saw him captain of Australia briefly in the summer of 1935-36, when he led the team to South Africa and returned with four massive victories and a draw. Bradman missed that tour because of illness, but took over from Vic as captain of South Australia and Australia the next season.

The last match of that South African tour lasted only two days, in which 694 runs were scored and 30 wickets fell. That was the way Vic played it.

He was aggressive and competitive, intolerant of fools, brusque and

The pioneering team of cricket commentators Arthur Gilligan, Alan McGilvray and Vic Richardson, with their wives. A team in every possible way.

Vic Richardson . . . a great sportsman and the greatest of the early commentators.

Johnny Moyes, *below*, who became such a household name in Australian cricket through the 'fifties and 'sixties, with Ray Lindwall.

Alan McGilvray with Brian Johnston, an entertainer in every sense, to the tips of his two-tone shoes.

Lindsay Hassett and Alan McGilvray . . . a formidable team at the microphone.

distant to many, but as loyal and as straight as it is possible to be. Some of those traits were later evident in his grandsons Ian Chappell, who became one of the great Australian captains, and Greg, who succeeded Ian as captain and went on to topple Bradman as Australia's greatest run-getter. Curiously, for all the straight-forwardness of his nature, I don't ever recall hearing Vic swear. His grandsons were a little less restrained in that area.

Vic's cricket came to an end after the South African tour of 1935-36. When the team returned they played a match on the Sydney Cricket Ground against an Australian XI captained by Don Bradman. It was a special fixture organised as a testimonial to former champions Warren Bardsley and Jack Gregory, and also as a tribute to the deeds of Vic's team in South Africa, which had done so marvellously well. We all knew it was Vic's last appearance in the Australian side, and perhaps his farewell appearance in first class cricket.

I played in Bradman's team that day, and fielded in the gully when the Australian side started its first innings. Vic opened the innings, and in the very first over, when that dreaded nought was still against his name, he steered a catch straight to me. These were days before I had done any broadcasting with Vic, but through the good graces of my first State captain, Alan Kippax, I had got to know Vic Richardson pretty well. I also had great respect for him. Most of the country did. He was a fair cricketer but an enormous man, one of those hard, strong, unshakeable types on whom the spirit of Anzac had been built.

It certainly did not seem right that his great career in top cricket should end with a duck in a testimonial match, particularly when he was still in charge of a fine Australian team.

I made a few quick decisions as that ball flew to me in the gully and decided he deserved a more fitting farewell. I deliberately dropped the catch. It was the only time I ever put a catch down on purpose. Bradman wasn't entirely sold on the idea, despite the circumstances.

'You dropped that deliberately, didn't you?' he inquired at the end of the over. I don't think he was really too upset, but he was the next Australian captain and he was determined to play the captain's role to the full. No mucking about, no matter what. I don't think I confessed anything to him, but I finished up doing a lot of running from third man to fine leg, nevertheless. The irony was it was no help to Vic. He still got a duck.

It had been the Sydney Cricket Ground where I first ran into Vic Richardson at the start of my Sheffield Shield career a few years earlier. He was a well entrenched Test player at that time, of course, and a man to be feared.

Kippax put me at silly mid-on to the first over of the South Australian innings. It was horribly close to the bat, I suppose, but not a position any different to that in which a thousand fieldsmen have placed themselves down the years.

Vic didn't find it acceptable.

'Nick off, lad,' he ordered. I stood my ground and said nothing. 'Did you hear what I said? Nick off!'

Still I stood my ground, offering a few nervous glances at my skipper, who showed no signs of rescuing me.

Down came the first ball. It was a little short and Vic jumped into it with relish. It screamed past mid-on with such power it hit the members' gate on the full, without ever gathering a great deal of height. When I worked out the angles later, some simple geometry put the flight path about an inch wide of my left ear.

Kippax walked over to me, full of the milk of human kindness. 'Perhaps you had better move back a pace or two, Sandy,' he offered.

Vic Richardson's strength and toughness were evident many times during our time together as broadcasters. He once rescued some teenage girls who were receiving unwanted attention from ten young hoodlums on an Adelaide beach. Vic engaged all ten in a few feet of water, and kept them occupied for the best part of twenty minutes while the police were summoned. He took a bit of a battering, but not one of the ten got the better of him, and all ten were present and accounted for when the police arrived to round them up.

He was marvellously dedicated to his broadcasting. He insisted on quality, he insisted on punctuality, yet he still had the free spirit to joke and make fun and add a very human touch to his commentary.

Charles Moses once put it into very sharp focus for me. 'McGilvray,' he said. 'Don't insult the public by trying to make jokes on air. Leave that to Vic. He has a sense of humour. You do it straight, and he can provide the light touches.'

Vic was also very good at plucking stories from the past and keeping everybody entertained during long hours of nothing. We had to accommodate Radio Australia, which had a world audience of millions, and the ABC was so locked into programming arrangements that occasionally we would have to keep our commentary going even when play had been washed out.

I recall one occasion in Brisbane when rain prevented the start of play. The teams had not been finalised, the toss had not been made—absolutely nothing at all had happened. Yet we were required to talk for forty minutes for the benefit of Radio Australia. After much pondering Vic and I decided we would talk about whether the batting captain should take a heavy roller or a light roller. It was about the only subject offering. We tossed for sides. I came down tails, so I argued the case for a light roller. Vic argued for the heavy roller. The debate raged. We got so involved in it we convinced ourselves of our arguments, spurious though they were. It was heated, involved debate.

When we had just about canvassed every possibility a dozen times Arthur Gilligan came into the box and Vic seized on him for quick relief with that famous line, 'What do you think, Arthur?'

'Well, I don't think I'd use a roller at all' came Gilligan's reply.

We had gasbagged for forty minutes of highly creative discussion without even considering that possibility.

There were many times in those halcyon days when broadcasting cricket was a hair-raising business. Often we would have to do our summaries from the city studios of the ABC. The Commission operated to a very rigid format. Timing was precise, tolerance almost unheard of. That post-match summary would often involve a breathtaking dash through town. Once, in Melbourne, Vic and I were still hurtling up Bourke Street, like a couple of Olympic sprinters, as the studio announcer began his introduction.

'And now,' he began, 'with their comments on the Test match between Australia and England at the MCG . . .'

About that stage we burst into the front door and attacked the stairs. ' . . . are Victor Richardson and Alan McGilvray'. It was somewhere about the 'and Alan McGilvray' part that we made the studio door and grabbed our seats. We were breathless and speechless. There followed two minutes of monosyllabic questions followed by monosyllabic answers. This buying of time embraced much heavy breathing as we regained our composure. But we had made it.

Vic rarely let his discipline drop. There was however, one occasion through the synthetic broadcasts of 1938 when a day's golf had been washed out and replaced by a hefty attack on a Scotch bottle at the golf club bar. 'Well it was raining, and I didn't think there'd be any play' was Vic's cheeky excuse when he arrived that night, obviously at the end of a big day. The fact that the rain was in Sydney and the cricket in London was, of course, irrelevant. Vic was dispatched to the ABC canteen, where he attacked an horrific meal of bread dipped in Worcestershire sauce. It was guaranteed, he declared, to get anybody going again.

For a man so devoted to his cricket, Vic Richardson hated talking about it after a long day at the microphone. He struck a very firm arrangement with me that once our broadcasting was done, cricket was taboo. We would have a meal, play snooker, drink . . . it didn't matter what we were doing, cricket was not to be discussed.

So determined was he about this that a fines system was set up whereby either of us found guilty of talking about cricket once we had left the ground would forfeit two shillings to a lottery ticket fund.

Vic would then send all manner of people over to me to ask what I thought of the pitch, or how many Bradman would get today, or whatever. Politeness demanded that I answer, as Vic knew it would. One Test match he launched such an attack upon me in this way it cost me more than £10—caught 100 times.

Victor Richardson was a man apart. His stature, his presence and his strength of character shone through in everything he did. He would have derived enormous pleasure had he lived to see the success of his two grandsons, though he would have claimed no credit. You could see a bit of Vic in each of the Chappell brothers. Ian had been a few years in the Australian team but was two years short of his captaincy term when Vic died in 1969. Greg had not quite made the Australian team at that stage, but was proving a very handy young Shield player. Whenever Vic was asked if his coaching had become an influence in the emerging career of the young Chappells, he would respond with a very sharp 'No'. They were the architects of their own lives, he would maintain. He didn't interfere with them. But they could hardly have missed his example.

Victor Richardson was a king of South Australian sport, a significant influence in a mighty era of Australian cricket, and a master pioneer broadcaster. Arthur Gilligan was a natural foil for him. He was the epitome of the English gentleman. Quiet, considerate, polite and exceedingly proper, he exuded a warmth that glowed. He didn't have the same direct, forthright manner that was Richardson's hallmark. His character was more mellow, his manner full of reason and understanding. He had a quiet assurance about him and an enormous presence. His knowledge of cricket, and his ability to encapsulate it and express it, were extraordinary.

The two personalities complemented each other splendidly. Their balance was very much part of their success. Arthur was as thoroughly English as Vic was Australian.

My passion for cricket had been born at the Sydney Cricket Ground in 1924 when Arthur Gilligan captained England against Herbie Collins' Australian side. I did not miss a ball of that Test, and the vision of Gilligan and Collins tossing for choice of innings is as vivid in my mind now as it was sixty-odd years ago. It was sheer magic in later years to meet and play with or against most of those men. Men like Collins, Bardsley, Ponsford, Taylor, Richardson, Kellaway, Hendry, Gregory, Oldfield and Mailey. Great men.

But there was something special about the day in Melbourne in 1947 when Arthur Gilligan made his way to the broadcasting box for the third Test between Bradman's team and Hammond's team. He had held in my mind the aura that schoolboys so often associate with their sporting heroes, and to broadcast with him was a considerable event in my life.

Rarely does the reality conform with the images built from schoolboy idolatry. But in Gilligan's case, the quality of the man exceeded anything my mind could have imagined. We broadcast twenty-five England-Australia Tests together, and built a bond in our commentary team that must have come across in the descriptions. Arthur, Vic and I were fortunate that our wives—Penny Gilligan, Peg Richardson and my own late wife, Gwen—became such firm friends as well. It was a special bond that only cricket, as the catalyst, could provide.

Arthur was probably the inspiration for the friendliness that existed between us. He insisted we were a team. Whatever we did, we did as a unit. Examples of his kindliness were legion. He once organised the Sydney Cricket Ground Trust to erect a tent on the SCG no 2 oval and play host to the blind and partially blind of the two World Wars. He knew there was a small army of people, whose sight had failed them for one reason or another and for whom our radio descriptions were the only way their love of cricket could be satisfied.

Arthur organised two shifts. The World War I veterans on one day, the World War II veterans on another. He appealed over the air for people with cars to pick them up, bring them to the ground, and return them home. He organised extensive hospitality from the SCG Trust, and rounded up players from both sides to present themselves when they were not involved in the play to rub shoulders with the blind people. When Keith Miller, Ray Lindwall and Denis Compton turned up, there was pandemonium. Quite a few blind men staggered out of the SCG on those days very happy, and very obviously so.

Gilligan had had a fairly tough war. He was heavily involved administratively with the Royal Air Force in defending Britain through the darkest days of the German Luftwaffe's onslaught. He had an abiding respect for those who had fought, and those who had suffered.

It was a common event through that tour of 1946-47 for Arthur to round up Vic and myself around 8.30 in the morning and take us off to a veterans' hospital. In the immediate postwar years there were some very sick and sorry boys in those hospitals, and their delight in having Vic and Arthur visit them had to be seen to be believed. They obviously identified with them very closely through the radio cricket descriptions.

Arthur's insistence on this type of community involvement was very much part of his nature, and won him enormous respect with the Australian public at large. At home he was no different. On my first visit to England in 1948 I spent a lovely evening at his home in Sussex.

I was fascinated by the letterbox. Arthur had a family of finches nesting in it. He nurtured those finches as if they were part of the family. The postman was politely asked not to use the letterbox while the finches were in residence, and had to make a considerable trek up the drive to deliver the letters by hand to the front door. So simple a kindness touched me to the extent that I tried to repeat the procedure in my own garden back in Sydney. Unfortunately I could not get the birds to co-operate.

Arthur was not without his impish touches. There was one occasion when Vic Richardson tied himself in knots trying to describe an over from Ernie Toshack to Cyril Washbrook. It came out 'Toshbrook to Washack'. Arthur took up the challenge with a Spoonerism or two of his own. Then came the telegrams by the thousands. We had sharvellous mots that produced bine foundaries, we had exquisite fatsmen whose strokes were too good for the bieldsmen. We had Bradser carving up Bedman. On and on they went.

The listening public saw it as some sort of contest. Eventually the Post Office came to us and asked us to call a halt. Much as they wanted the business, the decoding required to make any sense of the telegrams was taking up too much of their time. Things were grinding to a halt.

Vic and Arthur declared a truce, and we called 'enough' to the wild imaginings of our public.

Many commentators of real quality have graced the airwaves since cricket became a popular vehicle for serving sport to the masses, but none could match the particular place that Victor Richardson and Arthur Gilligan will always hold in the history of sport on radio.

THE COMMENTATORS

Since the days of Richardson and Gilligan, I have worked with a series of outstanding broadcasters. Men like Johnny Moyes and Lindsay Hassett, England's John Arlott, Brian Johnston and Christopher Martin-Jenkins, and many more. They were all different; they all had their peculiar strengths, but each of them added his own significant touch to a grand broadcasting era.

As a commentator I relied a great deal on the skills of the summarisers with whom I worked, the experts whose experience and knowledge bring the game to life for the listener. Having been brought up on the expertise of men like M A Noble and Arthur Gilligan, I well knew their importance.

In Australia I was fortunate to form very close partnerships with Johnny Moyes and Lindsay Hassett, and, in more recent times, Norman O'Neill and Max Walker. In England men like Freddie Trueman and Trevor Bailey were also a delight to work with, and they put their own particular stamp on radio cricket.

Moyes and Hassett were hard to beat. Both were very conversational in their style, easy to listen to and authoritative. Both were insistent on a team approach. We lived a lot of our lives together on tour, and I became firm friends with each of them. That in itself was a little curious, considering a dispute in which we became involved in the early 'fifties.

It surrounded the first Test of the 1952-53 series against South Africa in Brisbane. The Victorian off-spinner Ian Johnson was in the side and was asked to bowl 30 overs in the second innings of a match Australia eventually won by 96 runs. Doug Ring, another well-performed spinner of the time, had only 17 overs in the late stages and was virtually neglected.

Johnny Moyes made the comment that it wouldn't be Hassett's fault if Johnson didn't make the 1953 tour to England. Johnson had bowled for a very long time when others perhaps should have had a chance, and it was a natural enough conclusion to draw that such exposure in front of the national selectors could do his touring chances no harm.

Rather innocently, I supported Moyes. 'I fully agree, Johnny,' was all I said, and the matter dropped as the Test match continued.

Now there were those who considered Hassett was bowling Johnson more for Johnson's sake than the team's. I'm still not sure if Johnny Moyes considered it a deliberate ploy but whether the remark was an innocent conclusion to draw or not, it certainly raised the hackles of both Hassett and Johnson. They were, after all, both Victorians, both members of the South Melbourne Club, both long-term Australian players, and pretty good mates.

Their wrath did not become known to me until some weeks later when I was summoned to the office of the ABC General Manager, along with Johnny Moyes, to explain ourselves in the presence of Charles Moses and his deputy, 'Huck' Finlay. Sitting on the table in front of them was a very sinister-looking writ, filed by the South Melbourne Club in support of Hassett and Johnson, and claiming slander and defamation and all sorts of terrible things.

The ABC had worked out a simple solution. We would make heartfelt apology on the air, and that would be the end of it.

'No way ' said Johnny.

'Me either' I concurred. Johnny Moyes had been the news editor of a metropolitan newspaper in Sydney and was a very strong-willed man. He knew right from wrong, he knew truth from fiction, and he had an unswerving belief that he should stand by anything he said if he knew it to be right.

The matter eventually was resolved in Ian Johnson's home in Melbourne, some weeks later. I was in Melbourne for a Test match and was in bed after the first day heavy with cold and dosed up with rum and lemon juice, trying to sweat it out. The phone rang and Johnson insisted I see him there and then.

I staggered out to his home very much on the attack. I refused to enter until I felt I had been greeted sufficiently cordially, and the atmosphere for a time was extremely tense. In the end we all mellowed. Johnny and I conceded we might have chosen our words a touch more carefully, Johnson and Hassett conceded they may have over-reacted. By the time the night was out we were all mates again. Johnson went on to replace Hassett as captain of Australia and no great harm was done.

In later years, when I spent so many seasons sitting alongside Lindsay and absolutely revelled in his company, we would both think back on that confrontation with a certain amount of fondness. There is nothing like a good barney, amicably resolved, to encourage mutual respect.

Both Moyes and Hassett were ultimate professionals. Their

appreciation of cricket was such they were rarely unable to seize on a point that most others would pass up. They could chat away for hours on cricket without becoming dull. They were always clear and concise without the need of notes, or time to prepare their thoughts.

Moyes, a renowned journalist and sports author, did not have the advantage of being an international cricketer. He was a good one, mind you, having played for both South Australia and Victoria before moving to live in Sydney in the 'twenties. His attitude to life and cricket was perhaps exemplified in an innings for Gordon in Sydney club cricket when he hit 218 runs in 83 minutes. He knew and loved the game.

But he did not captain Australia as Lindsay did. He had no walk-up start so he had to earn the respect he enjoyed by making sure that what he said was spot on. He was not terribly tolerant of those with whom he worked whose knowledge of the game was significantly less than his.

One of the great passages of cricket commentary was delivered at the Adelaide Oval in early 1961 during the late stages of the drawn fourth Test between Australia and the West Indies. Australia had no hope of winning on the last afternoon, but looked very likely to lose when they lost their seventh, eighth and ninth second innings wickets in the space of three runs, with nearly two hours left to play. In fact, with Lindsay Kline last man in to support Ken Mackay, defeat seemed inevitable.

Even Norman O'Neill, bowling to Kline in the nets, had 'dismissed' him half a dozen times as he warmed up for his final, fateful innings.

It is now history, of course, that Kline survived the last 100 minutes of that game with Mackay to save the Test and, ultimately, the series. It was one of a series of breathtaking finishes to the Tests of that year. It was even more exciting than the famous tied Test in Brisbane a few weeks before, because the tension was spread over such a long period. The Brisbane action was over in a flash, the Adelaide action went virtually all afternoon.

Moyes found himself in the broadcasting box with Michael Charlton for the last twenty minutes of that Adelaide Test. Charlton was a brilliant radio man. He had a marvellous voice and a marvellous command of the language. He could turn his hand to anything and make it sound interesting. That afternoon, as Wesley Hall bowled the last over to Ken Mackay, the excitement and tension that Charlton and Moyes conveyed to millions of engrossed listeners all over the world was broadcasting 'in excelsis'.

It took something like that to convince Johnny that Michael Charlton was worth his place in the broadcasting box. Charlton's background in cricket was limited and so was his knowledge of what can be a very intricate game. Johnny was rather intolerant of that, and didn't like broadcasting with Charlton at all. That afternoon in Adelaide he found just a little more tolerance.

There were those, too, through the years who were intolerant of Lindsay Hassett. For my part he was the ideal man for his role. We developed a chatty style of commentary which I always felt the public liked.

Frequent changes in management in the ABC have often brought frequent changes in opinions. One such change decided at one time that Lindsay Hassett should go.

'I've got some bad news for you,' I was summarily told one day at the cricket. 'We're getting rid of your mate.' The news was delivered with some modicum of delight, more I fancy to upset me—for there were those who resented my influence on the style of cricket broadcasts—than because of any deep dissatisfaction with Lindsay. Lindsay's services were terminated, according to the dictates of this particular new broom.

Within a fortnight, the same gentleman was back, this time considerably contrite.

'Why didn't you tell me Hassett was so important?' he inquiried. Such a flood of protest had greeted Lindsay's demise, not just from the public but from some heavy influences up the line in the ABC as well, that the new broom had to plead for Lindsay's return. It took some hefty persuasion from me to get him back.

When Hassett finally retired some time later, I was the last to know. He wrote to me some three weeks after he had made his retirement a *fait accompli*. 'You would have talked me out of it if I had told you' he reasoned. He was right, too. I would have.

* * *

England in the summer of 1948 was to a cricket broadcaster on his first overseas tour something like Mecca is to a Moslem. To me it was, anyway. This was where it all started, where the game's greatness had been born and nurtured to the point where it had spread all that was fine to all corners of the earth.

The ABC and BBC had struck an arrangement whereby I was to join the BBC's commentary team and provide an Australian flavour for the people at home. This was the first tour by an Australian team since 1938. The War had bitten deep in England. A good part of a generation of cricket had been lost. Goodness knows what the Huttons and the Bradmans and the like might have done had the War not taken out a considerable part of their careers.

As Bradman's team arrived in 1948, Englishmen saw no point in crying over spilt milk. Now they could welcome an enemy of another kind, a kind they were happy to have along, and with whom the ensuing battles would be happy, joyful occasions, full of good sport and good humour. The atmosphere at the start of that tour was electric. The darkness was giving way to light as Englishmen and Australians alike started to get their lives back on an even keel.

My introduction to broadcasting cricket in England was at Hove, where the Australians were engaged in an early tour match against Sussex. I was very much bound up in the general high spirits that prevailed as

Bradman, out for a duck to Alec Bedser in the 1946–47 season. Bradman claimed this to be the best ball ever to take his wicket.

The dynamism that was Neil Harvey. A glorious stroke-player, he made a significant contribution to Australian cricket over several generations, both as a batsman and as a selector.

Len Hutton. He had a touch of Jardine about him the way he single-mindedly pursued victory.

I made my way up to the box and was greeted by Rex Alston, a well-known broadcaster and writer on cricket. The deal was that I would describe the last twenty minutes before lunch, then give a summary for Australia. Outside of that, I was available to the BBC team to use as they saw fit.

When my time came to broadcast, Alston was very careful to remind me that I was broadcasting to Britain, through the BBC, as well. Whether it was his meaning or not, I took his reminder as something of a warning. None of that colonial stuff here, old chap. This is England! I began my commentary, ready for a twenty-minute stint.

At the end of just one over Alston chipped in, thanked me, explained to everybody that I was the Australian broadcaster over for the tour, and commandeered the microphone. I sat waiting for an invitation to resume. None came. Then I heard the voice of John Arlott, whom at that stage I had not met, coming over the headphones from a ground in the north of England. He left little doubt as to what he thought of McGilvray's first broadcast in England.

'Rex, what on earth have you got there?' was the substance of his inquiry. 'You can't possibly let him broadcast.'

At that stage I admit to being somewhat confused and disillusioned about my role as a cricket commentator in England. Oh well, I thought, at least I can spend some time over here checking out shoe factories and buying some equipment for my father's business back home.

The substance of Alston's reluctance and Arlott's thumbs down was, as it turned out, a matter of style. At that time English commentators and Australian commentators did things very differently.

The English practice was to be terribly lyrical. They would talk about the birds, and the clouds and all manner of things. Their commentaries were rich with colour and atmosphere, but it didn't seem to matter if they missed a ball or two while they were discussing dress trends for the gentry in the Long Room.

My style was rather more direct. I would describe the ball, analyse every ball, give the score at least three times an over and often more, generally cover everything that happened. The BBC team saw that as being fairly dull. Certainly they weren't used to it.

By the end of that 1948 tour, though, my style, as practised by all Australian commentators since the very start of radio in Australia, had taken a considerable hold in Britain. We were getting an enormous amount of letters which indicated to the BBC that this new approach, which described every ball, was very popular. Others from Australia, of course, have done the same, but it is gratifying now to all Australian broadcasters who have been to England to see the way English commentary has changed. Strictly speaking, they now do it our way—the way Arlott and Co had found so distasteful that very first day at Hove.

Arlott was one of the first to recognise the value of a direct, ball to ball approach, and by the end of the tour was telling me that my style had found quite an appeal. I recounted his words that I had heard on the earphones at the start of the tour. Taken aback as he was, he smiled as if to say, 'We all make mistakes'.

One of the more eloquent supporters of our particular Australian method was the great Australian Prime Minister Sir Robert Menzies, whose abiding love of cricket went back to the days before World War I when Barnes and Foster were tearing through Australia's batting. Those were the days of Trumper and Ransford, of Bardsley and Armstrong, of Hobbs and Woolley. Sir Robert's boyhood love of the game, born in the midst of such superlative performers, never left him. During his record term as Australian Prime Minister, first in the early days of World War II and again from 1949 until he retired in 1966, Sir Robert won a reputation for his unswerving devotion to all things British. But when it came to listening to the cricket, he was very Australian.

'What we all like about you' he once told me, during an interview at Lord's on the occasion of the 200th Test between England and Australia, 'is that instead of regaling us on the state of the sky, or the condition of the flowers, or the seagulls on the ground or whatever, you always tell us the state of play. Who hit that ball, where it went, what runs resulted, if any, and what the state of the game is. And for that, sir, I thank you most profoundly.'

Sir Robert fancied himself as something of a coach as far as my broadcasting was concerned. As Australia's most brilliant orator, he made a study of words and their usage.

'The pause, Alan,' he used to tell me, 'can be almost as eloquent as any word. Use the pause. Slow down.'

I often tried to make the point with him that the pause he used so skilfully in the nation's forums when people hung on every word, was more difficult to employ when a ball had flown like a rocket to slips, a man had dived to take it, and a crowd was roaring itself hoarse in instant response.

I think deep down Sir Robert would have liked to have been a cricket commentator. Certainly he was a great champion for cricket. And, thankfully, he was a heartfelt supporter of the type of broadcasting I employed, and which at first found such little favour with my English contemporaries.

John Arlott, I must concede, did not endear himself to me on that first tour. I considered him fairly high-handed. But as the years have rolled on my respect for him has developed enormously, and these days we are good friends. He was not the most knowledgeable of cricket broadcasters, technically, but he had a unique command of the English language, and the way he has used it around England's cricket fields has given him a singular place in cricket folklore.

He could make a rainy day sound interesting. His colourful turn of phrase, his creative word pictures, could not be matched by any other commentator. You could close your eyes and listen to Arlott's commentaries and see everything as if you were sitting on the mid-on boundary.

His limited background in cricket occasionally came through, particularly early on. I remember Ray Lindwall taking him to task one day in 1948 because he had described Lindwall's deliveries as 'turning from the leg'. Lindwall was moved to explain to Arlott that he didn't turn the ball. He swung it in the air, perhaps cut it off the pitch, but he didn't turn it. He didn't want people back home to think he was turning it. That could mean he was bowling spinners, and I think Ray saw that as some sort of affront to his athleticism.

'Just a matter of expression, dear boy,' Arlott countered. 'Just a matter of expression.'

Arlott is a fantastic person. He won an enormous following as an expert on food and wine with *The Guardian* newspaper in London. He loved his wine and had literally thousands of bottles in his home in Sussex. He would always have a bottle with him at the cricket and, by the time he had dined at night, it was nothing for him to have downed seven bottles in an average day. He had a rule that he would not broadcast after lunch, a concession he made to his love of red wine.

I often wondered how Arlott would have handled the synthetic broadcasts of 1938. Ten years later, of course, communications had improved to the extent that direct broadcasts to Australia from London were quite acceptable, and the days of the synthetics had gone. But Arlott would have been marvellous in that exercise. Regrettably, we didn't see much of John Arlott in Australia. His distaste for flying and travel kept him pretty much at home. He received a standing ovation from the crowd and the players when he finished his final broadcast at the Lord's Centenary Test against Australia in 1980. I joined that ovation, heartily and without reservation, for he had been a truly great cricket commentator.

Brian Johnston was a similarly colourful wordsmith. 'Johnners', as he is known to just about everybody, looked upon his commentary as an entertainment first and an information service second. A brilliant personality, he always stood out in a crowd. From the two-tone brown and white shoes that adorned his feet to the garish yellow and orange of his MCC tie, Johnners played the role of the social English gentleman to a tee.

He always had a joke, was always full of laughter and high spirits. For a couple of generations he was the *bon vivant* of the commentary box, a broadcaster who could talk his way through a couple of hours' break in play with articulate tales of matches past, days at the theatre, horse riding in the country—it didn't seem to matter. Johnners was in the business of keeping people entertained and that he did brilliantly, in the box and outside it.

He had an enormous following, which he played to unashamedly. He would occasionally start the day by telling his audience how ghastly he felt. I recall on one occasion he went into a sorrowful tale about how he had run out of toothpaste and couldn't brush his teeth that morning. Next day toothpaste arrived in the broadcasting box by the bucketful.

Brian got on the air next morning to thank all the ladies who sent the toothpaste. 'But I seem to have lost my toothbrush' he complained. 'I'm afraid the toothpaste isn't much good to me without a toothbrush.' Next day a load of toothbrushes arrived from all over the country.

Johnston played to that sort of audience. He received gifts almost every day. Ladies would send him cake, fruit, sweets. Some days the box would be like a bazaar. And Brian would always acknowledge the gifts over the air, and in that way develop a personal touch in his commentaries that won him many fans.

The box was never dull when Brian Johnston was in residence. He loved to take me down a peg or two with practical jokes. His favourite was the cake trick. I had done my stint on air and was well out of the way at the other end of the commentary box, still with the headphones on listening to the commentary and with a microphone in front of me.

Johnners offered me some of the chocolate cake which had arrived in vast quantities that day. He waited until my mouth was full, and said on air: 'Now we'll ask Alan McGilvray what he thinks about that.'

There was nothing I could do but spit the cake into my hand and answer the question. Nobody heard my answer of course, because the whole commentary team was in uproar and Brian was explaining in explicit detail to the radio audience at large how I had been caught and mortally embarrassed.

I don't know how, but he actually caught me twice like that on successive tours.

That sort of bubbling good humour was Johnston's forte. He kept the commentary box a happy, frothy place, and endeared himself to millions of listeners with his infectious good humour. Cricket, to Johnston, could never be so serious that you couldn't find a good belly laugh in it. It was to be enjoyed, he reasoned, and that was the way he conveyed it to his listeners.

The other great wordsmith of my experience in cricket broadcasting was the South African, Charles Fortune, whose love of cricket eventually led him to be secretary of the South African Cricket Board when he retired as a broadcaster.

He was another who painted flowing, extravagant pictures with words. He would lose track of the game every so often, and he didn't often worry about such minor details as the score. But the words flowed from his mouth like a cascade of flowers, colourful and sweet-smelling and rich in warmth and character. He also was a highly emotive broadcaster, whose patriotism and pride knew no bounds, and were confined by none.

When Peter Van der Merwe's team won 3-1 against Bob Simpson's side in South Africa in 1966-67 — the first occasion South Africa had won a series against Australia—it provided the high point of Charles Fortune's life. Charles was on the air in the late stages of the final Test at Port Elizabeth when it became obvious that a South African win was inevitable. Charles had been on something of a high all day. He was twitchy and nervous. His self-control was obviously under strain as the emotion built within him.

Graeme Pollock and Tiger Lance quickly were moving towards the 170-odd run total South Africa needed to seal the series. The time came when Charles could hold on to himself no longer. He burst into uncontrolled sobbing. In fact, he almost convulsed. His body was shaking, as if in some sort of patriotic spasm. I grabbed the microphone to keep the commentary going. I ran through the scoreboard with Charles Fortune bawling his eyes out beside me. Chick Henderson, another member of the South African broadcasting team, was shaking Charles, slapping his face and trying to help him pull himself together.

Eventually he succeeded and Charles was able to take up the commentary again as the winning run was struck and South Africa triumphed by seven wickets.

That series parcelled up, South African cricket lifted to a new plane of excellence. Charles Fortune lived every moment of that success. Never before or since have I seen such emotion from a commentator at the result of a sporting contest.

Regrettably, not only for Charles and a whole generation of superb South African cricketers, but for the game as a whole, South Africa were to play only one more series before the ugly question of apartheid in sport, and South Africa's racial attitudes generally, brought them isolation in the cricket world.

The last series they played was against Bill Lawry's Australian team in 1969-70. They won that 4-0. It was the first time South Africa had won every match of a rubber. They won the last Test by 323 runs, the biggest winning margin of runs South Africa had ever scored.

This time a whole nation wept. No win, no glory, could console them for the fact that they had come to the end of the road. But at least, for Charles and a magnificent South African team who had so richly developed their talents, it was a glorious end.

Radio offered the opportunity to present word pictures as we saw them, without restrictions. The broadcasting boxes were always harmonious places in which all the broadcasters I knew had a real desire to communicate with their public. When television entered the picture, I could not see it ever providing commentators with that same scope for expression. The ABC asked me to do television, but I declined. I tried it a couple of times, but I hated having my commentary governed by the direction a camera happened to be pointing.

On one such occasion I noticed a commotion on the SCG Hill and suggested to the producer's assistant they might train the cameras on it. 'Ten o'clock,' I yelled, to give him the angle. He looked at his watch and said it was four o'clock. I just shook my head. The same fellow had a pad in front of him and was continually playing noughts and crosses. 'Who are you playing with?' I said. 'Myself' came the reply. 'Do you ever win?' I inquired. 'Yes, occasionally' he said. I decided there and then my future was not in television.

THE MIDDLE MEN

One of the best accolades I ever had as a cricket commentator was the puzzled look on one of my colleagues in Brisbane after I had called a dismissal. 'Goodness Mac, you've got good eyes,' he said, shaking his head in undisguised awe. He was not the only commentator through the years who was rather astounded by my speed in picking up something on the field. I would occasionally nominate the bouncer before it was bowled, explain with certainty that the finest of nicks was the ball flicking the pad, nominate a man out before the umpire's finger was up.

Before I sound like I'm singing my own praises as some sort of eagle-eyed fountain of knowledge, I have to concede some inside information. Most of those quick assessments of what had taken place were conveyed to me, quickly and certainly, by umpires with whom I had developed a comprehensive communications system. In the days of Col Egar and Lou Rowan, undoubtedly the best umpires I ever saw, as many as twenty signals were in operation. They kept me fully informed, quickly and accurately, on every eventuality. The signals were for each other, but they took me into their confidence and made sure I could see them.

A ball would go to the keeper rather sluggishly, and the batsman would be given out. Col Egar would casually turn so that I could see him, and nonchalantly rub away at his thumb. The message was clear – the batsman had been caught off his glove, and I could tell the world quickly and surely, without the often inconclusive aid of a TV replay.

Hands together might mean the ball had come off the pad, a touch of the ear might mean it went from bat to pad. Whatever the circumstance, Col or Lou would let me know pretty quickly, and the commentary was much better for it.

Throughout my time in radio I have also made a study of the idiosyncrasies of umpires. More often than not they telegraph their decisions before they actually make them. If I could read their intent, and get in with the decision before they did, I could call a man out before the crowd realised, so the swell of their roar built up behind me. That added so much drama to the broadcast. Egar, for instance, always drew his feet together, as if standing to attention, before he raised his finger to signal a batsman's demise. As soon as those legs came together, I knew. 'He's gone' I would say, beating the finger and beating the crowd.

It was an almost foolproof system, and one which I never let on about, lest Egar unconsciously changed his *modus operandi*. Other umpires had a habit of crouching before they gave a decision in the affirmative. Others let their hands drop to their sides first. Reading them, I reasoned, was one of the biggest aids to my broadcasting technique.

Rowan and Egar were most conscientious about our communication system. They thought it important their actions were quickly understood, for a start. And they said it relaxed them. Physically nominating the basis for each decision somehow crystallised it in their minds, and made them feel better. I made a point throughout my career of getting as close as I could to the umpires. With that pair it was very easy. They were great men with a great love of cricket, and our morning chats before play became a ritual.

For much of my career, too, I had considerable help from the players. Keith Miller would touch his forehead as he turned to bowl, thereby alerting me to the fact that he was going to let fly a bouncer. I was ready for it. Often I would get in first. A rub on the right side of his nose would nominate the inswinger, a rub to the left side would nominate the outswinger. I could call with certainty so many of the deliveries he bowled, particularly those that were in any way different. So it was with several players.

Occasionally we would get down to working out specific scenarios. I recall one such occasion in South Africa, where the Australian spinner Johnny Gleeson worked on a plan to dismiss Graeme Pollock. He reasoned that Pollock played away from his body a lot, and that if he bowled two or three of his stock deliveries, which would be the off-break to the left-hander, and tried to push him back, he might then be vulnerable to the floated wrong-'un. I happened to be having breakfast with Johnny as he mulled over his plan, and we determined he would need a gully fieldsman as well as a slip if it were to work properly. Off he went to see the skipper Bill Lawry, and duly returned to announce that all was in readiness. The plan was set.

Next day he had started an over to Pollock when he looked up to the commentary box and signalled that Plan A was in operation. The first ball went as scheduled, then the second, then the third. All was in readiness. Gleeson gave me the thumbs up and I began to describe the trap that was being laid. Alas! As Gleeson turned to bowl the ball he had planned for, Lawry pulled the gully away and stuck him somewhere else to fill a hole. Gleeson stopped in his tracks and turned to me, arms spread as if to decry the best laid plans of mice and men. I described Johnny's anguish at not having the fieldsman he wanted. As a broadcaster, I was able to give an insight into the play that not even all the players were able to appreciate.

That sort of communication, in which players, umpires, broadcasters, Press and public are integrated, sadly is not such a feature of modern cricket. Players are much more distant these days, seemingly less concerned for the public and the public appreciation of just what transpires in the middle. That's a shame. The happy communication that existed for the greater part of this century reflected a respect for the public and the role they play in the game. It also embodied a lot of common courtesy. And it was jolly good fun. I am glad to have lived through the cricketing era I did, for so many of the good things have been unnecessarily lost in the high pace of the modern game.

My relationship with umpires, and the considerable advantages it brought me, was something I kept to myself. I did not suggest working a signal system with other commentators because I felt we were stretching it far enough, and if it became a common practice, it would place simply too much stress upon the umpires' goodwill. I would never attempt such a relationship in England, either, where the umpires are much more mechanical.

English umpires, as a whole, are undoubtedly better than Australia's. There are probably any number of reasons for that, not least the fact that they have so much more experience. More even light, less glare, less heat and less pressure are perhaps other factors. I say less pressure because they are doing it six days a week, and therefore become terribly used to it. In Australia umpires do a little Shield cricket, then make the big step to Tests with comparatively little experience behind them. That builds a lot of pressure.

Australia, too, has asked more of its Test umpires than England. Never in England have the same two umpires stood for a full series of five matches, yet it has happened five times in Australia in England-Australia Tests alone. George Borwick, undoubtedly one of the best umpires we have produced, actually stood for all five Tests in three series. The last pair to be asked to stand for a full series of matches was Tom Brooks and Robin Bailhache in 1974-75. Both ultimately retired because of the pressures umpiring entailed.

An added pressure for Australian umpires these days is the dreaded TV replay. That has been around to thwart them for a few years, but it is infinitely worse now that it is available on a huge screen at the Sydney and Melbourne grounds, and available for all to see almost before the batsman has had time to turn and walk off. The sight of a dismissed batsman stopping to watch the replay on his way from the field has become commonplace. I am told that the England batsman Alan Lamb even went so far as to suggest, jokingly we all assume, that if the replay showed the umpire had erred, he was going to go back and demand another chance. The pressure those instant replays involve for umpires is awesome. It is different when the replay is on at home, and neither the umpires nor the players on the field know anything about it. But when it is there in front of them, immediate and obvious to all, it is setting the umpires up as sitting ducks.

I've watched a lot of Test umpires in my time, and I can separate seven of them as the best Australia has produced in that time. Those that stand out for me are George Borwick, Mel McInnes, Colin Egar, Lou Rowan, Tom Brooks, Robin Bailhache and Mel Johnson. All of them were subject to pressure of one kind or another. Egar had to wear the Meckiff affair; Rowan ran into some fierce arguments with John Snow and Ray Illingworth in 1970-71; McInnes was the target for unrelenting criticism in the England series of 1958-59.

McInnes had been a Test match umpire of the highest order for a very long time when he lined up for the fourth Test of 1958-59. There had been a lot of niggling from Fleet Street about Ian Meckiff and Gordon Rorke and the legality of their deliveries. The pressure already was on Mel when he turned down an appeal for caught behind against Jim Burke, the Australian opener, before he was 10. Mel was about the only man there who didn't think Burke was out. Burke batted for quite a time after that, and Mel's decision raised quite a debate. Worse was to come. Colin McDonald scored a century but retired hurt for a time and came back with a runner, Jim Burke again.

Burke had been running on the off-side of the pitch when McDonald took strike, then switched to the leg side. Unfortunately, umpire McInnes failed to note that. And neither Burke nor McDonald informed him. The very first ball McDonald faced after Burke swapped sides brought disaster for McInnes. Burke screamed down towards his line, level with the bowler's crease. McInnes turned away from him, looking for him on the other side. When the wicket was broken, Burke was yards short, but McInnes had his back to him and not a clue where he was. Unable to make a decision since he had not seen Burke run, he could do nothing else but give the benefit of the doubt to the batsman. It was a sad end for Mel McInnes. He retired after that game, somewhat broken in spirit. He had been an exceptionally good umpire, and deserved better.

Most umpires have their disasters. I remember one occasion when Lou Rowan ruled 'not out' to a catch behind against Bill Lawry in a Test. The Englishmen were dreadfully upset. I thought, also, that Lou was wrong, and so I suspect did just about everybody else involved. Later in the game, when Australia were fielding, Lawry was stationed at mid-on and had to make a long chase to the fence to retrieve a ball. 'Gee, that's a long run,' he said to Rowan when he resumed his spot.

'Why didn't you walk?' Rowan replied. At least they both could have a laugh about it.

Rowan and Egar in combination were the best umpires of my experience because of that seemingly imperturbable air. They worked at it. They would brush off any criticism from players, real or implied, with a 'Did I really?' or 'Go on, is that so?' They would not subject themselves to debate, or to the need to defend themselves.

The most dominant Australian umpire of my experience undoubtedly was George Borwick, who stood in Test matches between 1932 and 1948. He became such a fixture he was a sort of 'Mr Cricket' of his time. He upset me dreadfully on one occasion when I was captain of NSW and I was having a devil of a time trying to get one of my bowlers to appeal. He would never ask the question – he always gave the benefit of the doubt to the batsman. I explained he should give the umpire a chance to decide, that perhaps the umpire was in a better spot to judge. Eventually I harassed him into appealing one day. 'Don't be silly,' was George Borwick's response. In three words he undid about two year's work as far as I was concerned. He could have just said 'not out'. George was a good umpire though. He took no nonsense.

Umpiring is not any easy job. Most umpires worry a lot about it, searching their own souls and stewing over their mistakes. They make a contribution to the game that is seldom recognised. And for this commentator, at least, they have been marvellous allies.

GREEN FIELDS OF ENGLAND

To a lover of cricket, there is simply no place like England. In the natural order of things, it is fitting and proper that the game should have had its birth there. No other land, no other people could have contrived its lilting pace, its innate charm or its rich tradition as have the English. And nowhere else are those qualities maintained with quite the same diligence. My excitement at visiting England for an Ashes series was as intense on my tenth visit as it was on my first. That same knot in the stomach was there, that same buzz of anticipation. My life has been splendidly enriched by English cricket, by English ways, and by the warm friendship of English people.

The first thing that hits you on a cricket tour of England is the charm of the place. On my first tour there in 1948 a social match was arranged early in the tour for the Press. The Australians played against an English team led by Walter Hammond, who had retired as England captain only a year or two before. These matches became a tradition on English tours and were always splendid occasions, despite the fact I could rarely get a bat. We had some former first class cricketers like Jack Fingleton, who opened so courageously against Bodyline, and Percy Beames, who was a fine player with Victoria before he took up the pen as cricket writer with the Melbourne *Age.* Former players cannot resist the temptation in later years to show they still have some of their old skill, and we never seemed to lose more than three or four wickets in those Press games. The likes of Fingleton and Beames would bat for ages, and poor scrubbers like McGilvray would be left to twiddle our thumbs in the tent, and try to ward off the temptations of the refreshments.

The match was played at a glorious little village field in Gloucestershire, where the oaks and the elms encircled the ground, and the smell of freshly cut hay invigorated the senses. Spectators sat on haystacks around the boundary, and a 30-piece string orchestra was on hand to add atmosphere to the afternoon's proceedings. I recall standing in the field, gathering the rural scents in deep breaths and reflecting as music wafted over the field that this was cricket as it was meant to be played.

At the end of the game we had to head off to Manchester. I was travelling with Arthur Mailey, that impish spin bowler of the 'twenties who had taken to journalism with a flourish. Arthur said he had a friend whose home was on the way, and who he was sure would be able to find a bed for us for the night. It was a long drive, and breaking the journey seemed sensible, so I gladly concurred. When we arrived at his friend's home, it took my breath away. The 'home' was a huge mediaeval castle. Times were hard in postwar England, and the Duke and Duchess on whose estate it stood were forced to grow and sell vegetables on a roadside stall to help make ends meet. But their circumstances in no way impaired the grandeur and dignity of the place. Arthur's aristocratic friends gave us a marvellous welcome. We dined at a table that was almost as long as a cricket pitch, and which had adorned their banquet hall for centuries. The Duke sat at one end, the Duchess at the other, and Arthur and I at the middle on either side. We felt at times as if we needed a telephone to make conversation. We had a splendid dinner. Our hosts entertained us royally. They showed us the family heirlooms, which included a shirt worn by King James I when he had visited in the early seventeenth century. We slept in huge four-poster beds, and I recall my amusement at night, as a young fellow away from home for the first time, pondering on who might have slept there before me. The guest list over the centuries would have been mind boggling.

As we drove off next morning, England had taken on new lustre. What else but cricket could build such bridges? Arthur Mailey had grown up in the sandhills that encroached to within a few miles of the centre of Sydney at the turn of the century. He had been a glass blower and a Water Board labourer and all manner of things before cricket opened a whole new world for him. He started in Test cricket at thirty-five, was still there past forty, and had such unbelievable command of his leg spin and googly bowling that his thirty-six wickets against the England team of 1920-21 stood as an Australian series record for more than fifty years. He made two very successful tours of England, and his scalps down the years included such marvellous names as Trumper and Hobbs. In his final Test Mailey bowled Hobbs with a full toss, which in Mailey's armoury was an extremely dangerous delivery.

As a very young man I ran into Mailey one day playing club cricket in Sydney. Being Mailey, I was naturally cautious when I batted against him. The first ball he gave me was a full toss, which I gladly put away for four. The second ball was another full toss, which I again put away for four. The third ball was another full toss. It looked the same, and

I gratefully swiped at it again. But this time the ball dipped away from me at the last moment and I was well and truly stumped. After the match Mailey came to me and asked if I had learned anything. Treat each ball on its merits, he said. Assume nothing. Be patient.

I later came to appreciate that Mailey could make the ball do anything he wanted. He put so much spin on it you could hear it buzz in the air. It didn't even need to hit the pitch to be dangerous. Through that skill, Mailey had climbed from a battler of very humble beginnings to a confidante of Kings and Dukes. His wit and his charm won him an army of friends, and were undiminished in his declining years in Sydney, when my wife and I would take him on delightful Sunday afternoon drives. Whatever presence King James I commanded in that castle back in the early 1600s, he could not have been more warmly received than was Arthur Mailey nearly 350 years later.

That 1948 tour embodied thrill upon thrill for me. Apart from the excellence of Bradman's team and its historic performance, the tour introduced me to people and places that were legends. At a Lord's Taverners dinner I was privileged to sit with the mighty Jack Hobbs, and to talk with him and Herbert Sutcliffe about the greatest opening partnership in the game. I particularly remember a long chat with Maurice Tate, the champion fast-bowler of the 'twenties and 'thirties. I had met Tate previously in Australia in 1928, when the Great Public Schools arranged for the best performed batsmen and bowler of the GPS competition to meet the leading England players. I was introduced to Tate, and listened awe-struck to what he had to say. Incredibly, he remembered that meeting when we met again twenty years later.

Tate was dining with that great umpire Frank Chester when Arthur Mailey and I walked into the hotel dining room. As soon as I was introduced Tate recalled the schoolboy meeting of twenty years before, and we chatted away like old friends.

I had long admired a photograph in Vic Richardson's home, in which Tate was bowling to a field of seven slips. Batsmen of his era said he skidded the ball off the pitch faster even than Larwood. To now bump into people like Maurice Tate on an almost daily basis gave cricket a whole new meaning for me.

The grandeur of English cricket, of course, goes a lot deeper than the wonderful atmosphere of its grounds and the dignity of its traditions. England down the years has supplied in greater numbers than any other nation the most graceful and the most articulate players. There is a certain style to their play, an almost hereditary leaning towards the artistic. That leaning may have diminished somewhat since the demands of one-day cricket have exerted a larger influence on English play. But whenever the mind conjures up pictures of the most graceful and fluent players, Englishmen abound.

If I had to choose a solitary Englishman as the epitome of all that is fine in English cricket it would certainly be that prince of batsmen,

Denis Compton. He was the ultimate entertainer, a player of extraordinary ability who complemented his talents with an ebullient nature and a showman's flair. He was film star quality, and England loved him. He was marvellously aggressive, ever willing to jump down the wicket and attack. Compton would rather get out than just hang around and be boring. He loved the game as he loved life, and he captured in his batting a cavalier spontaneity that was sheer joy. Like all great champions, he did not do everything by the book. He made the delivery suit the type of shot he wanted to play. He would shuffle into position to dictate a bowler's line, and the exquisiteness of his timing and the strength of his wrists would reduce the best of bowlers to frustration. He picked up many runs on the leg side with an audacious sweep shot, and his cover drive was uncanny in the way it whistled through the gaps.

Compton first appeared against Australia in 1938. He kicked off with a century in the first Test and a 76 not out in the second innings of the second Test. From there he was not so successful against the wiles of an old-stager like Bill O'Reilly. He was out for one, for instance, when England declared at 7-903 in the final Test. But he had made his mark, and I recall Bill O'Reilly's warning me of his quality before he arrived in Australia with Walter Hammond's team in 1946. 'This boy's okay,' he said. 'He'll be a good 'un.'

Compton did nothing terribly exciting until he got to the fourth Test, whereupon he hit a century in each innings, the second of them unbeaten, in a consummate display of batting. With that tour behind him, he proceeded to hit an extraordinary 18 hundreds in the next English season. He took 3816 runs off a string of bowlers, whom he treated with equal disdain, and hammered the touring South African side into submission. By the time Bradman's team arrived in England for the summer of 1948 he was a very mature and accomplished batsman.

Compton scored 560 runs in the 1948 series against a very fine bowling attack indeed, headed by the redoubtable Miller and Lindwall. The respect Compton had for Miller's bowling was matched only by the respect Miller had for Compton's batting. Through the many battles they fought they developed an enduring friendship that flourished long after their cricket was gone. Both often talk about the first Test of the 1948 tour, when England faced a real battle after trailing by nearly 350 on the first innings. Compton put up a valiant second innings fight in a vain attempt to stave off defeat. As his score built past 180, Miller was fielding in the gully, urging him towards 200. 'Hit it . . . hit it!' he pleaded as Lindwall bowled short. Compton did not know whether he was trying to 'con' him or not.

Feigning some sort of deep-seated hurt at Compton's refusal to take his advice, Miller demanded the ball and a crack at the last line of England resistance. Miller then proceeded to remove Compton for 184 with what Denis often recalled as the most ferocious ball he ever faced.

'It came at me with such pace,' Compton recalled, 'it actually knocked me off my feet.' Compton had covered up, but the ball kept coming into him, forced him hard on to the back foot, then hit the bat so hard as Compton defended it sat him down on his stumps.

Compton's batting, as much as his nature, won him the respect and the friendship of the Australian bowlers. He would always give them a chance, and if he did get on top of them, he did it in such a manner that nobody could be displeased. There was no grim, negative defence. No nudging the ball here and there. He hit it with as much force as they bowled it, and they respected him mightily for that.

For a man as skilful as he was, Compton had a dreadful tour to Australia with Freddie Brown's team in 1950-51. He was doing it so tough at one stage, I am sure the Australian fast-bowlers contrived to give him a bit of a lift. Compton had scored only 31 runs in five innings when he shaped up to Bill Johnston for the second innings of the fourth Test. Johnston had dismissed Compton three times to that point, and I have not the slightest doubt he felt sorry for him. So much so that, Test match or no Test match, he decided he was too good a bloke to get three ducks in four Tests and should at least get off the mark. Johnston served up a rank long hop first ball which Compton thrashed as only Compton could. The ball flew towards square leg where the substitute fieldsman Sam Loxton threw out a left hand, more by reflex action than any considered design. The ball stuck and Compton was out for his third duck of the series. Johnston would never admit it, but I am sure he was doing his best to get Denis a start at least, in the best traditions of a game in the park, where good friends never allow each other the humiliation of a duck.

Eight innings for Compton brought him only 53 runs on that tour, which is almost unbelievable when measured against the mountains of runs his career produced. As is his nature, Compton took the reverses with the same modest good humour that he took the successes. Early in that tour the England opener Reg Simpson was having a similarly dreadful trot. Compton engaged me in earnest discussion with Simpson on the problem. 'Hey Mac,' Denis bade me, 'explain to poor Reg here how you Aussies get yourselves out of a bad trot, will you?' A little embarrassed, I offered the age old theory. Get yourself on the front foot and have a bit of a whack. Hit yourself out, I said.

Next Test Simpson's trot disappeared in a glorious innings of 156 not out, setting England up for their only win of the series. Simpson then engaged me in another earnest discussion with Compton.

'Hey Mac,' he said, 'explain to Denis what you Aussies do to get out of a bad trot, will you?'

Compton played in the Ashes-winning England team of 1953 and again in teams that retained the Ashes in Australia in 1954-55, and in England in 1956. He went out with an innings of 94 in the fifth Test of 1956. But, strictly speaking, Australians had been spared much of the dynamics that brought him 5807 runs in his Test career.

But the big innings had been something to behold. And the manner of them was something again. There was a splendour about him, and a flamboyant sort of dignity in his bearing. He never waited for decisions when he knew he was out. Nor did he ever embarrass an umpire or an opponent. He was a symbol, to me, of the spirit of sport, and the singular character England had given sport in the game of cricket.

I recall my first sight of Walter Hammond going out to bat. He had a bearing about him, a sort of majesty that lifted him above ordinary mortals. So it was with Denis Compton.

THE INVINCIBLES

Australia's dominance over England through the immediate postwar period was unarguable. From the MCC tour of 1946-47, through the English summer of 1948, and back to Australia in 1950-51, there was little England could do to stem the tide. Teams led by Wally Hammond, Norman Yardley and Freddie Brown succumbed one after the other, perplexed initially by the marvels of Bradman, the pugnacity of Barnes and the raw talents of Lindwall and Miller, and tormented later by Morris, Harvey, Hassett and Johnston. It was a glorious period in Australian cricket and a tough one for England, who had much ground to recover after the difficulties of a war at home.

It went sour for England from the moment contests between the two countries resumed at Brisbane in 1946. For a start, Hammond lost the first toss, leaving Australia perfect conditions in which to amass 645 runs. As soon as they had done so a murderous Brisbane thunderstorm swamped the ground. Efforts to protect the pitch when the Brisbane weather turns on its most spectacular shows are worthless. This was such a day, and as the tarpaulin covers floated about in the deluge, there was little doubt what the pitch would be like if Hammond and his men ever got back on it. As is Brisbane's way, a fierce sun followed the deluge, drying the ground sufficiently for play but leaving England to cope with the worst of Brisbane 'stickies'.

A further piece of poor fortune had befallen England early in the Australian innings when a very tentative Don Bradman, attempting a comeback after a long lay-off, was given not out at 28 to a catch by Jack Ikin in the gully. The umpire was right in giving him not out, but the Englishmen's insistence that they were hard done by stirred up a considerable hornet's nest. In such circumstances decisions can go either way. Had the umpire leaned towards England it might all have been over for Bradman, and perhaps Australia's confidence as well.

As it was, England had no hope chasing 645 on a wet wicket against bowlers like Lindwall, Miller and Ernie Toshack, and Australia were victorious by an innings and 332 runs. That set the course for the next half dozen years.

The disaster that befell England, however, was notable for one superb piece of cricket. I am often asked what I rate the best innings I ever saw, and one that always gets a mention is the innings Bill Edrich played in that game for 16. Batting is a diverse art which embraces many qualities. There are times when improvisation, courage and the sheer skill of survival offer as much to the connoisseur as the most ostentatious collection of fours and sixes. This was such an innings. In partnership with Walter Hammond, Edrich played through a tortuous hour before lunch in which avoidance became the supreme skill. When a Brisbane 'sticky' is playing true to form, the ball will do just about anything, and it will do it when you're least expecting it. Miller was quite frightening on this one. For Edrich the task was to make a quick judgment as to whether the ball might hit the stumps, and if it was not going to, try to make sure it did not hit the bat either.

Miller let a couple of deliveries really fly, but for the most part he pegged his pace back a little and let the pitch do the work. Bradman at one stage suggested he might bowl a little faster. Miller argued the point. 'If I bowl fast on this,' he said, 'I'll kill somebody.'

I shall never forget the sheer tenacity with which Edrich, particularly, resisted Miller's onslaught. It was the bulldog spirit at its best. When they went to lunch only three down, with the wicket drying fast, it seemed England might have been able to resurrect their position. Then Edrich had a rush of blood. Miller's second ball was nothing more than a loosener, a long hop outside the off stump which to Edrich, after so long a period of tormented concentration, was like manna from heaven. He thrashed at it, was caught in slips, and from there England plummeted to defeat. It was an ironic end for one of the most superb fighting innings I ever saw.

The Brisbane wicket dogged England repeatedly through those immediate post-war years. A similar situation developed at the start of the 1950-51 series, when Lindsay Hassett won the toss for Australia and Freddie Brown's bowlers managed to get them out for only 228 on a good batting pitch. Down came the deluge again, and in went Freddie's men on a mudpie pitch. Confronted with impossible circumstances in which to bat, Brown declared at 7-68 to get Australia back in under similar conditions. Not to be outdone, Hassett then declared at 7-32 leaving England just a little under 200 to score in the final innings to win the game. More importantly, there remained seventy minutes' play to survive that third day.

In the event, England managed 122. The pitch had improved a bit, thanks to Brisbane's famed horse-drawn roller, and England held back Len Hutton and Denis Compton to bat late in the order, when conditions might have been expected to be most suitable for their survival. Hutton played a glorious hand of 62 not out on the last morning, but the rest succumbed, and England again had fallen victim of the Brisbane 'sticky'. Twice they had been drubbed in circumstances that made mockery of the relative merits of the two teams. Thereafter more complete covering became the norm for Test matches in Australia, and Brisbane has been less of a minefield.

Through 1946-47 and 1948 the story had been much the same. Bradman, Barnes, Morris, Hassett and Co got the runs, and Lindwall and Miller, with some help from the Victorian left-armer Bill Johnston, got most of the wickets. England through the period had some fairly useful players, but Bradman's team developed into a side of such supreme power, coupled with a disciplined, fighting spirit, they were simply unbeatable. That period was perhaps the finest of Anglo-Australian cricket. It was a declining era for England, a rising one for Australia. England relied on a hard core of survivors from their pre-war team, while Australia had to build anew. They still had Barnes, Bradman and Hassett from pre-war days, but increasingly they came to rely on the new men like Morris and Miller, Lindwall and Harvey.

Neil Harvey was an enormously significant introduction to the Test side towards the end of the campaign against India in 1947-48. After a tentative start, he made 153 in his second Test, and at just nineteen years of age, it was already clear he would return from England a budding champion. Harvey went on to play 79 Tests for 6149 runs, second only to Bradman until Greg Chappell overhauled them both in 1984. He had a Test average of 48. Importantly, most of the runs would have been a joy to watch. Harvey was in the mould of Compton and Miller when it came to playing for the sheer joy of it, and he hit the ball with great flourish.

His 1948 tour was notable for a couple of innings. First of all he kept their unbeaten record intact when, against Yorkshire, he managed a highly valuable 18, including a straight six for the winning runs, as all fell about him. Australia had only three wickets standing, with just 31 runs to their credit and 63 to get, when Harvey set about his rescue operation. It made him something of a team hero, and when he finally got a chance in the fourth Test, he grabbed it with both hands. He started tentatively, failing to make contact to the first few balls he faced. Then Keith Miller took a hand. He shepherded the young Harvey through his settling-in period, farming the strike where he thought it necessary, encouraging, cajoling, drawing from the young newcomer his very best effort. It was a remarkable piece of team cricket. The accomplished 'old hand' taking an obviously nervous newcomer under his wing, settling his nerves and allowing confidence to grow until the fledgeling finally took flight, unleashing the glorious drives, cuts and pulls that became such a feature of international cricket for the next fifteen years. Harvey scored a fine 112 that day, and but for a slow start and a very careful passage through the nineties, it was marvellous batting. It also set Australia up for the chance to win on the final day, when Morris's 182 and Bradman's final Test century of 173 not out allowed Australia to score a record 3-404.

Harvey carried on in following years to be one of the finest left-handers the game has known. He took particular toll of South Africa down the years, scoring 834 runs in the 1952-53 series. It was also against South Africa he played one of his best innings, scoring 151 not out of an Australian target of 336 in the third Test at Durban in 1950. Rain had turned the pitch into a terrible 'sticky' while South Africa were batting in their first innings, so much so that the Australian captain, Lindsay Hassett, asked his bowlers to avoid dismissing the South Africans until it had dried out a bit.

Once the South Africans realised what was happening they threw their bats, were all out for 311, then proceeded to rout Australia for 75. By the time Australia had replied by dismissing South Africa for 99 in their second innings, the pitch was a mess, full of holes and assorted damage. Harvey treated it as though nothing was amiss. Those who saw his innings spoke of it as one of those rare treats which fall upon cricket perhaps once a generation. Australia won with twenty-five minutes to spare, but the innings, rather than the match, lives on.

For all the exquisiteness of his batting, Harvey had the odd rough deal from administrators. He was considered unlucky by many when Richie Benaud was preferred to him as captain in 1958. It proved an inspired decision as far as Benaud was concerned, but that can be said with the benefit of hindsight. Harvey was unlucky, and was ultimately given only one chance to captain Australia. That was at Lord's in 1961, when Benaud was injured, and he responded with a fine Australian win. Harvey also served as an Australian selector for many years after his cricket had finished, only to be unceremoniously dumped in 1979, an event which soured him more than any of the disappointments he might have had through his playing career. Thankfully, there were few of those. He was too fine a player to have had many setbacks.

From England's standpoint, the immediate post-war period was also significant for the emergence of Alec Bedser. Bedser played 51 Tests from 1946 to 1955 and in that time had 15 different partners as England's opening attack. He had 21 Tests against Australia and 10 different partners. Yet he still managed 104 wickets against Australia, taking five in an innings seven times, mostly against Australian teams that had the measure of England in most departments. For much of his career he seemed to be carrying the fight alone. How good might he have been had he had the assistance of a top class performer at the other end to maintain the pressure? Australian batsmen made a habit of merely trying to hold Alec out, confining their attacking shots, and therefore the greater risk, for the bowler at the other end. Late in his career, Brian Statham and Freddie Trueman happened along, but too late to be of great assistance to Alec's career as a whole. Bedser bowled a brisk medium-fast and was as strong as an ox, thumping that left foot down at the point of delivery and maximising effort on every ball. He relied on a sharp inswing, and was the sort of cricketer against whom few liberties could be taken.

The danger he represented to the best of batsmen is perhaps summed up in one ball he let go at Don Bradman in the Adelaide Test of 1946-47. Bradman had just come in, and Bedser's delivery swung very late from off stump to leg stump, then cut back to knock down the middle and off stumps. It meant a duck for Don. Bradman at the end of his career recalled that delivery as the finest ever to take his wicket. Bradman, in fact, regarded Bedser in the right conditions as close to the most difficult bowler he ever faced. So did a lot of other players, and had England had somebody to complement him in the fashion that Miller and Lindwall complemented each other, the face of post-war cricket could have been markedly different.

Jim Laker terrorised Australia in England, but suffered at the hands of Norman O'Neill in Australia.

Peter May, *below*, erect and correct in all he did. His on-drive was as near perfect as anything in the game.

Laker bowling to a packed field at Manchester, 1956, *top*. He achieved his 19 wickets on a horror pitch.

Norman O'Neill and the power that made him a joy to watch. He later became a fine commentator on the game.

THE WHEEL TURNS

Freddie Brown was a pugnacious man of extraordinary courage, and he deserved better than the 4-1 beating he took as England's captain in Australia in 1950-51. Brown laboured under a series of considerable misfortunes. First of all, his team was not particularly well equipped. The sprinkling of young men they had in their party did not measure up, and the load had to be borne by comparative veterans like Freddie himself, who at age forty carried a good part of the bowling load. Most of their better players were thirty-two or more, and when measured against the Australians their reflexes and their stamina ran a bad second, and their athleticism hardly matched at all. Injuries also dealt Freddie an unkind hand, taking the edge, for instance, off perhaps his most gifted batsman, Denis Compton, and reducing him to a Test average of seven.

Yet by the sheer tenacity of his leadership, as well as the courage of his own performance, Brown might have got them a lot closer. He was desperately unlucky to be thwarted in the first Test when caught on a Brisbane 'sticky', and worked himself into a sufficiently good position to win the second Test only to see it thrown away. Alec Bedser and Trevor Bailey had taken four wickets each in the first innings and Brown had backed up with four more in the second to keep Australia's batting under a fairly tight rein. Thanks to a handsome 62 from their captain, England had enough up their sleeve to require only 179 runs in the second innings, and they had left themselves more than three days to get them. My co-commentator Johnny Moyes remarked at the time that England probably would have got the runs had they had three hours to bat rather than three days, but in the event they pottered about without any real sign of taking the initiative and were dismissed 28 runs short. Lindwall, Miller and the slow-bowler Jack Iverson bowled extremely well, but they were helped mightily by some thoughtless batting. It was a terrible disappointment for Brown. A victory would have made it 1-1 and set up the series as something special, particularly as it had been thirteen years since England had won a Test match against Australia.

Thrashed in the third and fourth Tests, Brown at least had the satisfaction of achieving that long-awaited win in the final Test. He and Bedser took five first innings wickets apiece, and Bedser repeated the dose when Australia batted again. Those efforts, plus a marvellous 156 from Reg Simpson, left England victors by eight wickets. It was Australia's first defeat in 26 Tests. And it was a marvellous triumph for sheer courage and perseverance on Brown's part.

Australians are quick to recognise a man who will fight hard to win, yet accept defeat graciously if he has to. Freddie Brown was that kind of man, and his personal contribution went a long way towards making that visit one of the happiest and most good natured of all England visits to Australia. Such was the popularity of Brown's team, crowds actually willed them to win a Test. When they were beaten in Melbourne after looking certainties, Australia's win was received in comparative silence.

Brown's personal appeal was considerable. He had first come to Australia with Douglas Jardine's team in 1932-33 as a slow bowler, but bowled medium pace in his latter years. In the Sydney Test of early 1951 he was without Trevor Bailey and Doug Wright because of injury, and had to carry a huge slice of the bowling himself on a very hot day. Brown bowled 44 overs with spasmodic success as Australia built a big total.

I had dinner with Brown that night, and as I arrived at his hotel a policeman was in the process of booking him for leaving his car at the front door. I explained to the policeman whose car it was. 'Not that codger who bowled all day?' the policeman asked. Filled with admiration, he remarked it was no wonder he parked close to the door, and volunteered to stand guard over it while I arranged to have it moved. If need be, I'm sure he would have volunteered to park it himself, so markedly did he reflect the general respect that Brown's efforts had won.

He had the respect, too, of the Australian players. Again, Keith Miller comes to mind. When England batted in that same Sydney Test, they got away to a reasonable start to be humming along at 1-128.

Then Miller decided to take a few wickets. I say 'decided' because that is largely the way he operated. When he was really determined to do so, he could make inroads almost at will. He had Hutton, Simpson and Compton in quick succession. England slumped from 1-128 to 4-137 and in came Freddie Brown to stop the rot. On his way to the wicket, Miller accosted him.

'Hey Freddie,' he offered. 'There's a big crowd here looking for some action, why don't we give them a bit?' Brown looked at him quizzically.

'I'll give you three half volleys outside the off stump' Miller continued. 'Make sure you hit 'em.'

True to his word, Miller served up three juicy deliveries which Brown duly crashed through the covers. Three balls, 12 runs. The fourth ball Miller dug in viciously, and it caught Brown fair on the forehead. Stunned, Brown glared at his 'mate' who had been so full of compassion and good humour just a moment before. A wry grin came to Miller's face once he had been assured Freddie was okay. 'I said three balls, Freddie,' he explained. 'Not four.'

It was an exchange to exemplify the spirit that existed between the teams in that era. Highly competitive, totally committed, yet dignified, friendly and sporting. Rivals could be good mates, no matter how hard they played. It is, unfortunately, an attitude that has been largely lost in the higher strata of modern cricket.

By the end of that 1950-51 summer, England had turned the corner with a win at last, and a good section of the Australian team was moving towards retirement. The wheel was about to turn. When it did finally turn in England in 1953, it did so with a new man in charge and a very different attitude abroad.

Len Hutton was born and bred in Yorkshire, where the niceties of English life are traditionally less refined than they are in the Home Counties, to the south. Life is hard and tough, and the men grow up with fight in their bellies. When Len Hutton took over in 1952 as the first professional to be England's established captain, his resolve was firm. He must win. And if he couldn't win, he certainly would not lose.

Hutton had made it to the England team against Australia in 1938. He scored a century at his first appearance, and by the last Test had amassed an innings of 364 which surpassed Bradman's world record of 334, set eight years earlier. The war ate out perhaps his best cricket years, yet he returned to score 2428 runs in 27 Tests against Australia at an average of 56. At his best he was a superlative player, possessed of great concentration and, when the occasion warranted, a range of strokes to take the breath away.

As a captain, he was grim and unyielding, a sort of latter day Douglas Jardine. England teams had taken three successive series hidings from Australia in his time, and he was determined to restore the balance. England captaincy had been the preserve of the 'gentlemen' as the amateurs had been known, who more often than not had learned their cricket in the universities and lived their lives in the social embrace of one of the world's most class-conscious societies. English cricket for generations had operated in the atmosphere of the 'players and the gentlemen', where the professionals were virtual hirelings who changed in different rooms, took the field by different gates, and addressed their amateur team-mates as 'Mister'. It was a quaint and rather odd system that could exist only in the England of Empire.

By Hutton's time that distinction – discrimination if you like – had been worn away. All men were now on the one footing, and England's outlook was professional by name as well as by nature.

Hutton played it very hard. He slowed down the pace of the game, taking the initiative from the Australians who were traditionally more bold in outlook. Hutton won his first series as captain against Australia in 1953 by one Test to nil, with four drawn. The Ashes thus were returned to Lord's for the first time in nineteen years. They were Ashes by attrition.

One of Hutton's ploys was to so reduce the number of balls his bowlers delivered as to significantly restrict his opponents' opportunity to score. For instance, in 1953 England scored 2074 runs from 996 overs at about 2.08 runs per over. Australia scored 2289 runs off 836 overs at 2.74 per over. That meant 215 more runs to Australia off 116 overs fewer. In the fourth Test at Leeds, Australia bowled 177 overs and England hit 275 runs. England bowled less than half as many overs, 82, yet Australia managed 266 runs.

Hutton's attitude was simple. Don't let the Aussies win. Australia had some still useful performers in Hassett, Morris, Harvey, Lindwall and Miller, and some highly promising new blood in Richie Benaud and Alan Davidson. But they were simply ground out of it by England's attitude, more than their cricket, and the series triggered a particularly dull period in Tests between the two countries.

When Hutton's team arrived in Australia to defend the Ashes a year or so later, I challenged Len about his attitude. We were chatting about the relative merits of the two teams, and it seemed pretty clear to me that Australia had a distinct advantage. England had a couple of new and inexperienced fast-bowlers in Frank Tyson and Brian Statham, and some inexperienced batting in the likes of Colin Cowdrey. Australia, by contrast, had a well seasoned team of proven performers.

This theory I put to Hutton, who was moderately inflamed by the suggestion. 'No way! We will win,' he came back. I asked how he could be so sure. 'Because we'll give them less balls to hit than they give us' he replied. That seemed logical enough. Not in the best spirit of the noble game, perhaps, but logical, and as far as Hutton was concerned, effective.

In the event, he was pretty right. Australia bowled 759 overs at England in the series, and England took 2176 runs. Australia scored only 48 runs less – 2128 – but they had to do it from only 564 overs. That's a difference of 1664 balls. England through the series bowled about eleven-and-a-half overs per hour, while Australia rated better than 14. England's manipulation of the pace of the game undoubtedly was a factor in the series.

It was not the only factor, of course. Hutton took some brave decisions which helped. He reasoned pace was the means by which he could destroy Australia, and he decided to put all his eggs in one basket. After they had lost the first Test, he dropped the veteran fast-medium bowler Alec Bedser, who had almost single-handedly carried England's attack through the previous eight years.

Bedser took 1-131 in the first Test. Frank Tyson's figures were even worse, 1-160 off considerably fewer overs. Yet Hutton perceived that

Tyson's greater pace represented a danger Bedser's never could at that stage of his career. With the help of a famous English coach, Alf Gover, who was in Australia at that time, Hutton set about working on Tyson, shortening the run that in Brisbane had him almost at the sightboard, and generally tidying him up to make the most of his athletic speed.

The result was quite dramatic. By the Melbourne Test a month later, 'Typhoon' Tyson, the fastest bowler in the world, had emerged and Australia were on the run. Tyson took four wickets in the first innings, then a marvellous 6-85 in the second to dismiss Australia 29 runs short of their winning target. Australia never recovered from that. Tyson did even better in the third Test, taking 7-27 in the second innings to rattle Australia out for 111 and win easily. Statham was the ideal foil. Tyson took six wickets in the next Test, which England again won handsomely, and Hutton took his team back to England with a very handy 3-1 series win to his credit.

England cricket had risen again. To Len Hutton, the end had justified the means.

ART AND ARTFULNESS

The nearest thing to perfection I ever saw on the cricket field was the glorious execution of the Peter May on drive. With the exception of Greg Chappell, who played it almost as well, no player of my experience has approached the heights of excellence in any one shot that May did with that one. Of all the shots in cricket, I suppose my favourite has always been the cover drive, hit fluently and forcefully and placed so that it sweetly dissects the field. But the on drive has the same art about it when it is played well, and it is a more difficult shot to play. When May played it well, it was breathtaking. It would flash to the boundary, leaving fieldsmen helpless. May would stand and watch, erect, dignified, supreme.

Test cricket saw too little of Peter May. For me there have been few finer experiences than a Peter May hundred, for he captured the graceful elegance that was a feature of so many of the young England players of the 'fifties. Cowdrey had it as well, and so did Ted Dexter, but the pity was it never quite brought the rewards it deserved in terms of England performance.

May did get one fine hundred in the Ashes series of 1956, when he had taken over the England captaincy and was one match down approaching the third Test. He hit 103 at Headingley, and his partnership of 187 with Cyril Washbrook was a turning point of the series. Washbrook, a selector at the time, had not played for six years, but his return at forty-one years of age yielded an innings of 98 and proved most timely. But it was not the elegance of the batting that earned England a 2-1 series win. It was the bowling of the Surrey off-spinner Jim Laker, and more particularly one of the most horrendous pitches ever provided for a Test match.

Laker's capacity for wreaking havoc amongst the Australians was revealed at Leeds in the third Test, when he took good advantage of a difficult pitch to claim 11 wickets and wrap up the match by an innings. Perhaps that performance affected the judgment of the groundsman at Old Trafford, for when the Australians arrived there for the decisive fourth Test, the pitch was an abomination. Clouds of dust swirled about it from the first day, and the ball did such weird and unpredictable things the Australians could hardly lay a bat on it.

Laker was in no doubt as to how things might develop. He told me before the game, which started on a Thursday, that he thought it would be over by Saturday. Colin Cowdrey, too, made a very quick assessment of things. England had won the toss and batted first, and Cowdrey immediately took out the long handle. It was most uncharacteristic batting from him, lashing at everything. His partner, Peter Richardson, then the next man David Sheppard, did exactly the same. They knew they had to make hay while the sun shone, for they were going to be playing on a minefield before too long. I recall the puzzled look on the faces of the Australians when Lindwall's first ball brought up a cloud of dust. At lunch on the first day the groundsmen who took a broom to the batting creases were almost obliterated from sight by the dust storm they had caused.

England thrashed away to score 459. By the time the Australians went in all the unhappy portents had proved spot on. The spin was amazing. One ball to Lindwall was pitched on a reasonably good length. Lindwall went forward, then back, and the ball kicked so much it flew high over his head, over the keeper Godfrey Evans' head, and outpaced the slip fielder to the boundary. Laker bowled to the conditions splendidly. The pace, bounce and turn were erratic and impossible to predict. It was without question the worst wicket I have ever seen for Test cricket. Even the English were embarrassed about it. Sir James Barnes, a British Cabinet Minister at the time, bumped into me at lunch on the first day, denounced the whole thing as a disgrace, and said he was going back to London forthwith.

After play the Lancashire president invited Don Bradman, Bill O'Reilly and me to take a look at the pitch. 'What pitch?' boomed O'Reilly. 'There's no pitch out there.' He refused to go with us. But Sir Donald and I made the trek to the middle to confirm what we already knew.

'I wouldn't mind having a bowl on it' Bradman remarked. I found I could take the turf between my fingers and draw it up, much like a carpet. Nobody could offer any explanation. The pitch had been fine a few weeks before when Australia played Lancashire, but the groundsman apparently had given it a liberal application of marle, a fine manure that should be used many weeks before a pitch is due for play. Whatever inspired the preparation of that pitch, loaded as it was so heavily against Australia's pace and in favour of England's spin, will remain one of the more sinister mysteries of Anglo-Australian cricket.

Laker's 19 wickets there gave him 46 for the series, broke all sorts of records, and sent the Australians home with their collective tail between their legs. The series again had represented a turning point. May and the Australian skipper Ian Johnson believed in an adventurous approach and, compared to the previous series in England, the cricket was bright and lively.

When May returned to Australia two years later to defend the Ashes, he had a formidable team with him that everybody expected could do the job. It didn't quite turn out that way. First there was the influence of Richie Benaud, installed for this series as Australian captain. He injected a new enthusiasm into Australia's operations. They became a sharper, better co-ordinated group intent on the principle of team effort. They were alert and alive, and they drove each other relentlessly to achieve a 4-0 triumph. Not least of May's troubles centred on the skill of Benaud himself, and the left-arm all-rounder Alan Davidson. They ended up with 54 wickets between them, and with the frightening support of pace like Ian Meckiff's, Gordon Rorke's and, to a lesser extent, Ray Lindwall's, they at no stage let England off the hook.

Another factor which counted heavily against England was the swift decline in form of the scourge of '56, Jim Laker. Laker was a shadow of his former self. By the end of the tour he looked like he dreaded taking the field. The principal cause of his distress was the punishing batting of another young giant making his first appearance against England, Norman O'Neill.

O'Neill knew that Laker, with a 46-wicket haul to his credit at their last meeting, represented a huge danger to Australia. He decided there was a psychological battle to be fought, and he determined to get on top of Laker before Laker could get on top of him. O'Neill was chosen for his first look at May's team in an Australian XI which met the tourists in Perth at the start of their tour. He came to me in the billiard room of a Perth club before the game with a simple question.

'Is there any way I can get to Laker?' he inquired. I spoke to him for some time about Laker's bowling in England. We talked of the discernible change in action he had when he drifted a delivery sharply away in the air, and the dangers of picking the wrong delivery to attack. But O'Neill was determined to attack, and it had to be from the outset.

He dealt cruelly with Laker in that first game. I recall one straight hit struck with such power Trevor Bailey did not have time to move from his fielding position near the wheel of the sightboard to cut the ball off before it crashed into the wheel on the other side. It was awesome stuff, and Laker was visibly affected by it. O'Neill savaged him. There were risks involved, but O'Neill was good enough and powerful enough to overcome them, and by taking the initiative there and then he probably killed off the bogey of Laker for the series. Laker did claim O'Neill's wicket in that Perth game, but he was to get him only once again on the entire tour, in Sydney after Norm had compiled a very handy 77.

The tour embraced much controversy. Both Ian Meckiff, the Victorian left-arm opening bowler, and Gordon Rorke, a newcomer from Sydney, made heavy inroads into the England batting with their pace. The English Press claimed loud and long that Meckiff was a thrower, and they were none too happy about Rorke either, who bowled with a considerable drag. Some of the English batsmen reckoned Rorke was almost in their pocket before he let go of the ball, and he was terrifyingly swift. Certainly the bowling of that pair was a huge factor against the England performance, but the supreme quality that won the day for Australia was an unshakeable team spirit and an indomitable will to win.

Benaud maintained most of those qualities with an essentially rebuilt side that went back to England in 1961 and retained the Ashes. The pendulum had swung again. Having been denied the Ashes for nineteen years, England had held them for five, then lost them again. They would remain Australia's for eleven years.

England through the 'sixties had all sorts of trouble pulling together a winning combination. Many of their former champs had held on a little too long, and the normal process of gradual team-building had been dislocated. A lot of new players were required at once, and it was difficult to find the balance of experience and hope necessary to build a workable team. As so often happens with a team a little unsure of itself, the cricket became very conservative. Much of the cricket of the 'sixties was cautious, riskless stuff, in which a good number of inferior players were stretched merely to survive, let alone attempt anything heroic.

Australia through the period were under the command first of Bob Simpson, then Bill Lawry. They were opening batsmen of the highest order, who for a long time comprised one of the finest opening partnerships in the history of Australian cricket. But they had the approach of an opening bat in their captaincy as well. They ground out their matches. They were stubborn, defiant, riskless, dour. The qualities that made them such superb opening batsmen limited them to a captaincy approach that was unimaginative and lacked real flair. They made Australian cricket through that time extraordinarily secure in terms of not being beaten. Big scores and resolute batting were commonplace. But the winning of matches became proportionately difficult. Australia and England met in twenty Tests between the time Richie Benaud retired and Ian Chappell assumed control of the Australian side. Only six of those twenty Tests were decided—three wins apiece. Fourteen draws stood testimony to an attitude, on both sides, that kept the game on a very low simmer as far as excitement was concerned.

This was the decade of war in Vietnam, the protest movement and flower power. It was a decade in which a United States president and a potential president were assassinated, a decade in which man actually walked on the Moon. It was a decade of turmoil in which youth raised a vibrant new voice, and life took on new pace and new vitality. Measured against its time, the dull cricket of the 'sixties had become an incongruity.

That all changed through the Australian summer of 1970-71. Ray Illingworth had taken over as England captain in circumstances not totally accepted by his countrymen. He had taken over when the established captain, Colin Cowdrey, had to stand down with injury, and after some very handy performances in the role, was retained ahead of Cowdrey for the Australian tour. Cowdrey was immensely disappointed at missing the job. The backgrounds and the natures of the two men were very disparate and there was a wide philosophical gap, too, in the way they approached the game of cricket. Cowdrey was the complete gentleman who baulked at confrontation and saw cricket as a traditional thing, in which dignity was important and competitiveness had its bounds. Illingworth was in the mould of Jardine and Hutton. It is perhaps no accident that they were the last two England captains before him to win the Ashes in Australia. Illingworth was a highly combative man, strong, iron-willed and ready to do pretty well anything he felt necessary to win back the Ashes. He was the epitome of a Yorkshire fighter, and he welded into the better part of his team an obsessive lust for conquest.

That had its drawbacks, of course. It upset some of the more traditional elements of his team, and it certainly upset some Australian umpires and a good section of the Australian public. It also affected some Australian players, and perhaps so shaped the attitudes of a man like Ian Chappell that in time England found the boot on the other foot.

The tour started with a series of rather desultory draws. Both Illingworth and his counterpart Bill Lawry were careful not to make themselves vulnerable early on. But before the tour had reached the halfway mark, it was becoming increasingly clear that England had one major plus on their side that Australia could not match. That was the bowling of John Snow. He bowled superbly fast, but he also bowled with such aggression that he inspired a walk-off and near riot in Sydney, and was the scourge of the Australian umpiring fraternity, who warned him constantly.

Snow did bowl short a lot of the time, but in my view not as much as people came to accept. Like few other bowlers I have seen, he had the capacity to make the ball lift sharply from a good length, and he could intimidate without being intimidatory. Several times he cut a swathe through Australia, and it was he more than any other single factor that saw the Ashes won 2-0. Men like Derek Underwood, Basil d'Oliveira, John Edrich, Brian Luckhurst and Geoff Boycott all made their contributions. But it was Snow who won it for them.

I recall a young Ian Chappell explaining how Snow was forcing him to revise his whole approach to batting. His command of the rising ball forced Chappell into some hurried work with his brother Greg to develop defences against the delivery at the throat. The pair of them took to a concrete wicket in Adelaide and hurled a baseball at each other, short, quick and lifting, to better prepare themselves for a type of bowling that became commonplace.

Champions all. Young Greg Chappell, Doug Walters and Rodney Marsh, with their skipper Ian Chappell in England in 1972. It was the start of a great era in Australian cricket.

Bob Massie took 16 wickets on debut at Lord's in 1972, but collapsed thereafter, a victim of his own failing confidence.

Looking like something out of a rogue's gallery, Rod Marsh, Graeme Watson, Ross Edwards and Paul Sheahan recording 'Here come the Aussies', London, 1972.

Headingley 1975, and rival captains Tony Greig and Ian Chappell inspect the vandalised pitch that forced cancellation of the third Test.

Resentment built against Snow's bowling throughout the tour until the final Test in Sydney when the blow he struck Terry Jenner brought matters to a head. Snow was an intractable type for whom a warning seemed to be some sort of dare. Umpire Lou Rowan had a lot of trouble with him, and with Illingworth, and when the Jenner incident took place in Sydney, the confrontation spilled over. There was much finger-pointing and arm-waving as Snow, Illingworth and Rowan did battle. Illingworth argued that Snow's rising ball was not a bouncer.

'Well, there's somebody here bowling bouncers' Rowan offered, 'and it's certainly not me.'

The walk-off in which Illingworth risked forfeiting the last Test and the Ashes was a sad blot on the history of the contests between the two countries, and could so easily have been avoided had both Snow and Illingworth been less provocative. But it could not deny England's remarkable performance in the series. They overcame difficulties within their own party to win the series 2-0, and in the process Illingworth's sharp tactical appreciation, particularly in the use of his bowlers, and his uncompromising competitiveness were brilliantly portrayed.

The tour, though, ushered in a new era for Australia. In the first Test of the series a new wicket-keeper, somewhat overweight and seemingly a little slow behind the stumps, was introduced to the team. He earned the nickname Iron Gloves for a rather sloppy showing in the first Test, but selectors stuck with him and the name Rod Marsh was to play a huge part in Australia's fortunes of the next thirteen summers. By the second Test Greg Chappell had won a place in the Australian team. He began with a century. Like his grandfather and his elder brother before him, he was destined to claim an indelible place in the history of Australian cricket. By the sixth Test a lanky tearaway from Perth named Dennis Lillee had earned his spurs. Lillee had won instant recognition in the match against Western Australia when he greeted the redoubtable Geoff Boycott with a delivery that removed his cap. He took the first five of his 355 wickets in that first Adelaide Test. By the seventh Test, Ian Chappell had succeeded Bill Lawry as Australian captain. The Chappell era was underway.

THE SPIRITED SEVENTIES

Whatever Australia may have suffered at the hands of John Snow, they returned with interest under the spirited captaincy of Ian Chappell. By the second Test of the 1972 tour of England it was clear Australia had shaken off the shackles of the 'sixties and would quickly become a new fighting force in world cricket. Chappell welded in them a lively, competitive spirit not seen since Benaud's day. Through that drawn series of 1972, the 4-1 whipping of Mike Denness' team in 1974-75, through the World Cup tour of 1975 and Centenary Test of 1977, that competitive edge developed an abrasiveness not seen since the era of Jardine. Australia's cricket became fierce and uncompromising and more dynamically successful than it had been for more than a decade.

The second Test at Lord's in 1972 showed the way. For a start, it embraced an innings of 131 by the young Greg Chappell which he rated, even after he had topped Don Bradman as Australia's leading run-getter twelve years later, as his finest innings. It also forged a union between Dennis Lillee and Bob Massie which produced one of the best match performances in England since the days of Lindwall and Miller. Massie finished with sixteen wickets and Lillee with the other four, but Massie would concede his performance owed a great deal to the enormous pressure Lillee had exerted.

That was Massie's debut for Australia. He was close to unplayable in conditions which made his talents for swing and cut quite lethal. Curiously Massie was never to approach that sort of form again. He suffered from a distinct lack of confidence in his own ability, and in later seasons became highly vulnerable to anybody who took a long handle to him. Lillee, on the other hand, looked upon his 31 wickets of the 1972 tour as a launching pad. He worked hard on his game, set aside the effects of a couple of crippling injuries, and became the most successful, and the most feared, Australian bowler of his time.

With an ounce of luck, Australia might have won the Ashes on Chappell's first tour as captain. Having lost the first Test and won the second, they had much the better of the third Test until Chappell set England 451 to chase in 569 minutes in their final innings, and they refused to be tempted.

The fourth Test at Headingley produced another of those distasteful pitch controversies which seem to thwart Australia so often in England. I recall some mild surprise in the Australian team when we were at Hove shortly before the fourth Test and the England selectors hoisted Derek Underwood into their team. Underwood was a highly dangerous left-arm spin bowler on English wickets. He had taken 7-50 in the final Test against Australia at the Oval in 1968, thanks to the assistance of 1500 'groundsmen' who mopped up the field after a fierce rainstorm. That won the Test and levelled the series against Bill Lawry's team.

Greg Chappell regarded Underwood as the best exploiter of a suspect wicket of any bowler in England. But in 1972 there seemed no reason why he should suddenly be brought from nowhere to join the Test side. They had been travelling along reasonably well, basing their attack on the pace of John Snow, the seamers of Geoff Arnold, the medium-pace of Tony Greig and the off-spin of Illingworth. My first reaction when I saw Underwood's name in the England team was to assume they knew something about the Headingley pitch that we didn't.

I shall never forget our first sight of that Leeds strip. A group of Australian players, some Pressmen and myself went out together the day before the game to look at it. It was white and devoid of grass, and looked worse for the fact that it was surrounded by lush turf on all sides. I took a cricket ball and bounced it onto the pitch. It registered a dull thump, and would hardly bounce at all, rising to less than knee height. Ian Chappell just shook his head. Six inches off the pitch we could make the ball bounce chest high.

On every tour I have made to England there has been some sort of problem with the Leeds pitch. We accosted the groundsmen about it there and then. All sorts of excuses were put forward. There had been a rainstorm the previous weekend which flooded it and restricted use of the heavy roller; the pitch had been infested by a fungus called fuserium, which had killed off the grass. Amazingly, it did not seem to affect the turf around it.

Whatever the reasons, Underwood's selection proved a marvellous coup for England. He had four wickets in the first innings and six in the second, and England were simply much better equipped to take advantage of unusual conditions than were Australia. England won by nine wickets and the Australian dream of taking home the Ashes was lost.

It was some consolation to Australia that they won a superb final

Test at The Oval—a Test Ian Chappell often looks back on as the best he played in. This match was memorable for the efforts of the Chappell brothers, who scored a century each in Australia's first innings, five wickets in each innings from a marvellously hostile Dennis Lillee, and a tremendous, unbroken partnership of 71 from Rod Marsh and Paul Sheahan which gave Australia victory by five wickets. Marsh's war dance of jubilation as the winning run was struck summed up the new spirit in Australian cricket. He himself had had an innings of 91 in the first Test, claimed an Australian series record of 23 dismissals, and generally contributed largely to the vitality of the Australian effort.

From there, it was plain sailing for this rebuilt and revitalised Australian side. England toured under Mike Denness in 1974, and were simply never in the hunt against Lillee and his new comrade-in-arms, Jeff Thomson. Thomson was even quicker than Lillee—blindingly quick in fact when he got on a pitch that offered him any sort of encouragement at all. The first Test of that tour offered such a pitch, and by the time he had fired out the openers, Amiss and Luckhurst, with only 10 runs posted, the psychological battle of the summer had been fought and won. There followed a succession of broken fingers and broken spirits that saw England four Tests down before they climbed back in the final Test to win handsomely.

Mike Denness, Keith Fletcher and Tony Greig batted mightily in that final encounter. Denness had had to drop himself for the fifth Test, so poorly had he played, but came back for this one with a superb 188. Fletcher added 146 and Greig a spirited 89, and the Test was won by an innings. Significantly, Thomson did not play because of a damaged shoulder, and Lillee could bowl only six overs.

It was very much the summer of Lillee and Thomson. The more success they had, the more belligerent they became and, spurred on by crowds who had developed something of a blood lust, they were fearsome. The Englishmen could hardly disguise the fact that they feared for their health. The tour produced some grand examples of English courage, however, under the most trying circumstances.

The most striking was the effort of Colin Cowdrey, who was summoned to Australia a few days before the second Test because of injuries in the touring party. Cowdrey was forty-two years of age and the call to arms meant he was making his sixth visit to Australia with an England touring side. He had first toured as a very young man in 1954 with Len Hutton's team, and quickly established himself a player above the ordinary with a magnificent 102 out of an England total of 191 in the third Test in Melbourne.

Despite his enormous natural gifts and his long term in the England team, Cowdrey was an unlucky player. He was perhaps too much a gentleman. He could never muster the 'killer' that others could command. At times, he seemed almost apologetic about his great talent, as if it was a little unfair to the bowlers who bowled to him that he should be able to punish them so. Had he been a little more belligerent in his approach, he might have been even more prolific. As it was he was one of cricket's truly artistic players. He scored five centuries in twenty-seven Tests against Australia and was a joy to watch. Cowdrey suffered too by his willingness to move about in the order, batting at five, four, three and even as an opener on ten occasions. And he suffered immense disappointment in his ambition for the England captaincy, having tasted it in six different series at home between 1959 and 1968, and on three tours abroad, yet never having commanded the role permanently.

In short, he had already given England amazing and selfless service when he was called out of a winter at home to take on Lillee and Thomson in the fullness of their fury. It would have been so easy to leave the job to a younger man. But he did it gladly and gratefully, and at the end he said he enjoyed it. Though only in the country a couple of days and still suffering jet lag, he stood up to the pace in the Perth Test for 22 in the first innings and 41 as an opener in the second, and though he averaged only 18 for the series won everybody's respect for having a go.

Cowdrey was back in Australia in 1977, along with every other former Test player of either country who was healthy enough to stagger on to an aeroplane. The occasion was the Centenary Test at the MCG, the grandest of all cricket occasions, in which Melbourne in particular and cricket in general celebrated 100 years of Test cricket between the two countries.

It was the happiest of cricket weeks, an occasion to roll back the years and enjoy the company of so many great men who have made Anglo-Australian cricket Tests something special in sport. As befitted the occasion, the game was one of the finest ever played between the two nations.

Greg Chappell had assumed the Australian captaincy from his brother Ian, who retired as skipper after the World Cup series of 1975. That visit had been notable for three draws—two of them inspired by some of the slowest, most painstaking batting imaginable. John Edrich had taken nine hours to score 175 in the second Test, and Bob Woolmer hit a record slow century—six and a half hours for the 100—in the fourth to pitch them both into draws.

The brightest spot of that final Test came when a streaker took the field and hurdled both sets of stumps, much to the delight of photographers. Brian Johnston suggested in his commentary he could well have been no-balled for that!

The third Test of 1975 also finished in a draw, thanks to some vandals who dug up the pitch and poured oil all over it in support of somebody they felt ought not to be in gaol. Their 'Free Whoever-it-was' campaign was no particular business of the cricketers, but a handy publicity vehicle for the vandals which they had no compunction about using. The result in the end was three rather painful draws, and on top of other pressures it was enough for Ian Chappell to call quits.

England arrived for the Centenary Test under the leadership of Tony Greig who, by the strength of his personality and his all-round cricketing skill, had restored much of the bite to England cricket that had been lacking on their previous visit to Australia. He was a strong captain with a stomach for a fight, and England's efforts of the era reflected his drive. Australians had plenty of respect for him. He had scored a memorable hundred against the hostility of Lillee and Thomson at their best in Brisbane two summers before, and through home series against Ian Chappell's teams of 1972 and 1975 he had been a well-performed and determined adversary.

Greig made a considerable contribution to the Centenary Test, which in the event provided a standard of cricket and excitement for which the most supreme optimist could never have hoped.

England's bowlers did a sterling job first up to fire Australia out for 138, only to be fired out themselves for just 95. Dennis Lillee was their arch-destroyer with six wickets, and he and Max Walker, supplemented by some very hot fielding indeed, bowled superbly to restore Australia's position when they had looked very uncomfortable. Players on both sides agreed there was no physical reason the scoring in both first innings should have been so low. The pitch offered a little help, but nothing treacherous. The bowlers were simply terribly 'geed up' and the fieldsmen concentrated to the extent that not a chance went begging, and some that were barely chances were taken.

The one thing on which all were agreed was that the sense of occasion had affected everybody.

'It probably shouldn't be the case with Test players,' offered Tony Greig, 'but the occasion definitely got to some of the batsmen. I've never seen Greg Chappell miss a straight ball—I've seen him chop on one or two but never miss one. The guy was so tense trying to do the right thing. There were a lot of guys playing a game they would not normally play.'

Rod Marsh, who broke Wally Grout's Test record of 187 Test dismissals in the game, put it even more succinctly. 'Every time you walk into the Hilton Hotel you see 400 blokes who have probably been better cricketers than you, and you probably feel a little insignificant amongst all the greats,' he said.

Marsh had no need to feel insignificant. His 110 not out in the second innings, on top of superb work behind the stumps, saw to that. Marsh had a couple of times threatened to score a hundred against England. He was 92 not out in Melbourne in 1970-71 when Bill Lawry declared the innings on him, and he scored 91 in the Manchester Test of 1972. But now he had done it, the first Australian keeper to score a hundred in a Test against England. And as a result, Australia had built a lead of 462 as England started their second innings.

To win would have represented for England a feat greater than any side had ever achieved before them. In the event they finished just 45 runs short of the Australian total, leaving the match result identical to that 100 years before when the first Test also had ended in a 45-run Australian win. In achieving a second innings total of 417, England posted more runs for a fourth innings than any team of either country over that previous 100 years. Derek Randall scored 174 of those in his first Test against Australia. He survived a Lillee blow on the head, and was actually given out on 161 only to be recalled. Rod Marsh was quick to declare that the 'catch' which saw Randall heading to the pavilion had not carried, and the Australian captain, Greg Chappell, hurried after Randall to bring him back. It was typical of the sporting spirit of the occasion. Randall was an immediate crowd favourite for his effervescent good humour, and he very nearly pulled off one of the great wins of Test cricket.

Certainly the game's organisers were happy enough for the last day fight. The Queen was due on the final afternoon to meet the teams and when it appeared early in the piece the match might all be over in three days they were in a nice flap. They had gone to great lengths to organise an extra game of some sort to make sure there would be something on when the Queen got there. In the event the atmosphere could not have been better when the teams lined up to meet the Queen, affording the irrepressible Dennis Lillee the opportunity to steal the show by asking for her autograph. Many frowned upon that as somewhat improper but the Queen seemed to join the high spirits of the occasion, and while she declined his invitation there and then, she sent him an autograph later on.

At least officials were spared the problem of the Lord's Test in 1972, when the players were due to meet the Queen late on the fourth day. That was the match Bob Massie wrapped up for Australia with a day and a half to spare, so rather than appear at an empty Lord's the Queen invited the team to Buckingham Palace that evening. The Test win, of course, was the subject of great celebrations, and people like Walters, Chappell, Marsh and Lillee knew how to celebrate. Needless to say, the team was richly fortified by champagne and feeling a very healthy inner glow by the time they actually made the Palace.

This time in Melbourne there were no such difficulties, thanks largely to Randall, and the Queen and Prince Philip were privileged to be on hand for one of cricket's finest hours.

The game produced many heroes. David Hookes, just twenty years old and in his first Test match, smote the England captain Tony Greig for five successive boundaries in one over. Chappell later nominated this show of extraordinary aggression and confidence as the turning point of the game. And the crowd rose as one to the courage of Rick McCosker who, having been felled by a Willis bouncer in the first innings, came in to bat at No 10 in the second innings with his fractured jaw wired and heavily bandaged. He contributed a vital 25 and allowed the Australian innings to linger for what proved to be a decisive margin. It was, truly, a magnificent occasion in every respect.

With the benefit of hindsight, the only dampener perhaps might have been that some of the pressure under which the players were operating was not merely the atmosphere in which the match was played, but the secret negotiations for the establishment of World Series Cricket which at that stage already were well advanced. Still, nobody outside the players and their agents knew at the time, and for those of my generation, and for all the former combatants revelling in the nostalgia of it all, nothing could have destroyed what cricket had given us. And all of it seemed to be encapsulated in that one magnificent week.

Certainly the spectre of World Series Cricket ruined the next few series in which England and Australia met. By the time Greg Chappell's team was a month into the 1977 tour news of the clandestine developments that were to split the game had broken, and from there the pressures under which the players were trying to operate made a normal series impossible. The tour was shrouded in suspicion and dissent. Some players were worried whether they had done the right thing. Others were merely cashing in, at the end of their careers, and the last of their 'establishment' tours was of little consequence. Motivation was low, and the Australians became the centre of an administrative war that painted them as the enemy within. As the controversy raged, the cricket could not possibly command the concentration it deserved, and the Australians were handsomely beaten.

That is not to say they wouldn't have been beaten anyway, of course. They had a relatively inexperienced side, and England produced a couple of match-winning factors in the superb tactical skill of the new captain, Mike Brearley, and the resolution of Geoff Boycott as he moved inexorably towards his 100th hundred in first class cricket. Boycott had made 107 and 80 not out when recalled for the third Test at Trent Bridge, then hit a mighty 191, to the rapturous delight of his home crowd, to top the century of centuries in the fourth Test at Leeds. The resultant innings defeat for Australia returned the Ashes to England.

For Brearley, that triumph was to prove the start of an extraordinary run as captain of England. Brearley played in 19 Tests against Australia, and for 18 of them he was captain. He made his debut in the Centenary Test of 1977, then assumed the captaincy in England later that year when Tony Greig's involvement in World Series Cricket cost him the job. It must have been a difficult time for Brearley to assume control. Yet he did so with such comprehensive skill that his record shows him as the most successful of all England captains. He had the reins for 18 matches for 11 wins, only four defeats and three draws. Of those four defeats, three came in the 3-0 loss to Greg Chappell's team in a mini-series played in 1979-80 to celebrate the return to 'normality' after the World Series split. Even Chappell conceded he was mighty lucky to win those three Tests, having been favoured, for a start, with a toss in Sydney that allowed them to send England in on a damp pitch. Chappell did not want to play on that pitch, but Brearley did. Chappell told me later he thought Brearley had taken the odds there, hoping to win the toss, for Chappell was certain that if Australia had had to bat first Derek Underwood would have had

Ian Chappell came out of retirement to lead the Australians in the World Series Cricket breakaway. Never one for ceremony, his aggressive, sometimes abrasive manner was important to the new venture.

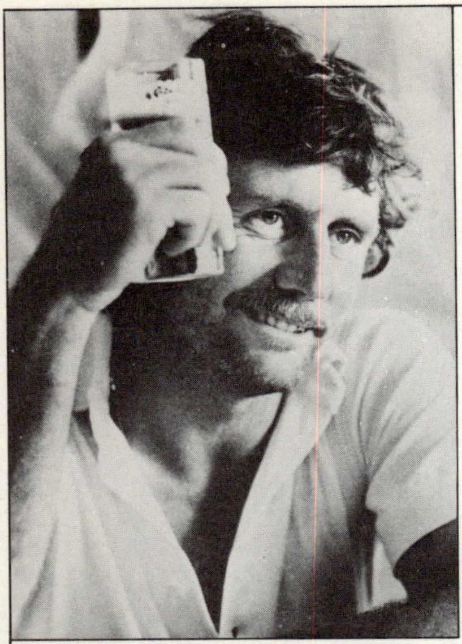

Chappell was at his best when relaxing with a beer, or informally dressed for a Press conference.

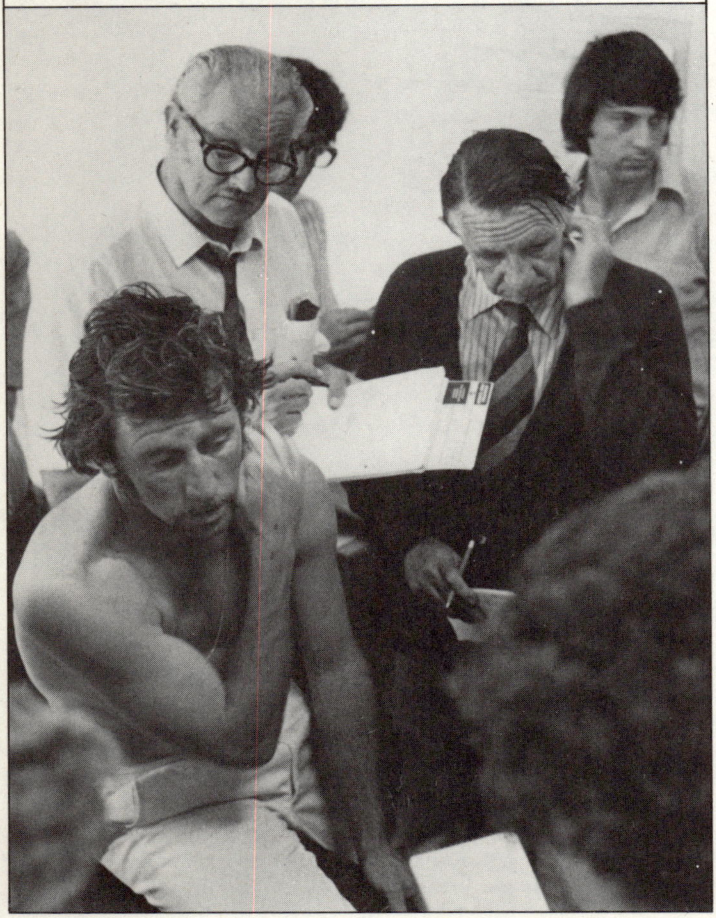

them out inside 100. That was a feature of Brearley's captaincy. He would play the odds, prepared to risk defeat if there was a good chance of a win. Throughout my experience, a certain amount of that sort of daring has been the hallmark of the truly great captains.

Brearley was a highly intelligent leader. An accomplished academic, he had scored a mountain of runs through his university days, but failed to fulfil the promise he showed when first given a chance with the MCC touring side to South Africa in 1964. He finally made it in his middle thirties, although I never considered Brearley totally worthy of a Test place on his batting alone. He scored 798 runs in his 19 Tests against Australia at 22.8 apiece, and topped 50 five times. He occasionally turned in a gritty hand which painted his determination a good deal more brightly than his ability. He hopped about the order a bit, too, playing 21 times as an opener and hovering between No 4 and No 7 for the rest of them.

But if Brearley never commanded as a batsman, there have been few who commanded better as a captain. Admittedly, he came at a good time for England cricket. He took over as the World Series ruckus began and played through a time when Australian cricket was in turmoil. His 5-1 series win in Australia in 1978-79, for instance, was achieved against a very second string Australian outfit under the leadership of Graham Yallop. But Brearley had the sharpest of cricket minds and the ability to make the most of even the slightest advantage. He also had a deep psychological understanding of the players in his side, and an extraordinary capacity for drawing out of them the very limit of their powers.

This was never better illustrated than in the 1981 tour of England. Ian Botham had led England for the first two Tests against Kim Hughes' Australian side, had lost the first and drawn the second, then decided that captaincy was not for him. Selectors brought back Brearley, and England went on to win the next three Tests and the Ashes. It was not merely the victories that indicated his ability, though, but the manner of them. In the first of them, he had the benefit of a poor decision by Hughes to force a follow on, which allowed England's bowlers last use of a deteriorating wicket. But he nevertheless drew a stunning performance, first from Ian Botham whose 149 in the second innings gave England a 129-run lead, then from Bob Willis whose amazing 8-43 chopped Australia off 19 runs short of the 130 they needed to win. Not since 1894, when England beat Australia in Sydney, had a side won a Test after following on.

In that Test and the next, Brearley dragged his team back from seemingly hopeless positions to win narrowly. It is a good captain who can manipulate victory with so little room for error. There was absolutely no doubt that Brearley was a very good captain indeed.

WINDS OF CHANGE

It was one of life's great ironies that the turmoil of World Series Cricket should burst upon us just a few months after the Centenary Test of 1977. Traditional cricket had been ambling along for more than 100 years with little more than cosmetic change, even if the attitudes of players had become somewhat more bellicose. The Centenary Test celebrations in Melbourne painted that century of tradition so well, with so many players of so long ago re-living their memories, replaying their battles. It seemed inconceivable that cricket as we know it was about to be turned upside down by what amounted to a sort of corporate raid by the Sydney media proprietor Kerry Packer, in collaboration with most of the world's better players.

Those who have listened to my broadcasts down the years would probably label me a traditionalist. Some modern players go so far as to say I am a 'square'. But the fact is I did not see World Series Cricket as the ogre which distressed so many of cricket's 'old guard'. Nor do I see the modern one-day phenomenon as the evil that so many traditionalists paint it. Cricket cannot stand apart from the world, though many would like to see it try. The attitudes of modern players in relation to the rewards they can earn from the game, and the changing attitudes of spectators who look for packaged action, only reflect our changing society. Cricket can change too, without sacrificing the basis of its long tradition. The pity is that the game could not effect this change from within. It required an attack from a television network to shake it up and teach it to cope with the changing attitudes of the late twentieth century.

The signs were there to be read for years before the World Series split came. I might well have been present when the first seeds were sown on Ian Chappell's last tour of England in 1975. A few of us were having dinner at Worcester. In the party were Rodney Marsh and his brother, Graham, who for years has been a well-performed player on the professional golf circuit. In relative terms, Graham would have been no better at his craft than Rodney was at his, but he earned a lot more money at it. The subject came up at dinner that night, and Graham Marsh made the point that the Australian players were silly to be making all the money they were making for the Cricket Board, and to be getting precious little of it themselves. There was no doubt the cricketers saw it exactly the same way.

Payments had been increased rather substantially through the mid-1970s, but cricketers still were poor relations in the money stakes when they compared themselves with tennis players, golfers and even the more sought-after club footballers. Clearly they were vulnerable to anybody who could promise them a better deal, and when Kerry Packer came along that vulnerability was starkly exposed.

There were many unfortunate aspects to the establishment of World Series Cricket, of course. For a start, there was the deceit of it all. It was a pity the secrecy of the operation eroded the trust long-standing friends had for each other. It was also a shame the whole operation became so polarised. When the initial split came, a certain amount of pig-headedness on both sides quickly turned it into a chasm.

In the end, though, now that those wounds are healing, has the game been so dreadfully damaged? The introduction of night cricket and the intensification of one-day internationals have drawn a whole new audience for cricket. A different audience, perhaps, less concerned with technique and cricket's finer points, but a new audience nevertheless, and they have given cricket an added dimension. And opportunity now is there for the players to be professional sportsmen in the true sense.

The challenge before cricket administrations is to strike the happy balance that will ensure the survival of Test cricket in its traditional form. To see that eroded would be a crisis, for nothing in sport quite matches the art of a five-day Test battle, in which punch and counter-punch are calculated with a subtlety that no other sport can match. There are dangers to Test cricket in the way one-day matches have been programmed in Australia in recent times.

Limited over cricket, by its nature, encourages different skills. A certain amount of defensive bowling, in which wickets are not important, and a different type of batting are necessary. I hesitate to say careless batting, for there is still scope for skill. It is just different skill. The opportunity does not exist to the same extent for establishing an innings, for building a score through sound technique and patient evaluation of the bowling. Therein lies a danger to Test cricket. Batting skills will not be developed to the same extent if limited over cricket shuts out the first class game.

The other point to be regretted is the proliferation of cricket to the point where the game seems devoid of its focal points any more. In Australia, it is literally hard to keep up with who is playing whom these days, and that can quickly lead to disinterest. There is much to be said for limiting cricket to the extent that there is still the traditional atmosphere of a Test match, that the game still has its peaks and climaxes to savour. The current overkill surely can be tempered without putting at risk the financial gains the game has made.

The one-day phenomenon has provided a few lessons. Its popularity cannot be denied and as a cricket form it is here to stay. In the spirit of compromise, I would suggest further amendments to the normal conduct of cricket in the first class arena that would ease the transition from one game to the other.

There is a case, in my mind, to confine first class cricket as we now know it to Test matches and special occasions. They would be the only games in which each team has two innings, and where the extent of a game is determined by time, rather than the number of overs bowled. Instead of the normal run of first class matches, like the Sheffield Shield in Australia and the County championship in England, I would substitute a competition in which matches were played over two days with 100 overs per side and one innings each. Statistically, more than sixty per cent of Test sides since the war have been dismissed inside 100 overs anyway. Containment would have no place in that game. Bowlers would bowl to dismiss batsmen, and batsmen would still have time to build their innings properly, without throwing the bat willy-nilly.

Containment as it is practised in one-day cricket today is an evil. To see Dennis Lillee bowling to one slip after two overs was dreadful. That took away all his strengths. It made him cannon fodder, for his greatness was his ability to take wickets, not to suspend action. A first class season of 100 overs-an-innings matches would develop and modify skills to suit both Test cricket and one-day cricket. There should not be the stark difference between the games that there is today.

Cricket is a game as malleable to change as any other. Nobody wants to see its art lost. And Test cricket should never change. But in many areas, there is scope for far greater imagination than has yet made itself apparent.

GREAT COMBINATIONS

Anyone who has played the game, be it in the local park or on the hallowed turf of Marylebone or Melbourne, will know that cricket is very much a team game. There have been detractors to argue the point down the years. But those who see cricket only as a collection of individual scores or individual performances understand little of its character. It is a game of dependence, a game in which one man's success provides another man's opportunity.

Throughout my time in cricket, the team aspect has been highlighted by some remarkable partnerships, by men who in tandem have achieved a height of performance they will acknowledge they could never have attained so well alone. The great teams usually revolve around individuals whose prime concern is doing something to make the job easier for their mates. How much better were Hobbs and Sutcliffe together than they would have been alone? How much did Grimmett revel in the success of O'Reilly, and Lindwall in the aggression of Miller? These were combinations which offered more than just physical support. There was a bond, an unstated concentration of forces that made them double trouble for anyone who faced them.

Clarrie Grimmett and Bill O'Reilly were bowlers of my vintage, and I doubt the world will ever see their like again. They remain unchallenged as the finest exponents of the spin bowling art cricket has known. Modern cricket no longer seems to embrace the subtleties which marked their particular brand of bowling.

Figures tell part of the story of their success. In fourteen Tests together, they took 166 of the 239 wickets to fall to bowlers. That's roughly seventy per cent. Grimmett took 88 of those and O'Reilly 78.

When they were in operation, other bowlers usually were there just to make up the number. They were each very thoughtful bowlers, quickish through the air, extremely accurate and absolutely relentless in their pursuit of wickets. At times they gave the impression they were racing each other to see who could clean things up more quickly. There was an affinity, and a rivalry, between them that drew the best out of both, and to face them together was to know not a moment's respite.

Grimmett was prepared to try anything. He would work on new deliveries in his backyard at home, with his dog painstakingly trained to retrieve the balls for him. One such delivery, developed from months of fastidious practice, was a top-spinner which would shoot off the pitch like a medium-pacer. Much later Richie Benaud won renown for his 'flipper', which was a similar ball, but certainly not new as many assumed. Grimmett bowled with a round arm and a leg-break action, but he concealed the variety in his bowling remarkably well. His top-spinner, however, was usually accompanied by a pronounced clicking of the fingers, which the better batsmen were quick to pick up. Stan McCabe once chided Grimmett about the top-spinner, to his cost.

'I can read you, Scarlet,' Stan declared triumphantly. 'You give that ball away with a click of the fingers. Whenever I hear that I know what's coming.'

Next time Grimmett bowled to McCabe he let go a big leg-break. The fingers clicked loudly, McCabe played for the top-spinner, only to be caught at slip as the ball turned off the pitch. Nonplussed, McCabe asked how he did it. 'I've got a left hand too, you know,' Grimmett laughed. He had clicked the fingers of his other hand, and fooled McCabe completely.

Grimmett was thirty-four before he made the Australian team and stayed there for eleven seasons, finishing up with 216 Test wickets at 24.21 runs apiece. He had been hugely successful in England, where his quicker delivery achieved results slower Australian spinners could not manage. He took 25 Test wickets in 1934—his third England tour—and despite a 44-wicket haul in South Africa in 1935-36 was not invited to tour England again. He never forgave the Australian selectors, and more particularly Don Bradman, for leaving him out in 1938. By then he was forty-seven and considered by many to be too old. His age, however, was the only figure to stand against him. All the others still suggested he was one of the best bowlers in the world, as he continued to prove in domestic cricket in Australia for another three or four years. His omission from that side, to me, remains one of the great blunders of Australian cricket.

Grimmett was an ageless character who played with his brain and with an economy of effort that suggested he might have gone on forever. Certainly Bill O'Reilly missed him on the 1938 tour. The man who beat Grimmett, Frank Ward, managed 0-142 in the Tests, and when the last Test was played at The Oval, O'Reilly was left to carry the burden pretty much alone, bowling 85 overs for three wickets in an England total of 903.

How often during that innings he wished he had the little fellow up the other end, weaving that special kind of magic they used to find together. Each believed he was a better bowler when the other was operating with him.

So it was, too, with Ray Lindwall and Keith Miller, whose athletic assaults upon England, particularly through the late 'forties and early 'fifties, are legendary. They played forty-nine Tests together, with Lindwall picking up 195 wickets and Miller 150. It is impossible to separate the pair when trying to evaluate their contribution to the Australian teams of their time. To all intents and purposes they were a unit. Lindwall was the more fluent bowler. He had a glorious action, beautiful control and a variety in the way he could move the ball in the air that made him very hard to play. Miller was more robust, more fiery, more unpredictable.

Comparing them was a rather pointless exercise because they were so complementary in the way they supported each other, but I recall a conversation with the great England opening pair Len Hutton and Cyril Washbrook which perhaps summed them up. 'Lindwall is a magnificent bowler' Hutton said, 'with beautiful control of the outswinger and an inswing yorker that is always a problem. You never really know when it is going to come. But when Miller is really flat out and trying . . . well, I would rather face six overs from Lindwall than one from Miller when he really lets go.'

Miller had a capacity to push himself that little bit extra, to almost will a wicket by sheer endeavour. The Australian team of the time readily recounts the story of the fourth Test against Hutton's team in 1955. England needed only 97 runs in the final innings to win, and the Australians were discussing before play a convenient time for their afternoon golf. The match, surely, would soon be over. A time was set in which everybody assumed England would comfortably get the runs.

'Make it half an hour earlier' Miller piped up. 'We can knock them over by then.' Team-mates knew Miller wasn't joking. He had a streak in him that made impossible situations that much more challenging.

Out they went. Miller bowled like a man possessed. He crashed through the defences of Bill Edrich almost immediately with a magnificent inswinger. He followed that up with the wickets of Hutton and Cowdrey before England had time to draw breath.

Suddenly, at 3-18, England's target of 97 was looking like a very tall mountain indeed. Miller then took a slashing catch in the covers, hurling himself to make the chance out of nothing, and Peter May was gone. In the end only a defiant 34 not out from Denis Compton kept England going. They were five down when they limped to 97, and Miller, virtually single-handed, had turned the game into a real battle for them.

Such was the brute strength and considerable fire with which Miller supplemented the more subtle skills of Lindwall. Miller was a physical bowler, as evidenced by his views on the bouncer. 'Bouncers are legitimate weapons' he used to say. 'The idea is to have a go at a guy . . . to get up around his head and make him duck and weave. When he gets the bat up anything can happen. I bowled plenty of bouncers. I got so many wickets bowling them when blokes tried to hook, I actually gave away the hook shot for fear of falling into the same sort of trap.' Miller conceded that he used to try to frighten batsmen out, and one can only imagine how much effect that sort of hostility had on Lindwall's figures.

As a youth, Miller was a very fine Australian Rules footballer with St Kilda and Victoria, and first won a place in Victoria's cricket team as a hard-hitting batsman. He had started to develop his bowling when the war came and he finished up stationed in England, flying with the RAAF. Keith put down much of his skill as a bowler to a fateful two minute discussion he had with the Derbyshire bowler George Pope, who played one Test for England.

'We were playing an AIF match at Blackpool on VE day' Miller recalls. 'It was a pretty social sort of game, and I was batting. A wicket fell, and while I was waiting for the next man to come in, I started chatting to George. I asked him how he held the ball, and he told me. Then he took off his cap. He was as bald as a badger, but inside his cap he had lashings of grease. For shining the ball he said. I learned more from George about bowling in the minute or two I was waiting for the next batsman than I would have learned from a hundred coaches. And I always used plenty of hair-oil.'

Miller became a world class bowler from that moment. He first teamed up with Lindwall in New Zealand in 1946—the first Test Australia played after the war. Miller vividly recalls his first meeting with Lindwall. 'He was a bright orange' Miller remembers. 'He had been in New Guinea in the latter part of the war and he had been taking anti-malaria tablets which left him an awful colour.' The pair hit it off from the outset. Both were established top-line footballers, Lindwall playing full-back for the St George Rugby League club in Sydney. An intense rivalry they were to develop through their later bowling exploits had its beginnings on that first tour of New Zealand with a football. A series of very competitive contests was organised to see who could kick the longest. Miller eventually won, but the battle was fiercely fought.

Lindwall was very intense in his cricket. He would bottle up his emotion on the field, turning a sort of angry white if a decision went badly against him, but saying nothing. He was also a very nervous batsman, and on his day a quite accomplished one. He was as intense about his cricket as Miller was outwardly casual, and the combination of the two was an unnerving experience for the best of batsmen.

Lindwall would stew for days over a batsman's foibles. Miller recalls the way Lindwall analysed the long-serving England batsman Tom Graveney. He reasoned Tom was a lazy starter. He organised Miller and made sure the pair of them warmed up properly in the dressing room before the game so they wouldn't need any looseners. Lindwall and Miller started like express trains, and Graveney was gone before he had time to get his bearings.

Lindwall kept a huge bottle of vinegar in his bathroom to oil up his muscles, and had an obsession about looking after his body. He would travel miles to find the right physiotherapist.

Miller looked after himself a little less carefully, and was less intense about the cricket, if no less determined. And if there was a race meeting nearby, his concentration was at definite risk.

On one such occasion in England the Australians were playing at Cambridge, and Miller had a very strong tip from one of his jockey mates for the Newmarket races, just a few miles up the road. Miller, conveniently it would seem, was out for about 20, did a quick change and was off to the races, confident his team-mates would bat out the rest of the afternoon. They didn't, of course, and Miller did not make it back to the ground until the Australians were taking the field. And then he made it only through the good graces of some kind friends and a very fast car.

One of the principal motivations of the Lindwall-Miller era was their determination to outdo each other. And on tour in England they performed some heroics through the long grind of county games, merely because they would decide a day on the golf course seemed more appealing than a day at the cricket. Opponents occasionally marvelled at the levels of their effort and hostility in meaningless midweek games which were traditionally a means of gentle practice.

To Lindwall and Miller, the simplest way to get some free time was to skittle the opposition as quickly as possible, and they would bowl as fiercely as if they were playing a crucial Test. The other big factor they had going for them as a partnership was their friendship. They roomed together, drank together, bowled together, and in the end they were one machine, committed to the destruction of whomever they happened to be playing.

Richie Benaud and Alan Davidson were another pairing which carried Australia's bowling through the late 'fifties and early 'sixties. They were each extraordinarily good cricketers, genuine all-rounders who could bowl a side out, or collar an attack, to turn a game. They were the principal bowlers of their era, and Benaud's leg-spin and Davidson's left-arm pace often operated in tandem, defying batsmen to settle into any sort of rhythm. Davidson took 166 Test wickets at 20.58 apiece, Benaud 248 at 27.03.

'Davo', as the cricket world knows him, had 84 wickets against England and Benaud 83. A significant part of their operation together was the cajoling which Benaud, as captain, saved for Davidson. His continual entreaties for 'one more over, Al pal' drew from Davidson some Hurculean efforts with the ball when, to look at him, he seemed spent and crippled. Davidson's career embraced a string of triumphs, few better than the double of 124 runs and 11 wickets in the tied Test against the

West Indies in 1960. He was a very good bowler, who later turned his hand to administration where he has served enthusiastically and well as president of the NSW Cricket Association, and as an Australian selector.

Dennis Lillee was the centrepiece of several successful fast-bowling partnerships. First of all, there were the fleeting glories of Lillee and Massie, whose exploits in England in 1972 went a long way towards putting Australia back on the victory road after some lean years. Towards the end, there was another enterprising partnership between Lillee and another West Australian, Terry Alderman. In seven Tests together they actually took 43 wickets apiece. But the partnership that will stand forever in the memories of those who saw it at its best, and more particularly those who faced it, is the pairing of Lillee and the Queensland firebrand Jeff Thomson.

This was a union of blinding pace and high aggression, a pairing to rank with Lindwall and Miller as the most successful of Australian cricket. They played only eleven Tests against England, but that was enough to win them some sort of immortality. Lillee had 56 wickets and Thomson 57 through that period, and their dominance was such England never stood a chance.

Statistically Lillee finished better than any of the great Australian bowlers. His world record of 355 Test victims, achieved in 70 Tests, is testimony to that. But if you break his figures down, he had 163 England wickets in 28 Tests, which compares rather well with Lindwall's 114 from 29 Tests. It is impossible to compare different eras reliably, and I would hate to have to say which was the better bowler. But no bowler, of either country, can compare with Lillee's success rate. He was a marvellous competitor.

Not least among the reasons for Lillee's success was his driving determination to better himself. I remember when he started off, a raw, unassuming rather quiet and very polite lad, who was ever searching for knowledge. He would seek out former fast-bowling greats like Keith Miller and Ray Lindwall and ask their advice. He was a listener and a learner, and he quickly applied the many lessons to modify his approach and his delivery, and add the complex subtleties of the fast bowler's art which quickly complemented his raw pace.

Pace—pure speed—is the first quality to make a great bowler. Lillee had that in abundance. It was natural, but it was undisciplined. He would be all over the place as he ran in and his accuracy suffered badly. He worked tirelessly on his delivery, concentrating on line and length, working on his variations, developing an economy of effort that would sustain him for long spells and lengthen his career. He also worked hard on his body, building himself up, and refusing to give in when some very bad injuries looked like prematurely finishing his career.

Another factor that proved an enormous help to Lillee and provided as fine a partnership as you would ever see was the emergence of the portly West Australian wicket-keeper Rod Marsh, who made first class cricket and Test Cricket at about the same time as Lillee. Their careers ran parallel, and achieved almost parallel laurels. Marsh, too, finished with a world record 355 Test dismissals. A massive 95 of those Test victims fell to the Marsh-Lillee combination. In all first class cricket, no fewer than 238 batsmen fell to that lethal scoreline, caught Marsh, bowled Lillee. They complemented each other superbly. Like Lillee, Marsh was a very determined worker who realised that success did not come easily. When he started, he was first noticed for his pugnacious batting. He kicked off with a maiden century for Western Australia, scored a lot of first class runs early in his career, and went on to become the first wicket-keeper to score a Test hundred. He had three of them, including a beauty in the Centenary Test, and was very close to a couple more.

But through those early days, only the most generous would have assumed his wicket-keeping could possibly have developed to the stage where it was without peer in the world. I recall being highly critical of the young Marsh on radio in the late 'sixties, when he played against India in his first season as West Australian 'keeper. He was overweight, and very slow to get over the stumps for returns. I met him for the first time later that night, and he challenged me about my comments. I think I told him he had no future as a 'keeper. Ten world records later, I am happy to concede my judgment was rather hasty.

But Rod's early experiences in big cricket taught him some hard lessons. He had a disappointing Test debut in Brisbane. His glovework was sloppy and earned him a lot of criticism, particularly in Sydney where local boy Brian Taber had been the shock omission from the Test side to accommodate him. Marsh took those reverses in his stride. He worked on his fitness first. He fined right down. He transformed from the slow and portly fumbler of those early days into the slickest, most athletic wicket-keeper in the game.

His association with Lillee was a joy. Not only could he read and anticipate Lillee's every move but he offered a fair bit of constructive advice, too. Marsh would suggest a ball here or a ball there to test a batsman's weakness. Greg Chappell will testify to their skill in a Shield match when Marsh signalled Lillee for a high bouncer down leg side. Marsh then stationed himself well away from the stumps on the leg side. Chappell hooked, got the finest of edges and Marsh was in position to take the catch yards wider of the wicket than he could ever have been under normal circumstances. Chappell couldn't work out how he managed to get there.

Between them Lillee and Marsh were a tremendous asset to their country's cricket. They were competitive, determined and industrious, and the success they achieved they earned through extremely hard work. Lillee, perhaps, did not endear himself to everybody with some of his behaviour. He let his competitiveness run away with him on too many occasions, resorting to levels of petulance that did him and his team no credit. That's a pity. Much of it perhaps was the result of unbridled enthusiasm, but much of his histrionics was pure bad form. To me, dignity is an important ingredient in cricket. It is one of my cricketing regrets that my admiration for Lillee as a supreme cricketer, and my regard for him as a man, were tempered by a row we had in an Adelaide hotel.

I had been invited to act as Master of Ceremonies at a testimonial dinner for Lillee in Brisbane. I accepted, but later withdrew. A similar dinner was on in Perth during a Test, and when I was not invited for that one, I felt I was being used for the other. It was a small point, perhaps, but such courtesies have always been important to me, and I would have felt uncomfortable about doing the job in Brisbane.

At the same time, Lillee got himself involved in a very distasteful confrontation with the Pakistan captain Javed Miandad, in which Miandad was kicked in the pants, Lillee was menaced with a bat, players shaped up like boxers, and umpires had to step between them. It was hardly dignified behaviour, and in my view an insult to so many great players who had graced the game before them. I said so on television.

A week or two later I ran into Dennis Lillee in a hotel in Adelaide. I was having a drink with some friends when Lillee spotted me. He launched into a tirade of abuse. It was a very heavy salvo indeed, and it upset me greatly. Dennis was not only hot under the collar because I suggested he be suspended over the Miandad affair, but I think he misinterpreted also my reasons for pulling out of his Brisbane dinner. The Press, too, assumed I had dropped out there as some sort of protest at Lillee's involvement with Miandad. That was simply not the case, but Dennis was in no mood for any explanations when our paths crossed in Adelaide. That exchange is one of my great regrets in cricket. I admired Dennis greatly, and for the greater part of his career I got on pretty well with him. I certainly enjoyed his cricket very much. He was truly a great performer.

England, too, had their best rewards from bowling partnerships of high calibre. When Alec Bedser bowled so well for them, for instance, he could find nobody to help much at the other end, and success was consequently hard to come by. He did a sterling job, and might have been a real giant with help, but he had to battle through with fifteen different partners, so he was pretty much on his own. When Brian Statham, Frank Tyson and Freddie Trueman happened along, all about the same time, England suddenly had bite from both ends, and their fortunes changed dramatically.

Tyson was something of a one-tour wonder, but his partnership with Statham through the Australian tour of 1954-55 absolutely shattered Australia. Tyson had most of the wickets then, and his pace was extreme, but the Australians were quick to pay credit to Statham, who was pretty nearly as quick in those early days anyway. He was also supremely accurate. His line and his length were immaculate, his movement off the pitch disconcerting, and he offered nothing loose that gave a batsman room to manouevre.

When Trueman added his Yorkshire belligerance to Statham's relentless control, batsmen of all persuasions felt their sting. They played eleven Tests together against Australia for 74 wickets between them. Through their period they were dynamite for England, complementary in nature as well as in deed. Statham was the essence of reliability, bowling long periods without flinching. Trueman was the firebrand, aggressive, unpredictable, as accomplished at getting a laugh as he was at getting a wicket. He was one of the game's real characters. He would find a funny story for each of his 307 Test wickets.

The wicket Statham will remember most, however, is the one he didn't want to take. It was on the England tour of Australia in 1962-63, and the Australian Prime Minister, Sir Robert Menzies, had prevailed upon Sir Donald Bradman to turn out in a Prime Minister's XI against the touring side. It had been fifteen years since the fifty-four-year-old champion had played his last Test innings, but he agreed to play—just this once.

When the time came for him to bat 10 000 people had packed the small Manuka ground in Canberra to see another glimpse of the immortal Bradman. Many who had never seen him knew only the legend. The air was heavy with the excitement of it, not least among the England players. Bradman played one straight drive for four off Tom Graveney and a couple of defensive shots, then faced up to the fateful ball from Statham. The ball pitched outside the off stump and Bradman met it with a defensive bat. The ball flicked off the bat, on to his leg, and somehow managed to rebound to the stumps with just enough force to dislodge a bail. There was universal remorse. Statham was shattered. Umpire Alan Davidson was too stunned to call no-ball, and as the prince of batsmen made his way off the field for the last time, thousands of people who longed for a few runs at least, were left to lament. Nobody was sadder than Brian Statham.

Of the other successful bowling partnerships of my time, three stand out. Tony Lock and Jim Laker formed a formidable spin pairing for England, skittling Australia in one series, but their success at the national level was short-lived compared to that they enjoyed with Surrey. The West Indies produced two superb bowling combinations in the pace pair Charlie Griffith and Wes Hall, and the spinners Alf Valentine and Sonny Ramadhin.

Laker and Lock won the Ashes of 1956 in two stunning performances at Leeds and Manchester. They shared eighteen wickets at Headingley and all twenty at Old Trafford, where Laker's nineteen wickets took something of the gloss from the considerable contribution made by Lock. Each was the ideal foil for the other, and together their immaculate control won many victories.

Spin bowlers have to be good to succeed in England, and when the West Indies pair Ramadhin and Valentine finished the 1950 Test series with fifty-nine wickets between them, they clearly were a partnership out of the ordinary. That England series was their debut in Test cricket, and to say England were somewhat taken aback is an understatement. They never achieved quite the same success in two series in Australia, although they were always a danger, and particularly so when Lance Gibbs was added to the West Indies spin armoury in 1960-61. Together Ramadhin and Valentine played ten Tests against Australia for fifty-one wickets—31 to Valentine and 20 to Ramadhin. Against all countries together Valentine had 113 and Ramadhin 111 in 29 games.

They played through a time when West Indies cricket lacked the direction it later acquired under captains like Frank Worrell and Clive Lloyd. In the Melbourne Test of the 1951-52 series, Australia still needed 38 to win when Doug Ring and Bill Johnston came together for the last wicket. At that stage three wickets had fallen for four runs and Australia looked to be beaten. As Johnston and Ring pegged the target back, the West Indies panicked. The captain, John Goddard, lost control, arguing with Jeff Stollmeyer and Gerry Gomez about who should bowl. Ramadhin simply got fed up with it and walked off the field, with Australia still a few runs short of victory. Valentine and Ramadhin had taken eight wickets in that innings to have Australia on the run, but the confusion within the West Indies ranks thwarted the victory. It was not the only time that lack of direction in West Indian cricket of the era counted against the talents of Ramadhin and Valentine.

Keith Miller, *top left*, was the complete cricketer. He bowled and batted with tremendous skill and aggression, and had a brilliant 'feel' for the game. Ray Lindwall, *top right*, . . . one of the finest fast bowlers of all time.

Together, Keith Miller and Ray Lindwall were unbeatable and great mates, on and off the field.

Sonny Ramadhin and Frank Worrell, *top left*. Worrell lifted West Indies cricket to international level.
Everton Weekes, *top right*, the West Indies batting champion who fell foul of Lindwall and Miller.
Cricket in the West Indies . . . as much a game for boys on the street as for champions in the stadiums.

THE GAME OF GAMES

The Royal Hotel in Bridgetown, Barbados, sprawls down to the beach. The water is a striking emerald green, and the sand is white enough to be taken for snow, but for the waves that lap upon it and the ebony bodies that cavort there. The hotel itself has an enormous rock swimming pool that must go for 150 metres or more. On one side are the rooms, with verandahs opening on to the water. On the other side is an exotic tropical bar and breakfast room, where rum and coke are consumed in vast quantities and peals of laughter drift into the air all day.

I made sure on my three tours to the West Indies I had one of those rooms with the verandah. It was about six paces to the water, and a swift, invigorating swim to breakfast was an ideal way to start the day.

The idyllic setting and the holiday atmosphere of that hotel were typical of my first impressions of the West Indies. The islands, generally speaking, were happy, carefree places where life was for living and enjoying on a daily basis. Nobody worried too much about tomorrow's problems. Tension, pressure and a variety of other modern commodities had no place there. A cold rum and coconut water, a game of cricket with the kids on the beach—these were the high points of existence in countries where summer sun and happy grins were taken for granted.

On my first trip there in 1965 I was asked to help educate a commentary team who were about to present cricket live on television for the first time. I spent four days working with a quartet of broadcasters who obviously knew little of their craft, but seemed willing enough to learn. At the end of it I was rather pleased with the progress we had made. Came match day, and four new commentators turned up. The lot I had been working with had the day off. That is the sort of people they were. They did not seem to worry too much about anything at all. So long as everybody had a good time.

In later years it was heart-breaking to see much of that splendid good nature eroded. External and internal pressures of all sorts seemed to get to the very heart of the West Indies character. Economic difficulties, unemployment and an inevitable pre-occupation with racial differences so soured the West Indies community as a whole that on my last tour there, in 1978, I actually feared for my life. I was asked to leave the West Indies for my own safety. I vowed never to return.

But those unhappy days were a long way off when I first became involved with West Indies cricketers in the Australian summer of 1951-52. The West Indies at that time were still comparative newcomers to the expanding world of international cricket.

The various nations that comprise West Indies cricket were still somewhat disparate. Cricket was the thing that gathered them together best. But as they moved from the umbrella of British protection and carved an independent spirit, they inevitably clung to differing philosophies and the jealousies and suspicions that neighbours develop became apparent.

That attitude has tended to spill into West Indies cricket for much of the time since their introduction to the Test scene in 1928. The cricketers have always got on all right together. But their varying backgrounds seemed to undermine their common effort. So often, when the crunch came, there was not that ultimate competitive edge that develops only when there is something to fight for, and the fight is fought with unity and total harmony.

Certainly in the early tours to Australia the rich and natural talents that abounded were never welded into a unified side. G C Grant's team in 1930-31 had some wonderful players like George Headley and Learie Constantine, but could never really get their act together against a fine Australian team under Bill Woodfull. They lost that series 4-1.

Again in 1951-52, the skipper John Goddard could not successfully tie together the talents he had at his disposal. Their side was never totally disciplined or unified, and they also lost 4-1. Yet this was the team of Weekes, Worrell and Walcott, the famous three 'Ws'.

Frank Worrell ultimately went on to turn the tide for West Indies cricket. Prior to his taking over the captaincy in 1960, West Indies had used ten captains over a period of fifty-five Tests and won only twelve matches. Worrell and later Clive Lloyd, who helped develop one of the finest cricket teams the world has ever known, had the capacity to drag West Indies cricket together. They succeeded where others failed in making brilliant teams out of a collection of talented but undisciplined players from different countries. And they each succeeded in producing some of the finest international cricket the world has seen.

The West Indies came of age as international cricketers under Worrell in the early 'sixties, but much of their new competitiveness was undoubtedly born on that tour of Australia ten years earlier. Everton Weekes took a battering from Keith Miller and Ray Lindwall in the final Test and the lesson that Test cricket was a very different animal to the happy-go-lucky cricket of the islands would not have been lost on Worrell.

Weekes was a magnificent batsman. He was small in stature but big on courage, and had a sense of timing and strokeplay that set the tone for many West Indies champions who followed. I can remember him in his forties, when he had long retired from competitive cricket, playing a match in the West Indies with an under-19 team. He made quite a few runs against the young bowlers, but such was the quality of his batting it was often quoted to young players who followed as the 'perfect' innings. It was virtually mistake free, full of exquisite judgment and precise timing, and still with a great deal of the power that had marked his time on the Test match stage.

Weekes' most devastating shot was the hook shot. He whipped the bat across his brow like a fly-swatter. He would peel the ball virtually from his eyes, roll the wrists over the shot and crack it hard and low towards the square leg fence. He played that shot with relish against Lindwall and Miller in Brisbane in the first Test of the 1951-52 series. He made 70-odd in the second innings, and made them with such defiant flourish that he seemed certain to have an enormous summer.

As it turned out, he did not have a particularly good series. But Lindwall and Miller could not shut from their minds the pasting Weekes had dealt them at the start of the series. They simply had to finish on top. They were, after all, the finest fast-bowling combination in the world and the most devastating since Harold Larwood and Bill Voce almost disintegrated the British Empire twenty years before.

In the last Test in Sydney they let Weekes have it. The series had already been won, and there was certainly no need to introduce any nastiness into the final stages of what had been a pleasant summer. But Lindwall and Miller gave Weekes a frightful peppering. Almost every ball was a bouncer. Weekes had made a duck in the first innings, and although he stood up to it for a while in the second innings, he took a terrible hiding. He made 21, caught behind off a Lindwall flier.

Many argued that the end justified the means. Miller took five cheap wickets in the first innings and Lindwall five in the second. But it was not good to look at. I felt they were out of order and I said so on the air. That raised a few hackles in the Australian dressing room. I was invited down for a chat to be greeted by a very angry Ray Lindwall at the dressing room door.

'You had no right to say those things' he thundered at me. 'I ought to thump you in the nose.' It was hardly a very pleasant greeting.

'Hit me and I'll fall down,' I answered quickly. 'But I'll get up a gentleman, and you won't be.' It was all I could think of quickly. Without waiting for him to consider his next move, I removed myself from the dressing room as fast as I could.

It is often a source of amazement to me how blind patriotism colours people's thinking on simple matters of right and wrong. I had no doubt in my mind that the treatment Miller and Lindwall dealt to Weekes was wrong in concept and hurtful to the game in its execution. I could find few who agreed with me.

My 'attack' on Lindwall and Miller became headlines. When I went to an ABC farewell party that evening I was made feel like a leper. It was made very clear to me that my comment was considered to be some sort of treachery against the Australian team. Miller and Lindwall were folk heroes at the time, national figures of the most revered kind. When I finally broached the subject with them, the heat had died down and they laughed at me for worrying about my remarks. They are now both firm and lifelong friends.

But I still believe they were wrong to attack Weekes the way they did, and I suspect Frank Worrell felt the same way. Certainly by the time he returned in charge of the West Indies team of 1960-61 he was totally committed to winning, and to competing with Australian cricket on Australian terms.

Frank Worrell had a strength of character that set him apart. He was a very intelligent man with a keen understanding of people. He was the product of an era where consideration and courtesy were important qualities, and his kindness endeared him to all who met him.

He knew the battle he faced in making a united team out of the West Indies, but it was a problem he was prepared to address and one he attacked with supreme skill.

The tour did not start well for Frank. The run around the States prior to the first Test brought him one win from seven games. It was hardly an encouraging start. But Worrell refused to capitulate. One by one he identified the difficulties the West Indies faced, and one by one he solved them. He did so with such emphasis that by the time the team left Australia, at the end of the greatest series of them all, they were national heroes.

The turning point of the tour came in Melbourne against Victoria a couple of games before the first Test. Rohan Kanhai hit a magnificent 252 in this game and Sonny Ramadhin picked up 10 wickets with his looping spin. Those performances gave confidence, and in part proved to the West Indies players that they had the equipment to beat Australia if only they could use it properly.

The more significant result of that match for Worrell was the performance of Victorian leg-spinner Lindsay Kline. He took 4-93, and bowled with enough command to again raise the question in Worrell's mind as to whether his batsmen were totally 'psyched out' when it came to confronting slow bowling.

His concern grew very large indeed after the Sydney match against New South Wales, when the Australian captain Richie Benaud ripped into them with 6-61 and NSW won by an innings and 119 runs. Worrell knew that he had to somehow convince his team that Benaud and spin were not necessarily the bogy his batsmen seemed to think they were.

That became his mission for the first Test. He had to prove that Benaud could be handled. Talking to his team got him nowhere. I recall some long evenings where we sat and chatted. Frank would simply shake his head. 'How can I convince them? How can I make them believe Benaud is not good enough to get us out?' he would ask.

Frank was expert at reading his players' minds. He could tell what they felt, how they felt. He could see it in their eyes. In this case he could see that no amount of talking was going to solve anything. Benaud's psychological edge over his batsmen was too entrenched. His only recourse, he reasoned, was to show them.

Worrell went in in the first innings of the first Test when the West Indies had lost 3-65. Gary Sobers was at the other end. Worrell's primary concern was for the tour, and despite the precarious nature of their position, his main object remained proving to Sobers and the rest of his side watching from the dressing room that Benaud was not the great bowler they assumed.

He shepherded the mighty Sobers through the early part of that innings. Worrell took as much of Benaud's bowling as he could possibly organise. The concentration he summoned was extraordinary. Sobers was sufficiently impressed to go on to score 132. Frank was out for 65, but not before he had added 174 runs with Sobers for the fourth wicket and virtually guaranteed that the spectre of Benaud's leg-spin would not hang over them all summer. Benaud finished with 0-93 off 24 overs in that innings and took only one wicket for 162 in the game. He finished with 22 wickets for the series, but by no means did he dominate as the West Indies at first feared. For Worrell that first Test performance made the difference between a good tour and a bad tour. He could now see some real light at the end of the tunnel.

That match, of course, became the famous tied Test. Each team scored 737 runs with the final Australian wicket falling to the second last ball of the match. It was a game in which everything that cricket has to offer was wrapped in one dramatic parcel and dropped on a nation's cricket-lovers as the game's ultimate offering.

The match was gripping from the start. There was Worrell's duel with Benaud; there was a splendid innings of 132 from Sobers. Alan Davidson, that great Australian all-rounder, became the first player to score 100 runs and take 10 wickets in a Test match. He was magnificent. Norman O'Neill thrilled the crowd with an innings of 181; Wesley Hall was athletic magnificence of a rare kind as he crippled the Australian batting in the second innings to take 5-63.

Had the match not ended in a tie and thus won itself an indelible place in the history of the game, it would still have been notable for the quality of its cricket. The drama at the end, of course, is now legendary. In that last over seven balls were bowled, five runs were scored to bring the scores level, one batsman was caught, a catch was dropped, an attempted run out failed, and the last two batsmen were run out when the scores were level.

It had looked all over for Australia when Hall had ripped through their second innings to leave them 6-92. Australia was chasing 233 and things looked grim. Then Benaud joined Alan Davidson, and the value of a couple of good all-rounders was never better in evidence than in their partnership of 134. That took the score to 226—seven runs needed to win. A brilliant piece of work by Joe Solomon ran out Davidson. New man Wally Grout took a single off the first ball then faced Wes Hall for that last over. As might be said these days in the vernacular of modern television and the one-day scrambles, the equation then read: Runs needed 6, balls remaining 8, wickets in hand 3.

History has well recorded that last over. I have listened to the tape of Clive Harberg's description over and over again. It is magic cricket.

First Ball: Grout hit on leg. No time to worry about that however, since Benaud calls him for a single with the ball stationary about a yard from the stumps. They make it. The equation now reads five runs wanted, seven balls remaining, three wickets standing.

Second Ball: Hall lets fly a bouncer. Benaud swings to hook. A faint touch of the glove and 'keeper Gerry Alexander roars his appeal for the catch. Benaud out for 52. Still five runs wanted, six balls to come, two wickets in hand.

Third Ball: Ian Meckiff plays it without a run. Still five runs wanted, five balls left.

Fourth Ball: Meckiff fails to make contact and Grout, taking off like Jesse Owens, calls for a bye. Four balls left, four runs to get, still two wickets standing.

Fifth Ball: Grout goes on to the back foot looking for his favourite hook shot. The ball is too far up for it but still he swings and the ball flies high into the air at square leg. Kanhai moves to get under it but ducks out of the way as the big frame of Wesley Hall comes at him trying to make the catch. Hall drops it. The batsmen scurry through for a single. Three runs wanted, three balls to go.

Sixth ball: Hall, somewhat heart-broken, moves in again. By now a certain amount of pandemonium has broken out in the crowd. This time Meckiff swings across the flight of the ball, somehow manages to connect and the ball flies high towards the mid-wicket boundary. Clive Harberg calls the four. The match looks over. But the grass in the outfield had not been cut that morning and a patch of clover slows up the ball sufficiently to allow Conrad Hunte to field. The batsmen have completed two and turned for three as Hunte picks up. It looks safe enough. Meckiff has the speed but Grout hasn't. The ball flies to Alexander's gloves and the bails are off before Grout, diving full length, is anywhere near his crease. The batsmen had crossed for their third run, so two counted and the scores were level. Two balls remain. One wicket standing.

By this time confusion reigned. The scoreboard attendants had no idea what was happening. The players weren't sure how many runs were needed. But the umpires Col Hoy and Colin Egar, whose poise and concentration were unbelievable through those final overs, had command of the situation throughout.

Lindsay Kline joined Ian Meckiff for the seventh delivery.

Kline played it towards mid-wicket. Meckiff called him. Solomon gathered fifteen yards out. There was nobody at the wicket to take his throw. Alexander, standing back to Hall's pace, had no hope of getting there. Frank Worrell saw that and raced to the bowler's end and called for the ball. It was a certain run-out at that end since Kline had been late in responding to Meckiff's call. But the noise at the time was deafening. The crowd was screaming. The players were screaming. Solomon had no hope of hearing his skipper's call. He threw to the wicket-keeper's end. He had the width of no more than one and a half stumps to hit from his side-on position.

In perhaps the most significant piece of fielding in the history of Test cricket, little Joe Solomon's throw homed in on the stumps like a laser beam. Meckiff was still a yard short and umpire Hoy's finger went up. Australia all out 232. Scores level. Match tied. The first tie in Test cricket.

In the pandemonium that followed few people realised it was a tie. The West Indies players dashed off the field thinking they had won. Worrell was shouting at them 'No, we haven't won'. Nobody could hear him. The Australians thought they had lost. Meckiff was furious with himself for getting run out. Benaud ran on to the ground to shake Frank Worrell's hand. The skippers knew the result, and as it sank in all over the country, the success of Frank Worrell's tour was assured.

Now I can assure you my account of the last moments of that Test is a faithful one. As I said, I have listened to the broadcast a hundred times. I have discussed that final over with every man who took part. I have listened entranced to their various accounts of it. Through the rest of that tour we talked about it again and again. If I didn't raise the question of it to satisfy my thirst for information as to what actually went through the players' minds, they made sure they related the drama of it to me. And they did so with a touch of sadistic pleasure.

For the fact is I missed it. I wasn't there. In what must rank as the greatest error of judgment in my life, I left the ground with a couple of hours to go on that fateful afternoon to catch an early plane back to Sydney. My broadcasting commitments had finished for the day, and with Australia heading to a seemingly certain defeat in the early afternoon, Keith Miller and I decided we would head back to Sydney on the last flight, rather than wait in Brisbane the extra day. As we neared Sydney the hostess in the aircraft volunteered to us the news that the match had finished 'even'.

'You mean it was a draw?' Miller asked. 'No, it wasn't a draw' she replied. 'Then the West Indies won?' Miller offered. 'No, nobody won it' she said. 'I'll go back and find out.'

By the time she returned with confirmation Miller and I had canvassed the possibility of the only other result – a tie – and were in the process of attacking a bottle of Scotch and convincing ourselves it simply could not be.

It was, of course, and I don't think I have ever really got over it. I have spent nearly twenty-five years being furious with myself for leaving Brisbane that day. Never again have I left a Test match early.

AUSTRALIA BY A WHISKER

By the second Test match in Melbourne the West Indies had run off the rails a little. As often happens when gifted players of real flair suddenly scent a chance against a team considered better than they are, they changed their approach entirely. Gone was the dashing band of batting cavaliers that had taken the Australian bowlers by the scruff of the neck in Brisbane and enthralled a nation's cricket lovers with their daring. In their place was a bunch of tentative fumblers, hellbent on tight defence whose conservative appraisal of every ball rendered them dull and ineffectual.

The disaster their change in attitude brought was compounded by having the worst of very difficult conditions. Their bowlers had to toil in temperatures which reached 103 degrees Fahrenheit in the shade, and were hovering somewhere around 150 degrees in the centre. Big stands at the Melbourne Cricket Ground make for big crowds, but they act as a windblock and make it hell in the middle on a hot day.

The end result was that the West Indies played like a rabble. They were out for 181 in their first innings and had to follow on. Then came three wickets in four balls from Johnny Martin, that bubbly little left-arm spinner from NSW whose big-hitting sixes were as much a part of his game as his prodigious spin. Those wickets—Kanhai, Sobers and Worrell—put paid to the West Indies.

By the third Test in Sydney, Frank Worrell had quietly worked himself into a position of supreme command. For the first time in their history, the West Indies had become a coherent, workmanlike band of international cricketers. Their play was co-ordinated, their competitiveness thoroughly established. They played with a precision that brought the first signs of the machine-like cricket that became their hallmark in Clive Lloyd's day, twenty years later. But for all the new purpose and direction, they had taken a firm decision not to alter their outlook. The conservative nonsense in which they had indulged in Melbourne was gone.

It was not an easy scene for them. They had been soundly beaten twice by NSW on the SCG pitch, and defeat here would have sent the tour into decline. But from the time Conrad Hunte got hold of the first ball from Alan Davidson and slammed it through the on-side for four, it was clear what their approach would be. Thanks to a magnificent innings of 168 by Gary Sobers, and some splendid second innings spin bowling by Lance Gibbs and Alf Valentine who shared nine wickets, the West Indies won by 222 runs and the tour was alive again.

The fourth and fifth Tests were triumphs for cricket. The West Indies could easily have won both games and finished the series 3-1 victors against Australia. Certainly they should have won the fourth. This was a match in which their cricket had matured to the point where they were in command all the way. Rohan Kanhai had picked up a century in each innings, Lance Gibbs had added a blaze of excitement with a first innings hat-trick. Everything they did was done with composure and polish. Everything, that is, but the finishing touch.

When Worrell declared closed the West Indies second innings, leaving Australia 459 runs to chase, it seemed they had plenty of time to wrap up their victory. They were thwarted by that legendary last wicket stand of Ken Mackay and Lindsay Kline which lasted for nearly two hours. It was an afternoon of unbelievable tension. Messages came back to us that streets were emptying through the cities of Australia as people ran to a radio to listen to those last overs. The quality of the match, and the courage with which the battle was waged, were best summed up by Wes Hall's last ball to Ken Mackay. Rather than risk anything by allowing the ball to touch the bat, Mackay thrust out his chest and took it on the ribs. As the ball fell dead at his feet, the match over and safely drawn, Mackay's ribs felt like a knife had been plunged into them.

But, again, the two teams had produced a match and a finish that would live on as long as cricket was talked about. Like the tie in Brisbane, it was pure magic.

The final Test was hardly less exciting. The teams had level-pegged throughout until, on the last afternoon, Australia had just three wickets standing with four runs still needed to win. Then came a sad incident that may or may not have affected the result, but which will forever leave a question mark on the ultimate Australian victory.

Once more the tension was terribly high as Alf Valentine bowled to Wally Grout. Grout jammed the ball through slips and took off. Valentine pointed to the ground, where the off bail had fallen. Gerry Alexander stood with his arms spread, appealing for a 'bowled' verdict against Grout. That would have left Australia eight down with four runs still needed—a remarkably similar scenario to that which had resulted in the Brisbane tie. From there, anything was possible.

Umpires Hoy and Egar did not see how the bail was dislodged. They conferred and decided they could not give Grout out. According to the letter of the law they were well within their rights. But, clearly, Grout should have been on his way. There was really no way the bail could have fallen off the stumps except by the action of Grout playing his shot. The circumstantial evidence against Grout was enough to hang him. By a process of elimination, the ball, surely, must have grazed the off stump. I asked Wally later what he thought had happened. He theorised that the ground around the stumps had been breaking up, and that when he jammed down hard on the ball some flying turf may have hit the stumps.

Certainly he did not feel he had touched the stumps, either with his bat or his foot. Nor did he hear the ball hit the stump, although he conceded it could have. But the tension had been such at the time, he wasn't really sure what had happened. I suppose nobody will ever be sure. Grout had enough doubt to feel obliged to throw his wicket away next ball, but the two runs were crucial and Australia duly sealed the series by two wickets.

No series could ever have been so closely contested. Significantly, the argument that raged about the Grout 'bail affair' was conducted only among the public and the media. The cricketers themselves forgot it in an instant. They had played in a magnificent series that had captured all that is fine in cricket. They had enjoyed good fellowship; they had conducted themselves with absolute courtesy and decorum; they had played brilliantly and fairly, and they had richly entertained an adoring public. I often wonder how modern players might have treated an incident such as that in which Grout was the centrepiece. What might some of our modern Australians have said to Viv Richards, for instance, if a similar circumstance had occurred today? Thankfully the acrimony and poor behaviour that seem to be part of the make-up of a good number of modern players was not part of the scene in those days.

When the final presentation was made of the Frank Worrell Trophy at the end of that game, a huge crowd remained to watch. When Frank Worrell was introduced they burst into a spontaneous and raucous version of 'For He's a Jolly Good Fellow'. That just about summed everything up.

The Australian captain Richie Benaud, who had completed his 50th Test match in the Melbourne encounter, was lavish in his praise of the West Indies. Of Worrell he said: 'Frank will remain in the hearts of cricket lovers in this country for many a long day.

'It is a magnificent moment for me to stand here in front of all you people and to be able to say that, having played in this my 50th Test match, I have never played in five more memorable, nor more enjoyable games, nor have I and my team ever played against a finer bunch of cricketers than these West Indians.

'I've come to know Frank pretty well in this past season, and I would like to tell you that it has not only been a pleasure to play against our visitors and against Frank, but to play in a series as captain against Frank Worrell has been a privilege'.

Sir Donald Bradman described Worrell as a great cricketer of the artistic mould. Frank himself was terribly overcome. Despite what must have been a bitter disappointment on that final afternoon, he was humble and sincere in his congratulations to Benaud and the Australian team. He presented Benaud with his cap, his tie and his blazer as a poignant symbol of the spirit in which the series had been played. Cricket, as a sport, had never shone so brightly.

It was a mark of the esteem in which Frank Worrell was held that the Australian Board of Control, as it was then called, decided to institute the 'Frank Worrell Trophy' for perpetual competition between the two countries. Mounted at the top of the trophy was one of the balls used in the tied Test.

Melbourne reflected Australia's respect for the tourists—it was almost love—by turning on a fabulous motorcade through the city in which hundreds of thousands of people paid homage. It was an expression of a nation's thanks for the finest sporting contests in which they had ever become embroiled. It was a singularly moving event.

Under Worrell, West Indies cricket had turned the corner. And cricket itself had found a new peak of excellence.

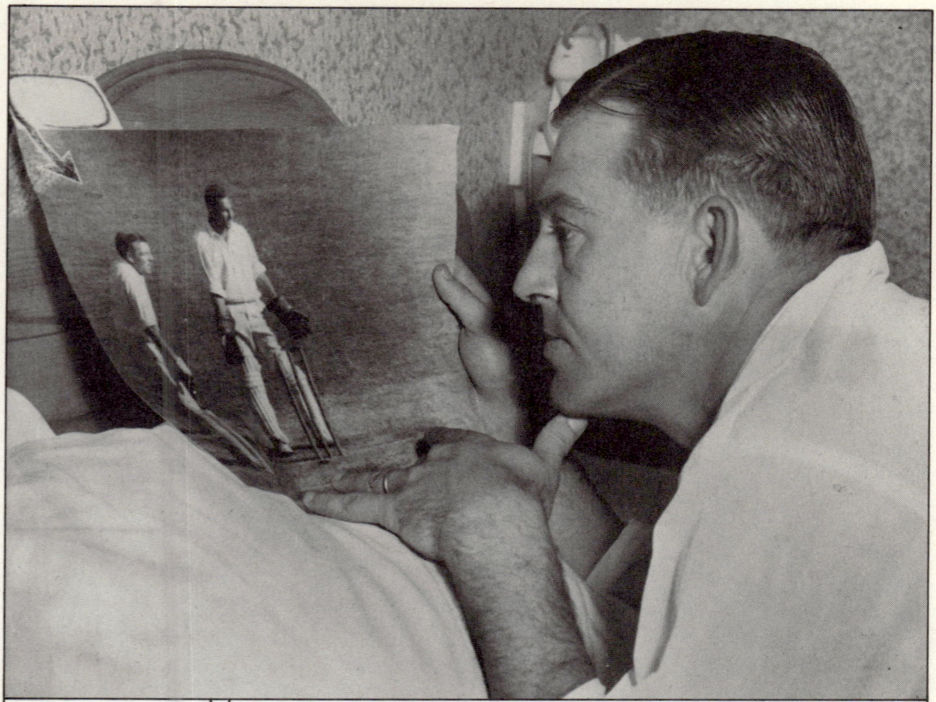

Wally Grout examines the photograph of the famous bail incident at the MCG in 1961. The mystery of how the bail ended up on the ground has never been satisfactorily solved.

Laurie Mayne . . . he twisted the tail of the tiger in the West Indies in 1965.

Gary Sobers, *above*, ranks among the finest batsmen cricket has seen in any era. His captaincy, however, did not quite match his other talents.

Charlie Griffith, the 'tiger' at the centre of a throwing controversy which inflamed relations between Bob Simpson's team and Gary Sobers' side.

A SOBERING EXPERIENCE

Garfield St Auburn Sobers, in the right mood, was majesty at the batting crease. He had a range of shots and a fluency in his strokeplay that only a handful of international cricketers could claim. He was a batsman to destroy bowlers. He would wind up like a coiled spring, wielding the bat in a full and extravagant arc that dragged every ounce of power out of his lithe frame. To some of the finest bowlers of his time he was a ruthless carnivore. He would simply gobble them up, as if they existed only to be his personal fodder.

Sobers ended his Test career with more than 8000 runs to his credit, and most of them would have been scored with the singular flourish that was his alone. With Gary Sobers there was never any pussy-footing around. He went for the jugular, and if runs were there to be scored, they would be scored dynamically.

A couple of Sobers' efforts stand out in my mind. I first saw him on the 1960-61 tour of Australia, where his centuries in Brisbane and Sydney were supreme efforts. In the Sydney game he scored 168, and I can still see in my mind the six he hit off Ian Meckiff's bowling with the new ball. Meckiff at that time was a very slippery operator. He was later banished because his bowling action was considered dubious. He had been the centre of an enormous 'chucking' furore when Peter May's England team had been in Australia in 1958-59.

Whether he threw or not, he certainly made the ball travel very swiftly, and he was not in the habit of being hit for six when he had a firm new ball in his hand. But this was no ordinary six. The ball was pitched about off stump and was short enough to force Sobers on to his back foot.

I can still see the vision of Sobers, on his toes and reaching for his full height, whipping the bat through to hit on the up. He connected with such awesome power the ball flew high, slightly to the on-side of a straight hit, and careered into the Sheridan Stand at the SCG. If ever there was a shot to break a bowler's heart, it was that one.

There was also the occasion of Sobers' innings for the Rest of the World against Australia at the MCG in early 1972. The series had been an emergency arrangement, hastily organised to replace a South African tour which had been cancelled because of the then gathering argument over apartheid in sport. The Rest of the World team, of which Sobers was captain, was something of a hotch potch of players from several countries who performed with various levels of competence.

In Perth they had been well and truly cleaned up by an emerging young talent named Dennis Lillee. Lillee had taken 8-29 on his favourite Perth wicket as the Rest of the World XI caved in for an inglorious 59. It was never a tour to really capture great heights. Some of the players seemed to be taking it all fairly casually. But it reached one of those rare high points when the caravan reached Melbourne. Sobers took personal control of the match with an innings of 254 that will forever rank amongst the great batting performances.

Sir Donald Bradman, not often given to handing out high praise, described it as one of the finest innings he had ever witnessed. So did just about everybody else who saw it.

The longer Sobers went, the harder the bowlers tried. Dennis Lillee and Bob Massie bowled like lions trying to stem the tide. They took a hammering for their trouble.

Curiously, I am convinced that innings developed almost by accident because of Sobers' total lack of concern as to how many runs he finished up with. The pressure was not terribly intense. It was a manufactured series, without a great deal hanging on it, and Sobers went about his batting with the freedom of approach that he might have expressed on a beach back home, with a few of the boys. He hit out with abandon.

It was the best expression of unbridled talent I ever saw. There were no inhibitions, no restrictions. He played without thought of risk. And every shot was struck truly and gloriously. It was an innings upon which it would simply be impossible to improve. Those efforts stand out among many fine hands by Gary Sobers. He was without doubt a supreme master of the batting art.

By the time the Australian team reached the West Indies in 1965 to renew contact, Sobers had taken over from Worrell as captain of the West Indies. This was the first series since the epic of 1960-61, and everybody was looking forward to it.

Frank Worrell had said at the farewell in Melbourne five years before that he hoped the West Indies could wrest back the Frank Worrell Trophy in a series that would be played in the same friendly and exciting way. In the event, the tour was anything but friendly.

Batsman supreme Sobers may well have been. But as a captain he lacked the ability Worrell had possessed to forge a common bond in his team. He was very much his own man. As often happens with those who have extraordinary ability, he found it hard to accept lesser talents in others. His commitment to his team did not have the same obsessive strength about it that Worrell had shown.

In later years the West Indies fell into much of their old ways under Sobers. In Australia in 1968-69, for instance, I well remember one afternoon at the SCG, on the eve of a Test match, when the West Indies' final practice was notable for the absence of their skipper.

The West Indies were not travelling particularly well on that tour, and they needed all the cohesive effort they could muster. Sobers arrived at that final practice as the rest of his beleaguered team were packing up. He presented himself for a Press conference in the SCG Members' Stand resplendent in green slacks, straight from the golf course. His talent was sufficient to get away with that sort of thing, personally. But as captain, it had a mortifying effect on his team.

Bob Simpson was captain of the 1965 Australia team in the West Indies, and unlike the happy relationship of a few years before between Worrell and Benaud, there were unhappy vibes from the start.

In the very first Test in Kingston, Jamaica, Sobers was out in the second innings for 27, caught by Simpson at slip off the bowling of leg-spinner Peter Philpott. He was clearly out, and umpire Douglas Sang Hue gave him out. Sobers disputed that. He stood and glared and made very obvious his thoughts about the decision.

Now that sort of thing to a West Indies crowd is dynamite. They did not actually riot. But they were very nasty just the same and the incident immediately soured relations between the two camps. More particularly there was an obvious friction between Simpson and Sobers. They were both strong-willed men who were not given to accepting second best about anything.

In retrospect the rival skippers were facing an uphill battle anyway. It was simply impossible to expect that, for sheer charisma, this series could even approach that of 1960-61. Nevertheless, so much was now expected of a West Indies-Australia series that the captains must have felt hefty pressure to produce something outstanding.

On top of that, events in the West Indies were tending to exacerbate the difficulties the separate nations had always experienced in getting themselves together. Trinidad, along with neighbouring Tobago, and Jamaica had been granted independence from Britain since the 1960 tour, and their new found status as fully-fledged members of the Commonwealth put them in a different bracket in some ways to the other nations.

Frank Worrell had become manager of the West Indies team, but it was not a position from which to command the same results he had achieved while captain. Ultimately the subject that made the tour quite nasty on the field was the matter of short-pitched bowling. I remember discussing it with Worrell at the start of the tour, and I vividly recall his frustration in trying to curb it. There was general agreement that excessive bouncer bowling was undesirable. Certainly it was as far as Frank was concerned. 'I have told my boys no more than two per over, and two it will be' Worrell had told me at the tour's start.

But the trigger to what became a very sordid affair came in the first Test in the form of West Australian paceman Laurie Mayne. Mayne was an aggressive type who looked for wickets any way he could get them. He gave the West Indies batsmen as much curry as he could, and to do that he bowled a lot shorter than most of Australia's batsmen would have considered safe, considering the armament the West Indies had available for retaliation.

Mayne finished the first Test with eight wickets. Australia lost the game anyway, but thanks to Mayne's approach they were to lose a good deal more before the tour was over. 'I can't control my boys' Worrell confided to me after play on the first day. 'Mayne is bowling bouncers, we bowl bouncers.'

Mayne bowling bouncers, of course, was a very different kettle of fish to Wes Hall and Charlie Griffith bowling bouncers. The West Indians were yards faster and infinitely more dangerous. But, as far as the West Indies were concerned, what was good for the goose was good for the gander. The tour degenerated into a bumper war of distasteful proportions. You can imagine what some of the Australian batsmen, sporting bruises and cuts more suited to a prize fight, thought of Laurie Mayne's bowling tactics of the first Test.

Retribution was taken with interest.

The principal vehicle of that retribution was Charlie Griffith. He did not gather a great number of wickets through the series, but he bowled with blinding speed and let go more than an acceptable number of bouncers. There was also widespread belief in the Australian team that he threw. Certainly there was an almighty kink in his elbow not long before the moment of delivery, and certainly his bowling action was unconventional and highly suspect.

In the event, he absolutely terrorised the Australian batsmen. They showed enormous courage in standing up to him, but he exerted such pressure that batsmen became easy fodder for Griffith's supports. They would see an over off from Griffith, their blood pressure up and their brows sweating. An inevitable relief led them to chase less frightening bowlers like Gary Sobers and Lance Gibbs. They would let their concentration slip, they would chase the runs they could not possibly take from Griffith and to a lesser extent Wes Hall, and they would get out. That applied pretty well throughout the series, and for the first time they went down to the West Indies, two Tests to one.

The argument that raged over Griffith's delivery became the overwhelming feature of the tour. The Australian team, if not unanimous in their opinion that Griffith threw, certainly gave themselves the benefit of any doubt, and a large majority of them considered he did. All the travelling journalists were convinced he threw. Richie Benaud, by that time the cricket correspondent for the Sydney *Sun*, armed himself with a pile of photographs that painted Griffith's delivery in a very poor light indeed.

The only defenders of Griffith in an Australian contingent that developed great hostility on the subject were Keith Miller and myself. I maintained Griffith was conforming to the letter of the law. Certainly his action did not look right, and certainly it was very close to a throw. But the conditions drawn up for the tour expressly decreed that so long as the arm was not straightened 'immediately prior' to release of the ball, the action was legal.

Throwing at the time was a delicate matter in the international cricket world. Ian Meckiff had been unceremoniously dumped just the previous season after being called for throwing in a Test against South Africa. The game's legislators at the International Cricket Conference had spent a good deal of time working out just what was and what wasn't fair.

As far as I was concerned, Griffith conformed with the formula they came up with. His arm was bent until it reached about the shoulder, then it straightened quickly and remained straight for perhaps half a metre of its travelling arc before he let the ball go. I didn't think that was 'immediately prior'. I said so. My responsibility was to be fair, not parochial, and while I didn't like the way Griffith bowled any more than anybody else, I was obliged to endorse his right to bowl within the law. Unfortunately, I was again painted as some sort of subversive within the Australian camp.

Keith Miller stuck by me. Keith was not averse to a bumper or two of his own in the old days, and he respected the right of fast bowlers to summon as much aggression as they could. They were legitimate deliveries in his book, aimed at disturbing a batsman's concentration and composure. He maintained Hall and Griffith were merely trying to frighten the batsmen out, and that was OK by his standards.

They did a pretty good job, too. But Miller wrote in his newspaper reports back to Australia, as I did in my radio reports, that Griffith was operating within the law. At the edge of it, perhaps, but within it. It became something of a *cause célèbre* within the Australian team. The manager Bob Parish called me to his room at the peak of the controversy and presented a pile of photographs to support the 'Charlie's a chucker' theory. I remained unconvinced.

Bob Simpson got into a fearful argument with Miller over the matter. They went at it hammer and tongs. Miller stoicly defended his opinion, and his right to it, by pointing out that he had gone around once or twice in the heat of Test match cricket himself.

Even the ABC back home baulked at my attitude. They secured some film of Griffith bowling, invited former umpire George Borwick into the studios, and came up with the opinion that Griffith did in fact throw, and I was off beam. I was a little annoyed about that. Had I been given the chance in debate, I am sure my case would have stood up.

There were those, of course, who agreed. I had one cable from Sir Hudson Fysh, then the chief of Qantas Airways, which arrived about 3 am following the night that I had first defended Griffith.

It was despatched from the ABC, and my first thought was 'This is trouble'. I could see myself being called home because of another bout of that 'unpatriotic' attitude that my comments occasionally were seen to be when they were unpopular.

'We are all proud of your excellent summary given tonight, upholding the best traditions of sportsmanship,' the cable read. What a relief! A victory for fair comment? I looked upon it as such, for again the point had been rammed home to me that patriotism, or parochialism, often clouds the judgment of so many when it comes to questions like these. Charlie Griffith's bowling was off, and in the broad sense probably was a throw. But it was the letter of the law that was at fault, not Charlie. He simply took advantage of it.

The debate still lingered when I returned to Sydney. The next season I was sitting in front of the ABC box at the Sydney Cricket Ground with Don Bradman when Richie Benaud joined us. 'Have a look at this, Mac,' he said, offering his book with another selection of those Griffith photographs. 'What do you think of it now?' The photos had been arranged in a sequence to cover the full range of Griffith's delivery. They didn't alter my opinion on the matter. Bradman had a look at the book.

'Doesn't that prove something to you, Mac?' he queried. 'It proves nothing' I retorted. 'Just have a look at his feet.'

The placement of the feet in the range of photographs made it clear they were not all taken of the one delivery. They made Griffith look bad, but they weren't conclusive. I'm sure Bradman and the rest of the Board of Control at the time were convinced Griffith had done us unfairly in the West Indies. But they couldn't do a thing about it.

The Griffith saga had a terrible effect on the tour. It inevitably soured the relationship between the sides. It probably finished Brian Booth as an international cricketer. Booth scored 117 in one Test, but was black and blue at the end. He did not have a hook shot in his armoury, and he was virtually defenceless to the ball that jumped at his throat.

Under the circumstances the tour uncovered a lot of courage in the Australian side. In the fourth Test in Barbados, for instance, Bill Lawry scored 210 and Bob Simpson 201 in an opening stand of 382. Bob Cowper then scored 102 and the Australians amassed 650 runs. Cowper stood up to the Griffith onslaught better than anybody. As a left-hander he found Griffith's deliveries were slanting across him and fading away on the off side. Cowper finished with 400 odd runs at an average of 52 and avoided most of the strife.

'I don't know what you blokes are all on about' he used to say, chiding his team-mates in jest about the bruises they were taking. Eventually Charlie Griffith hit him on the instep with a full toss, a very painful blow indeed. It was an injury of which his team-mates made cruel capital.

Bill Lawry, too, showed enormous courage in confronting Griffith. But while the Australians summoned all they had to stand up to the shock tactics, other bowlers took advantage when they relaxed. The Australian bowlers Graham McKenzie, Neil Hawke and Peter Philpott stuck to the job throughout, and in the end Australia did well to get out of it with a 2-1 defeat.

It was not a pleasant summer's cricket. There were plenty of arguments and plenty of acrimony. At the end of it I sought interviews with Sobers and Simpson to tape and send home. Each agreed to an interview, but neither would do it until the other had gone first. For a time it was an impasse. Eventually Simmo relented. The interviews reflected the bitterness of the series, and the unhappy feeling between the two captains. That bitterness and feeling were so obvious, in fact, I decided not to send the interviews back to Australia. Some things are better left unsaid.

It was a shame that the attitudes on the field did not match those off it. The West Indies people as a whole were hospitality itself. The homes we visited, with their magnificent gardens and generous, friendly atmosphere, were memories to treasure. Their love of cricket, too, was something to be seen. At the grounds they would climb up trees, telephone posts, anything to get a vantage point. Many a ground there, with a capacity of about 15 000, will drag in 25 000 for a Test match.

The initiative of some of the children is extraordinary. At Kingston, Jamaica, one group of young boys had a flourishing business going organising 'black market tickets' for the ground. One young fellow of about thirteen or fourteen had organised a ground entry system whereby he placed a plank of wood over a 44-gallon drum. He found a spot beside the wall of the ground and underneath a quite large tree.

For a price, young fellows in their dozens would take turns to stand on one end of the plank, while the entrepreneur climbed the tree. He would leap from the tree on to the other end of the plank, thus catapulting the customer to the top of the wall. Once there, the young fellow who had paid his money had to contend with jagged pieces of glass that were embedded into the top of the wall to prevent the very sort of thing in which these boys were engaging.

I could see all this taking place from the commentary box in the Kingston Ground. Some of the injuries were horrific. Boys were getting cut to pieces as they clambered over the wall, but plenty of them got in and most seemed to regard their injuries as an acceptable price of entry.

The police eventually cottoned on to the racket. They would arm themselves with long bamboo poles, and as the boys' heads appeared over the wall, the police would give them a clout. Back they would go, gather their senses, hop back on the plank and be launched skyward again. I tried to tell the kids what was happening inside the fence, where the policemen formed the second line of defence. They simply didn't care. They just kept coming. The fellow jumping out of the tree must have made a fortune that day.

The people's involvement with cricket, and their intensity, had its drawbacks. In the match against Guyana on that 1965 tour one of the local umpires had run foul of the mob for decisions with which they did not necessarily agree. Their response was to ambush him several times as he tried to ride home on his bicycle after play. They gave him a considerable working over, sufficient to discourage him from putting himself forward when the third Test was played there later in the tour.

The word, too, had got around. One appointed umpire simply refused his invitation to stand. By the time the Test match was ready to get underway, only one umpire had turned up. Nobody could really blame the non-arrival. Umpiring was a dodgy business here at the best of times, but on a tour in which tensions had run pretty high, and before a crowd who took it awfully seriously, it was downright dangerous.

Into the breach stepped Gerry Gomez. At that time he was a West Indies selector, having been a West Indies Test player and an extremely capable and popular manager of the 1960-61 tour of Australia. He was also doing some broadcasting and writing for a newspaper. To that considerable portfolio he now added the role of emergency Test match umpire.

Now that embodied a few hazards. Gerry, a great friend of mine and one of the real gentlemen of cricket, had spent most of his life trying to make West Indies cricket great. He had a deep and emotional involvement in the team and all it did. West Indies cricket to him was an abiding love. To push all of that into the background and stand in judgment in a Test match was asking a lot. In the event Gerry was scheduled to fill the breach only for a day until somebody could be imported, but he decided to continue and did a pretty good job.

The only flaw in his operation was an occasion when Bill Lawry was given run out for twenty in the first innings. Gerry's response to the sharp return from the field which arrived at the wicket about the same time as Lawry was to leap excitedly into the air, both arms raised in appeal. It was a natural, instinctive reaction. Lawry saw the two hands in the air. He knew it couldn't be a signal for a six, so he took it to mean he was out. By the time Lawry was making his way off the field, Gerry's excitement had calmed a touch. Embarrassed, he considered again the verdict, and stuck by it. It was, however, the only time I have seen an umpire appeal for a dismissal in a Test match.

Broadcasting at Georgetown was far from easy. The crowd's animation made it difficult to make yourself heard above the noise. They were all around there, drinking their rum, singing their songs and beating out their rhythms on the backs of chairs. They also had a terrible habit of listening to the cricket on their transistors right in front of us, causing a feedback that would put a piercing whistle into the transmission.

When it became obvious that I was finding it very hard and looking particularly frustrated, a giant of a man waltzed up to me with an offer I could not refuse. 'You having trouble, Mr Alan?' the giant inquired. 'My name's Charlie, and if you like I can help you.'

Well, Charlie was not the sort of fellow you argue with. He was massive. His face looked like it had been chipped out of a coalface, and he had arms like tree trunks. 'Yes Charlie, I am having some trouble and I don't know what to do about it,' I answered, as politely as possible. 'You bring me a bottle of rum each day, and I'll see that the crowd doesn't interfere with you' Charlie offered.

That sounded fair enough to me. Next day Charlie reported for duty. He looked like rum was really the last thing he needed, but I got him a bottle to keep him happy. 'You point out anyone who is making too much noise and I'll fix it,' he demanded. After a considerable time I eventually pointed out somebody whose transistor was coming back at us. I assumed Charlie would speak to him. Explain the problem. Ask them to co-operate.

Charlie's contribution was to grab hold of the poor unfortunate I had nominated, fling him to the ground and kick him fair in the face. I couldn't believe it. Blood poured from his nose. I was nauseated, not only by the ugly scene unfolding in front of me, but more particularly by the sickening realisation that I had sentenced this poor chap to so unseemly a fate.

Charlie seemed fairly pleased with himself. I never again dared use his services, though his very presence maintained a quite orderly environment around the broadcasting box for the rest of the match.

CARIBBEAN CRISES

To the average cricket administrator of the late '70s, World Series Cricket was like a red rag to a bull. It was galling and humiliating to established cricket that so huge a concept could be dropped on them as a *fait accompli.* It was particularly heart rending for them to accept that most of the world's best players had been covert accomplices to one of the most devastating revolutions from within that sport had ever experienced.

Cricket's administration might well have brought much of the problem upon itself. There has always been a reluctance within cricket officialdom to move with the times. Men who make up cricket boards are usually former players – seldom Test players – or long-time devotees of the game who live by standards so long entrenched that they are simply old fashioned and out of date. These men are always well meaning, and their love of cricket is without question. But their outlook is essentially conservative and resistant to change. High and honourable motives sometimes are interpreted as high-handed and pompous autocracy.

When the World Series Cricket revolution came about it was crystal clear that administration had let itself fall out of touch with the players. The game was experiencing a new commercial restlessness, and top players were becoming increasingly dissatisfied with their lot, financially. They knew they were drawing big gates and, by the standards of other professional sports, they felt they were not getting a lot in return.

They were, then, extremely vulnerable when Australian media magnate Kerry Packer tempted them with a brand new world of riches. That players from Australia, England and the West Indies could sign themselves away to this alternative cricket under the very noses of the established administration hit the game like a bombshell. The day it all became public at Hove, on the Australian tour of England in 1977, battle lines were quickly drawn. Cricket officialdom had been caught with its pants down, and this left no room for negotiation. Kerry Packer and those who sailed with him were the enemy. Subsequent negotiation was little more than a series of threats and counter threats.

Kerry Packer certainly was not going to budge and neither was cricket's ultimate governing body, the International Cricket Conference. Each vowed to destroy the other, and caught in the crossfire was a whole generation of the world's top cricketers.

This was the backdrop for Australia's tour of the West Indies in 1978. The International Cricket Conference had decreed that anyone signed to play with the Packer organisation after October 1 1977, was ineligible to play Test cricket. Australia went along with that. The Chappells, Lillee, Marsh, Walters and what amounted to virtually the first and second Australian XIs went off to play World Series cricket. Bob Simpson, ten years retired as Australian captain, answered an SOS to lead a new team of young tyros in their stead.

They got through a home series against India very well, then took off for the Caribbean where the situation was far less clear cut. Australian administrators were very hot under the collar about World Series Cricket and had conformed with the English view that there could be no compromise. The West Indies, on the other hand, did all they could to marry the two areas of the game. They had all their top players contracted to the Board and, whatever might happen subsequently, they saw no reason to withdraw those contracts. Their attitude, broadly, was that if their best players wanted to go off and make some money playing World Series Cricket, that was fine, so long as they could fit it in with their commitments to the West Indies.

So when Bob Simpson's team of young hopefuls arrived in the West Indies in 1978 they were confronted with a fully-fledged West Indies team under Clive Lloyd that was just beginning to reach for its ultimate status as one of the finest cricket sides the world has seen. It was the greatest mismatch of modern times.

Australia were up against it from the start. They lost the toss for the first Test, and when rain delayed the start they were made to open their innings two minutes before the luncheon adjournment on a very dangerous pitch. By the time Craig Sarjeant took strike and watched the first ball fly over his head, they were a couple of minutes into the luncheon break. They were out for 90, beaten by an innings, then badly beaten again in the second Test.

From there the tour turned into a war of attrition. Cricket, as the game I had known from my boyhood, embraced all things fine for me. It was tragic now to see cricket so sullied by the wrangling and the hatred that overwhelmed the rest of the tour.

The double-booking of World Series players sooner or later had to catch up with the West Indies Board. Their initial attitude was that the players could continue to play with the West Indies until they made themselves unavailable. While the Australians were there no conflict existed. But the West Indies were facing a tour of India after the Australian series. This would conflict with the World Series commitments in Australia. Decisions had to be reached. There was really no doubt in anybody's minds where the West Indies players would be going. The big money was in Australia and that was the end of it.

But the West Indies Board gave them the right of choice. They set a deadline by which the players had to declare whether they were available for India or not. That deadline fell between the second and third Tests. The players asked that it be extended so that they could talk the matter over. Kerry Packer actually flew to the West Indies to discuss the matter with the Board. It was a stalemate.

The West Indies had undertaken to the International Cricket Conference they would not negotiate or take any action that might undermine the ICC's authority. They decided that if their players would not go to India, they were out. That meant Clive Lloyd, Gordon Greenidge, Andy Roberts, Viv Richards, Joel Garner and Colin Croft dropping out of the West Indies side.

West Indies spectators are not too fussed about the intricacies of international cricket administration. They know they have a lot of good players, and their only interest is to see those players on the field, giving a hiding to any team that happens to be passing by. They took very unkindly indeed to the news that their very best players were now barred from playing against Australia.

Their first wave of attack came in the form of a boycott for the third Test in Georgetown, Guyana. Alvin Kallicharran took over the West Indies captaincy from Lloyd, who was Guyanese and very much a home town hero. That inflamed the locals for a start. The West Indies Board and the selectors were made to be the villains of the piece. The population at large didn't bother to consider the rights and wrongs of the matter. They simply didn't care. They wanted their best players and that was the end of it. The atmosphere for that Test was intensely bitter. There was talk of riots, and all manner of retribution against the Board and the selectors. That did not come to pass. Instead there was a sort of passive undercurrent of contempt. Hardly anybody went to the game, and the atmosphere in the ground was cold and grim.

I felt for the West Indies Board. They were in a no-win situation, and I cannot see anything else they could possibly have done. Had they capitulated and allowed the players to do as they wished, they would have been turning their backs on the international cricket community that was trying to cope with a problem of immense proportions.

The pity was that negotiation could not have been conducted in a more meaningful way right at the start. I thought then there was room to schedule the seasons and the first-class program so as to allow Kerry Packer his piece of the action and retain the traditional Test matches virtually in tandem. Neither Mr Packer nor the ICC seemed terribly keen to bend. The West Indies thus were caught up in it all and could not bend either, no matter how much they might have wanted to.

Australia managed to score 362 runs in the second innings in that third Test, despite three ducks among their first six batsmen, with grand centuries from Graeme Wood and Craig Serjeant reaping a win. But the cricket had been pushed into the background by the chaos. For the rest of the series it went from bad to worse.

The bitterness was reaching dangerous levels by the fourth Test in Trinidad. The boycott of the game this time was organised, with pickets outside the ground and a lot of tough-looking characters making ground entry very difficult indeed. First they would ask you not to go in. Then they would tell you not to go in.

I was confronted by a very big man at the gate whose eyes narrowed as I tried to debate the matter with him. The fact that I was Australian and had to broadcast back home in no way impressed him.

'You're not going in there,' he told me. He looked like he would break me in two quite happily. Thankfully he didn't, but as I brushed past him to enter I was roundly abused and jostled by a horde of protestors who found very little argument from most of the people they had turned away that day. It was a horrible experience, and it became clear to me then that the tour wasn't going to get any better.

By this time I was starting to feel the strain. I saw my responsibility as reporting fairly and accurately to Australia all that was taking place. The local crowds were not exactly covering themselves with glory, and I said so. In fact, I was utterly disgusted with some of the behaviour in which spectators had indulged throughout the tour. Their attitude was an abuse of a fine game. My broadcasts were for Australian consumption, but the local stations often picked them up and used them locally. The result was that I was fairly universally looked upon by people in the West Indies as an infiltrator from abroad poisoning minds against them.

The commentary box in all the Test grounds in the West Indies is directly opposite the Members' Pavilion, so each day at start and close of play, and at the adjournments if I was game enough, I had to cross the field to get to and from the box. Those short walks became increasingly harrowing. I was abused and reviled and generally made to feel most uncomfortable.

The final Test brought matters to a head. The most terrible riot erupted on the last day. The game ended in a hail of house bricks and amidst volleys of gunfire.

It all started when Australia were pressing towards victory on the last afternoon. The West Indies had lost eight second innings wickets and still had 38 balls of the last 20 overs to play when Vanburn Holder was given out, caught by Steve Rixon at the wicket off the bowling of leg-spinner Jim Higgs. Holder stood and considered his position. There was no doubt he was out, and I think Holder lingered as much for his disappointment as for any dissatisfaction with the decision. But he did linger as if to dispute the verdict. That was enough for the crowd. Tension had been high for weeks, and the double disappointment of not having their better players, then seeing Australia in a position to win, was too much for them. Holder later was mortified that he had not left the field immediately. He simply did not consider the consequences. Holder is a good man and a very fair man, and the last thing he would want to do was in any way to trigger the sort of mayhem that followed his reluctance to leave the crease.

First of all came the missiles. There were bottles seemingly by the truckload, oil drums, chairs, bricks, literally anything that could be torn up and hurled. The bricks were travelling close to 100 metres from the perimeter of the ground. I reasoned they must have had some sort of slingshot arrangement to fire them that far.

The players gradually retreated from the pitch towards the Members' Stand. At first the former West Indies captain Gerry Alexander and the Australian manager Fred Bennett went out on to the field to try to calm things down. They had no chance.

The police joined the fray, pistols drawn. There was sporadic gunfire. Fred Bennett said later that the police had told him they were only firing blanks. I spent enough time in the army to know that blanks don't make the whistling noise I heard the bullets making that day. They were only aimed in the air, but bullets are bullets, and the fact they were fired at all emphasised the critical stage matters had reached.

When the players eventually took the decision to run for their lives, they were showered with bottles and debris. I remember describing the scene back to Australia. I said they were being rained with bottles, and it would be a miracle if someone was not seriously hurt. The only injury as it turned out was a small cut Gerry Alexander suffered to his head. The Australian players were extremely lucky.

I watched it all from the elevated broadcasting box. I had a briefcase packed with papers in front of my face as a shield as I spoke into the microphone. A crowd had gathered below us and were making it very obvious we were the enemy and what we were saying in our broadcasts was not to their liking.

Eventually the riot police arrived. They wore shields and protective gear and were armed with automatic weapons. I remember thinking: Hell, if someone pulls a trigger here it will be carnage. Thankfully the riot police were better trained than that. But for a time it was an extremely dangerous scene. Eventually we had to consider the dash across the field from the broadcasting box to the Members' Pavilion. I made several attempts to negotiate the twenty or so steps down to the ground. Waiting at the bottom were half a dozen men armed with bricks.

'You get back inside, man,' they demanded. I was in no position to argue. Half a dozen times I tried to make my way out of that box, and half a dozen times I was threatened and turned back. I apparently had upset the locals by describing the scene in some detail, and bemoaning the fact that the machine-guns were necessary at a cricket Test. I felt that my duty.

An hour passed before I even looked like getting out of the box. Jackie Hendricks, a former West Indies wicket-keeper who had been in Australia with Frank Worrell's team, was in the adjoining box. I sought his assistance in getting across the field. 'No way man,' came his reply. 'No way.' He intended staying there all night if necessary. He would not venture out while there were any remnants of the rioting mobs below.

We eventually made our break when only two or three people remained below. Once we reached the ground however, they came from everywhere. Jackie and I were separated. A mob of about forty people surrounded me, jostling and jeering. Jackie was having the same sort of trouble with a mob of his own. I used my briefcase as a sort of shield cum battering ram to get close to the Members' Pavilion, where I was rescued by a policeman.

'You crazy fool' he rebuked me. 'You could have been knifed out there, and you wouldn't have known where it was coming from.' That, I admit, I had not considered. I was naturally very apprehensive about the whole thing, but I don't think I was actually frightened until the policeman put it like that.

The Australian players had been barricaded in their dressing room. They were still being pelted with missiles of all descriptions.

Once in the pavilion Fred Bennett grabbed hold of me. 'Come with me Mac,' he beckoned. 'We're having a meeting with the President in the committee room and I want a witness.' The President of the West Indies Board was Mr Alan Rae, and he was mightily upset by everything that had taken place. Four or five policemen flanked him and he was very agitated. His main concern was that the match be extended into the next morning so it could be completed. He reasoned it would be wrong if Australia were robbed of their winning chance. The riot had knocked the pitch around but that didn't seem to worry him. So long as they could make it playable, he wanted everybody back next morning to wrap things up.

While the debate raged I joined Jack Anderson, a well-known and very fair-minded Jamaican journalist for a much-needed drink. He was as upset about events as I was. The problem, in fact, probably bit more deeply for Jack, because he had to live with it constantly. Life in Kingston was pretty tough at that time, and the difficulties at the cricket were symptomatic of many social problems the island of Jamaica itself was confronting. Jack apologised that he had to leave. His wife was cooking him a roast, he said, and we agreed to have a farewell drink next day, since it seemed the cricket would be resumed.

The ride back to the hotel from the Kingston Ground normally was no more than ten minutes. I was driven back that evening through the mob that still lingered outside the ground. They were harrassing any car that carried an Australian. They thumped at the windows, stood in front of the vehicle, generally made things as difficult as they could. It took forty-five minutes to make the hotel.

On the way a newsflash on the radio announced that Jack Anderson had been shot and killed on the way home. I couldn't believe it. I had been drinking with him not an hour before. Whatever effect the riots had had on me to that point now paled against the horror and revulsion I felt. When I reached the hotel I rang Jack's son. He confirmed that his father was dead. He had been machine-gunned.

By now I was shaking. I don't know whether it was rage, or hate, or fear. It could have been all of those things. But to think that so simple and so honourable a pursuit as cricket, which I loved so dearly, could be surrounded by such madness made the blood run cold. I was wrestling with these emotions when I had a visitor. He introduced himself as a representative of the Australian government and without beating about the bush explained that they would like me out of Jamaica.

My reports of events, though 100 per cent accurate as far as I was concerned, did not paint the West Indies well and were considered inflammatory. And since they could not guarantee my safety, they'd rather I wasn't there. Somehow it didn't seem right and I started to argue. The cricket was to continue next day after all, and it didn't seem right to run. But he was very persuasive. I was out of the hotel early next morning and spent the hours before the first available flight in the comparative security of the airport. I was a very relieved man when that flight reached Miami, Florida.

I vowed I would never return to the West Indies. It was a heart-breaking farewell. I had met so many wonderful people there, and been entertained so often and so royally through those tours of 1965 and 1973. That it should end like this was one of the saddest experiences of my life in cricket.

As events transpired the final Test did not resume on the next morning. Umpire Ralph Gosein decreed that to play an extra day was in contravention of the law and the tour conditions. He simply overruled the Board and refused to stand. Whether the rule, or the fear of more trouble, was his prime consideration I suppose we will never know.

But the damage had been done. I don't think anybody would have had much of a stomach for cricket that next morning.

It was a shame that a new generation of young Australian players had to be exposed to the turmoil of that tour. Peter Toohey, for instance, scored a century and a 97 in the fifth Test and looked a player of rich promise. He never really attained the heights expected of him. I remember Greg Chappell complaining a year or two later when World Series Cricket had run its course and the game was united again. 'Toohey is a big disappointment to me' he said. 'He is a sort of poor man's Doug Walters, with a lot of ability, but his technique is amiss.'

Craig Serjeant was another for whom the tour became a cricketing Waterloo. Who knows how much that experience affected them?

I felt grateful that I had been introduced to the game in less troubled times. Even when we were surrounded by Great Depressions and World Wars, cricket at no time surrendered its grace and its serenity. Even the trials of Bodyline were a mere hiccough compared to what was going on in the late 'seventies.

THE ACHIEVERS

Cricketers through the ages have fallen into several well-defined categories. There are those who are richly talented and use that talent well. They are extremely few. There are many more who are very talented, and rely on that talent alone to achieve their success. They usually achieve moderately, and never reach their full potential. There are those who have little talent but an enormous capacity for work, who achieve a great deal more than the more talented people they overtake.

In the middle there is a large group whose talent is moderate, but who, by their iron wills, their big hearts and their determination to succeed, make the most of every ounce of talent they possess. These are the real achievers, the ultimate competitors on whom most great teams are built.

Max Walker was such a competitor. Max has an outlook on life that reflects the power of positive thinking. In my last years as a Test match broadcaster I had the pleasure to work with him. He introduced to ABC broadcasts the brightness and good humour that were his trade-mark when he was an Australian fast-bowler. He was beside me, in fact, for my last stint at the Test match microphone in Sydney at the end of the West Indies-Australia series of 1984-85. He had to rescue me at the end when a speech of farewell by the Australian Prime Minister, Bob Hawke, was broadcast over the public address system and somewhat undermined my composure.

As a cricketer, Max seemed to do most things wrong. Wrong as far as the text books go anyway. He had an awkward bowling action that unwound like a windmill at the end. It earned him the nickname 'Tanglefoot', later abbreviated to 'Tangles', very early in his career.

Walker burst on to the Test match scene against Pakistan in 1973 and cleaned them up in Sydney in only his second Test. Dennis Lillee had injured his back and was bowling under great duress. Tangles slipped into the breach, grabbing 6-15 in Pakistan's second innings. He took five wickets for three runs off his last 30 deliveries and Pakistan were all out for 106 when they had only needed 159 to win the game. They were the sort of odds on which he seemed to thrive. He bowled on his courage.

When Ian Chappell's team reached the West Indies in 1973 that courage was to be fully tested. The Australian team was extremely well equipped in the pace department when they started off. Dennis Lillee and Bob Massie had put England to the sword the previous year, and Walker was merely their backup. In the event Lillee and Massie broke down and it was left to Walker to pick up the pieces. Lillee played only in the first Test before the stress fractures in his back that very nearly ended his career put him out of business. Massie did not play a Test at all.

Walker was confronted with some hot batting talent, uninviting pitches, and a considerable lack of experience as a front-line new ball bowler. To Max, they were mere challenges. He finished the series with 27 wickets, three times took five wickets in an innings, and was the principal factor in a 2-0 series win which reflected great credit on an improvised Australian team.

It also reflected great credit on the skipper Ian Chappell, who was at his absolute best in this series in moulding a relatively unlikely bunch into a winning outfit. It was a tour in which skilful improvisation won the day. He managed to drag the best out of everybody.

By the fourth Test in Guyana, Australia held a shaky 1-0 lead, but were battling injuries and illness and knew they would need to perform well to stay in front. On the morning that match started I was waiting for a cab to the ground. Max Walker arrived in the hotel foyer at the same time. He was barefoot, and walking on his tip toes. The backs of his legs were a mess. Blood vessels had burst. He was black and blue and generally in a dreadful state. It looked as if it would be impossible to get a boot on, let alone bowl in a Test match.

'Max,' I said. 'You can't possibly play in that condition. You'll do yourself terrible damage.' His reply was the story of the tour. 'Somebody has to do it, mate,' he said.

Australia lost the toss and were in the field that morning. Walker bowled 38 overs in the first innings, his feet packed in foam rubber, then another 24 in the second, and finished with five wickets for the match. That performance typified the outlook of that side. They would do anything for Chappell and they would leave no stone unturned to win. Walker's effort was true grit. He could hardly walk, let alone run, yet he shut the pain from his mind and bowled as well as it was possible for him to do.

Chappell even managed to draw some exceptional bowling from Doug Walters on that tour. Chappell had long known Walters' value as a medium-pace bowler and used him intelligently in short spells throughout their time together. On that tour he really used him only once, and Walters responded with a match-winning five wickets in the first innings and two in the second. 'It's taken a bloody long time for him to realise I'm a match-winner' Walters jokingly complained later.

Walters meant a great deal to Australia's dominance over the West Indies through the series of 1968-69 and 1973. For a start he was an enormous ally for Chappell. The pair were the best of buddies from the time Walters entered the Test scene in 1965-66, and when Chappell took over the captaincy five years later, Walters was very much in his corner. I never heard Doug complain seriously about anything. He always had a happy grin and a bright word, and the job he did in the field encouraging his team-mates and lifting their spirits when things were grim was worth hundreds of runs.

His batting, too, took a particular toll through that period. Against Sobers' team in the Australian summer of 1968-69 he was absolutely dynamic. He scored four centuries in that series, including a double of 242 and 103 in the final Test in Sydney. He scored six fifties in consecutive innings and took the long handle generally to an attack that, by general consensus, was a season past its usefulness. Wes Hall and Charlie Griffith again led the attack in that series, but were past it.

By 1973, Walters still had plenty to offer. The West Indies, for instance, had a pace bowler named Michael Foster, who bowled a difficult legside line and was extremely hard to get away. He was a fairly negative bowler, but if Australia were to win they had to make sure he couldn't tie them down.

Chappell used Walters as his storm trooper here. Dougie was never one to do everything completely by the book anyway, and he found it no real problem to take a couple of quick steps well wide of his leg stump and crash his leg theory bowling through the open spaces on the off side.

Similarly Chappell decided he had to attend to the potential the long-serving off-spinner Lance Gibbs had for undermining a team. Chappell's answer to Gibbs was to jump yards down the pitch to him and crack his drives as straight as possible. Like Worrell had determined with Benaud years before, Chappell reasoned that if he didn't get on top of Gibbs, Gibbs would get on top of them. It was a ritual that whenever Gibbs bowled to Chappell, Chappell would jump yards down the pitch and attack. He got away with it. I asked Ian later why he hit so straight.

'If he puts his hand down to stop them it won't do his spinning finger any good' he offered. To Chappell, psychological destruction seemed much more likely if those crashing drives were whizzing past Gibbs himself. Hit elsewhere, no matter how many runs they acquired, they would not have the same impact.

That was the way Chappell thought out his cricket. He was single-minded and aggressive, but he never closed his mind to the offerings of his team.

The West Indies at the time had Roy Fredericks opening the batting, Fredericks was a fine player of the square cut, and he could place the ball beautifully to avoid the fieldsmen. Georgetown has an almost rectangular Test match ground, and it seemed to me Chappell was putting all his eggs in one basket in trying to cut off that Fredericks cut shot. The fieldsman was either too fine or too square, leaving a thirty-yard area in one direction to cover, when there was a spot in between that would have allowed him a fifteen-yard option either way.

I talked it over with Max Walker. Walker, of course, was an architect, and he delved deeply into all he had learned at the Royal Melbourne Institute of Technology to work the whole thing out trigonometrically. We gathered all the ground measurements. Max got to work with pen and paper, and worked out slide rule calculations of mind-boggling complexity. The speed at which a fieldsman could travel was computed. In the end we drew up an equation which suggested the fieldsman should be moved an appreciable distance from where Chappell had him.

Our case thoroughly prepared, we put it to Chappell. He listened patiently and attentively. Walker explained it all in terms of high mathematics. He presented Chappell with diagrams and projections that he had spent hours drawing up.

At the end of it we waited expectantly for Chappell's response.

'What a load of rubbish' he volunteered. Actually his words were a little sharper than that, as was Ian's occasional habit. Max was crest-fallen. So well-researched a theory deserved a better fate. Curiously, next time Fredericks was at the crease Chappell applied the Walker plan exactly as we had prescribed it. I'm sure he went back to the table when we weren't looking and retrieved the diagrams. That was Chappell's way. He would listen to everybody, so long as he could see reasonable sense in what they were saying. But he made his own decisions in the end.

That tour was a much happier one for the Australian side than it was for the West Indies. When it started, Gary Sobers had had an unbroken run of eighty-five consecutive appearances for the West Indies. He had been captain for the last thirty-nine of those Tests. Yet he did not make an appearance through the series because of a silly wrangle with the West Indies Board of Control.

Sobers had a knee cartilage removed in England the previous year. At the start of the West Indies season he had captained Barbados through a Shell Shield match, but limped badly and was clearly unfit. Before they would choose him for the first Test the selectors required Sobers to have a fitness test. He refused. He maintained his record for the West Indies was such that if he said he was fit, that should have been good enough. All sorts of people tried to persuade him otherwise. The West Indies Board went to extraordinary lengths to induce him to have the test. The Prime Minister of Trinidad even got into the act, stirring up quite a hornet's nest. The more the debate raged, the more intransigent Sobers became.

He took no part in the Tests, leaving the captaincy to Rohan Kanhai. It took an edge off the series.

Kanhai, marvellous player that he was, was never a very good captain. But he was a top class fellow, and this time there was an easy, happy rapport between the two teams. Much of the damage that had been done in relations between the two sides in 1965 was happily repaired.

My memories of the West Indies, their cricket and their people, were so splendid at the end of that tour. Even the tragedy of later events could never change that.

THE SPRINGBOK PHENOMENON

Jack Fingleton, the gritty Australian opening batsman of Bodyline days who later became a celebrated cricket author and critic, once made the mistake of provoking the England pace bowler Harold Larwood. Jack was batting in the second Test of the Bodyline series at the Melbourne Cricket Ground, and after only one ball of the innings he walked down the pitch and patted the turf just three or four yards in front of Larwood. Vic Richardson was sitting with some of the non-playing Englishmen at the time. 'Oooh, Lar won't like that,' he recalled their saying. 'Watch him now!'

From that moment Fingleton took one of the most fearful batterings from a pace bowler in the history of cricket. He was pummelled for two or three overs and finished the day dreadfully bruised. When he arrived at the dressing room at the end of it, Richardson chided him about his exaggerated protest at the length of Larwood's bowling.

'Well, that'll teach you a lesson, Jack,' Vic said. 'Never kick a tiger when he's quiet.'

That lesson might well have applied to Syd Smith, the veteran president of the NSW Cricket Association, after his speech of welcome to Jack Cheetham's South African side in the summer of 1952-53. South Africa to that point had played seven series against Australia in the preceding 50 years. Australia had won 22 games and South Africa one.

On their previous visit to Australia they had taken a mauling from Bradman at his best. The Don had finished up with 806 runs in the series at an average of 201.

Smith looked back on all this and made a sympathetic speech of welcome, in which he suggested to Cheetham and his men that the tour would provide a good lesson for them. It would give them the opportunity to learn how to become real competitors. It was a patronising welcome which clearly had an effect on Cheetham's team. For the next four months they played cricket like their lives depended on it. They finished up drawing the series at two Tests all, despite Neil Harvey's scoring a record 834 runs against them, and fought like tigers throughout.

But for a minor aberration against Ian Craig's team in 1957-58, South Africa have been pretty much on top of Australia ever since. They have won 10 Tests to Australia's seven, with seven drawn, and when the plug was finally pulled on exchanges between the two countries in 1971, their last series had been a 4-0 whitewash of Bill Lawry's team. Syd Smith, for sure, had kicked a sleeping tiger.

I have nursed a soft spot for South African cricket since Vic Richardson regaled me with tales of the team he captained there in 1935-36. That tour was a 4-0 triumph for Australia, but more particularly it was perhaps the most stunning victory for the art of slow bowling that international cricket has experienced. The triumph belonged very much to that pair of artful dodgers Clarrie Grimmett and Bill O'Reilly, who between them took 71 out of the 98 South African wickets to fall to bowlers in the five Tests. Grimmett had 44 of those wickets, and O'Reilly 27, and it is fair to say they mesmerised South Africa with their guile. Vic used to speak in absolute raptures about the scope their bowling gave a team. Grimmett was forty-five years of age when he perplexed South Africa's batsmen on that tour, and he was still bowling pretty well in first class cricket as he nudged fifty. The remarkable success of bowlers like Grimmett and O'Reilly in those days is hard to measure against the rip and tear pace that is such an obsession in the rather more athletic cricket of today.

When the shutters came down on South African cricket at the end of the 1969-70 season, they were clearly the best team in the world. I put their team of that time among the three best sides I have seen play. Don Bradman's 1948 team is unsurpassable, but the 1970 South African team, with players like Barry Richards and the Pollock brothers, Eddie Barlow and Tiger Lance, would have run them close. With Clive Lloyd's 1984-85 West Indian team, they rate as the finest of post-war cricket.

It is a tragedy for the game that their international participation was cut short. South Africa to me had always been a friendly place, in which hospitality for visiting sporting teams is simply unsurpassed on the world circuit. There is no denying they have incredible problems, and the path they have chosen to deal with those problems is unacceptable to many. But whether sport should be a vehicle to exert political pressure is open to debate. My own view is that it should not. There is a universal quality to sport that breaks down barriers of race, creed and culture. It is a means of communication which the world should be encouraging, rather than shutting off. Closing the door on sporting contact is the politics of confrontation. There has to be a more agreeable solution.

In any event, South Africa's loss is cricket's loss. One can only wonder at how that 1970 side might have dominated the world stage through the early and mid 'seventies. How much of an impact would men like Barry Richards and Graeme Pollock have made if they had been allowed the same exposure as their contemporaries of other lands? Would a player like Mike Procter, barely introduced to the world of international cricket when expulsion came, have established himself as one of the finest all-rounders of all time? I think he might have. And I have no doubt whatever that the cricket world was deprived of watching a side that would have been talked of for generations as one of the very finest to grace the game.

Australia's clashes with South Africa have always managed to attract headlines and heartache. The most devastating was the day in late 1963 when Australian fast-bowler Ian Meckiff was called by umpire Col Egar for throwing. It was the first Test of the series at the 'Gabba in Brisbane, and Meckiff opened the bowling in partnership with Graham McKenzie as South Africa set after the Australian total of 435.

Meckiff had been occasionally labelled 'suspect' from the time he first commanded international attention by ripping through Peter May's England side in 1958-59. A left-armer, he bowled with a very front-on action, and his arm had a definite kink at the elbow for the greater part of its journey. It sometimes looked worse when he was tired, for the kink seemed to grow more exaggerated as he struggled for pace under duress. But to say it was a throw is very difficult indeed.

The laws at that time were not terribly clear. They merely stated that the delivery had to be fair, 'not thrown or jerked', and if the umpire was not 'entirely satisfied of the absolute fairness of a delivery in this respect, he shall call no-ball'. Later on the International Cricket Conference went to great pains to clarify the laws regarding the legality of a delivery. They inserted clauses to identify the instant of delivery, and exactly when a straightened arm constituted a throw. It is doubtful whether they could ever phrase the law in such a way that it was not open to some variance of interpretation.

At any rate, as far as Colin Egar was concerned that Saturday afternoon in Brisbane, all he had to go on was the law as it was then written. And on four occasions in that first over from Meckiff, he decided he was not 'entirely satisfied' with the 'absolute fairness' of the delivery. The benefit of any doubt, in other words, went with the batsman and against the bowler.

Four times Egar's arm went out at square leg. It was like the guillotine for Meckiff. To be called for throwing in a Test match four times in your first over was as good as having your papers marked: 'Beware this man throws'. In simple terms, Egar, in those four sharp, definitive movements, effectively killed off Meckiff as an international cricketer.

Everybody at the ground was stunned. I was not in the broadcasting box at the time, and in the event I was glad not to be. It was a very trying moment for everybody. The over was completed in virtual silence. It had the ring of an execution about it as Egar kept calling 'no-ball', and players and spectators alike looked on with mouths agape. Charles Fortune was doing the commentary at the time. It was terribly hard for him, as it must have been hard for Trevor Goddard trying to bat through a scene in which the Australian's distress was so obvious.

When the over was completed and it all started to sink in, a buzz of excited chatter went around the ground. The theme of most of it seemed to be 'could this really be happening?' And there was great expectation as to whether the Australian captain Richie Benaud would put the matter to the ultimate test and bowl Meckiff from the other end, where Lou Rowan would have had to make a judgment. Benaud did not. That was very wise of Benaud. I am sure Rowan would have done exactly the same thing. In fact, he told me later he would have.

There was much talk at the time that the word had come down from the top that this was the match in which the axe would fall on Meckiff. I don't believe that for a moment. Egar, for a start, was not the type of man to be used in that way. If the Board of Control had suggested to him that he should call Meckiff, he would simply have told them to do their own dirty work. The judgment was there for the umpires to make, and neither Egar nor Rowan was the type of man to shirk a responsibility.

Looking back, I can recall sensing that something was on. Egar was more than usually tense and preoccupied before the match. I am sure he and Lou Rowan had talked about Meckiff's bowling many times, and watched him very closely through many matches. I think they merely decided that this match was his ultimate test. That they would watch his action particularly closely, and if that doubt was still there, they would defer judgment no longer.

Looking at it that way, it was merely the luck of the draw that Egar was left with the decision. Had Meckiff bowled from the other end, Rowan would probably have made the same judgment.

It was certainly a big decision to make. I still can't decide in my own mind whether Meckiff actually threw. I recall thinking at the time: Oh Colin, how can you be sure? But it was not a decision made lightly. Egar knew it would finish Meckiff. He retired at the end of that game. It was also an unhappy exit for Richie Benaud after a most distinguished term as Australian captain. Benaud missed the next Test with injury, then handed the captaincy over to Bob Simpson for the rest of the series before retiring altogether.

Of all the men I have met in cricket, I would know none better than I know Colin Egar. We have been extremely close friends for more than twenty-five years. Yet, even now, I cannot draw Colin on the events of that December Saturday in 1963. He would not speak of it then, and he will not speak of it now. I am sure it was the toughest decision he ever had to make in cricket. But it is a measure of the stature he held

The Ian Meckiff affair dominated the start of the South African tour in 1963. Photographs tended to condemn Meckiff, but there was always an element of doubt.

Meckiff, and the umpire who called him for throwing, Colin Egar, had no hard feelings after the dramatic Brisbane confrontation.

Peter van der Merwe . . . he had a significant change in approach when Bob Simpson's team arrived in South Africa in 1966.

Ali Bacher was a hard captain, and he led one of the finest sides the world has known.

as an umpire that he was prepared to make it. He did not walk away from what he saw as a very clear responsibility.

It was a sad end for Meckiff. He had begun his Test career sensationally as a key man in Richie Benaud's triumphs against Peter May's team of 1958-59. His 6-38 in the second Test of that series had made him a national hero. He had figured in the tied Test against the West Indies in 1960, having been run out off the second last ball of the match to claim a unique piece of history.

Meckiff had suffered throughout his career from those who never let up about his action. In England, particularly, where he was victim of a vitriolic attack by the Fleet Street Press writers after the 1958-59 tour, he was crucified. Meckiff was an extremely charming fellow who fell victim to a bowling style that was different. It was completely natural to him, and because of the way his arm was constructed, impossible to alter. But it was different, and for this he paid a harsh penalty indeed.

It was a very distressing day for all concerned, and not least for Colin Egar, who was left to make a very lonely judgment.

The Meckiff incident apart, that 1963-64 series was not a terribly exciting contest. Eddie Barlow did wonderfully well for South Africa with a couple of centuries and a double century, and his partnership of 341 with the then nineteen-year-old Graeme Pollock in the fourth Test was marvellous stuff. Pollock hit 175 that day, on top of 122 in the previous Test, and we had our first glimpse of an emerging champion. But those efforts apart, it was a dour series. The South Africans had learned to play it the hard way. They had developed a new competitiveness and a new will to win, and occasionally that meant sacrificing some of the niceties of cricket that had marked their earlier visits.

Sheer stubbornness had motivated Cheetham's side back in 1952-53. There were no stars in the team. Russell Endean, in fact, was the only player in the party to score a century, and the only batsman to top 400 runs. Yet they still managed to draw the series against an Australian team in which men like Hassett, Morris, Lindwall, Miller and Johnston were starting to make the downhill slide. In the process they produced an off spin bowler in Hugh Tayfield who took 30 wickets and should have warned Australia of danger to come. He was the first to expose Australia's vulnerability to that sort of bowling, a vulnerability that cost them dearly in the next few years when Jim Laker got to them in England.

That same stubbornness was evident as Trevor Goddard's team squared the 1963-64 series 1-1. The competitive streak grew to the point where in the two series Australia played with South Africa after that, each resulted in handsome wins for the Springboks.

It was obvious to me that South Africa were going to play it very hard when I arrived in South Africa for the tour of 1966-67. Peter Van der Merwe had been appointed captain. Van der Merwe had been on the tour of Australia three years before, and had been a constant visitor to the broadcasting box. I doubt I have ever met a more inquisitive man.

He was always quizzing the various commentators about players, their strengths and their weaknesses. He was a charming enough fellow, though, and we didn't mind paying host to a young man who seemed to be taking his cricket pretty seriously.

I was astonished to find a very different Peter Van der Merwe when we reached South Africa at the start of that 1966 campaign. First of all, he didn't want to know me. And even when he finally remembered the many hours he had spent with us in Australia, he was most arrogant and disdainful in his attitude to us. Clearly, Australia were now simply the enemy, and this was war.

That attitude was reinforced in the late stages of the fourth Test when Australia went to tea on the final day with just two second innings wickets standing, and still 41 runs to get if they were to avoid an innings defeat. Ian Chappell was in the midst of one of his finest fighting innings—13 not out—as a huge thunderstorm threatened the New Wanderers Ground in Johannesburg. The thunderstorm represented Australia's only real hope of saving the series. They were already two Tests to one down.

While the players were at tea and the black clouds gathered, I was playing host to umpires Kidson and Draper, and the president of the South African Umpires Association, in the broadcasting box. We were chatting away towards the end of the tea break when Van der Merwe led his team on to the field. It was a slightly comical scene, with the South African team on the field waiting to wrap up a Test series, and the two umpires sitting with me in the commentary box, chatting away about all manner of things.

The tea adjournment still had four minutes to run, and Van der Merwe's early arrival at the pitch was nothing more than an intimidatory ruse to get the umpires there early and try to beat the thunderstorm.

'What are they doing out there? I've never seen a team on the field before the umpires' I said. Kidson and Draper looked slightly fidgety. We checked watches and I told them that if they started early they would leave themselves open to much criticism. To their credit, they kept everybody waiting a full minute after they reached the wicket. As it turned out, only three balls were possible before the rain started anyway, and Australia were saved.

But if Van der Merwe had had his way, they might have had that few minutes extra that could have been decisive. I considered it to be outrageous cheek at the time, but typical of the obsessive drive South Africa had now acquired for victory.

Van der Merwe's capacity for insulting Australians was further in evidence on the 1969-70 tour when he was writing for one of the larger newspapers. Australia were making heavy weather of that tour against Ali Bacher's men and Van der Merwe was led to write: 'If some of the Aussies want to learn how to play the hook stroke, it can probably be arranged for any reasonable club batsman in Johannesburg to show them how.' The hide of him. Coming from a former South African captain I considered that to be the height of rudeness.

That hard, competitive edge again was evident in 1969-70, when Bill Lawry led a bedraggled Australian side through a 4-0 shellacking by Ali Bacher's team. At the start of the second Test in Durban, Bacher approached Lawry thirty-five minutes before play and suggested they toss early. Lawry agreed, and Bacher won the toss. As soon as it was completed, the Australians were astonished to see the ground staff out on the pitch, giving the wicket a final cut and roll.

According to the rules, the pitch can be cut or rolled up to thirty minutes before play. By tossing thirty-five minutes before the start, Bacher was within the letter of the law. But clearly, since the toss is not normally effected until a few minutes before play, the spirit of the game decrees that the pitch should not be touched once it is determined who is to bat and who is to bowl. In that respect, Bacher's action in ordering a final trim was out of court. Many in the Press box believed a new wicket should be prepared, so seriously did they view Bacher's action.

In the event, things panned out very nicely for South Africa. Barry Richards expressed his delight with the quality of the pitch by putting together a classic 140. Graeme Pollock gave it a very healthy vote of confidence, too. He hit a majestic 274, and figured in a 200-run partnership with Tiger Lance for the sixth wicket that was the ultimate in punitive batsmanship. At the end of it all, South Africa had a very handy first innings tally of 622, and bleats from the Australians about how they had been 'had' fell on universally deaf ears.

That was the way South Africa's approach to cricket had toughened up. It was certainly a very different South African game to the one for which Syd Smith had felt compelled to feel so sorry eighteen years before. Like their Rugby teams who for years had ground opponents into the turf through awesome, uncompromising power, they had developed a lust for victory and a national will to win that had made them the best.

Both of those Australian tours, in 1966 and 1970, finished up 'no contests'. South Africa were too good in all departments. In 1966-67, South Africa scored 2811 runs for the loss of 74 wickets; Australia managed 2431 for the loss of 92 wickets. That about summed it up. Wicket-keeper Dennis Lindsay was freakish, finishing the series with 606 runs and 24 dismissals. He hit three centuries. So dominant was he, he completed one of those centuries by jumping into the first ball Dave Renneberg bowled with a new ball and thrashing it over his head and out of the ground for six. There was nothing Australia could do to prevent South Africa winning their first series against Australia and their first series at home.

The series also introduced the brilliant talents of Michael Procter, who finished with 15 wickets from his three Tests and left little doubt he would be a champion of the future. What a pity he was to play only seven Tests.

By 1969, matters had only got worse as far as Australia was concerned. But in fairness to Bill Lawry's team, they were given little chance by a ridiculously taxing program with which administrators should never have saddled them. The Australians played through a five-Test program in India before flying direct to South Africa for a further four Tests. It was like asking somebody to fight a ten-round warm-up against Joe Frazier, then putting him straight in against Muhammad Ali. I remember meeting the Australians at Jan Smuts Airport in Johannesburg when they arrived from India. They looked haggard. Their eyes seemed to be standing out of their heads and some of them looked positively yellow. At an early tour game in Pretoria I wandered past the Australian dressing room about half an hour after the start of play. The openers were batting, and about eight of their team-mates were sitting on the benches in front of the pavilion. Most of them were asleep.

That fatigue, coupled with the awesome strength of the South African side, made the tour something of a mismatch. South Africa won all four Tests in a relative canter. Figures again paint the picture rather starkly. South Africa scored 2704 runs for the loss of 67 wickets. Australia could manage only 1775 for the loss of 80 wickets. Graeme Pollock hit 517 runs in the four Tests, Barry Richards 508 and Eddie Barlow 360. Yet Ian Redpath's 283 was the best Australia could do. The normally reliable Bill Lawry could gather only 193 runs in eight innings, and the young lion Ian Chappell managed only 92 all up. It was dismal stuff.

Good as South Africa were, and I would not seek to diminish their triumph, Australia's performances were clearly severly affected by fatigue. Graham McKenzie, for instance, finished with one wicket from 111 overs for 333 runs. And even the wicket he had was the result of Ali Bacher's stumbling onto his stumps as he played his shot. Those figures were not real, and the tour was a very frustrating one for the Australian players. It was particularly frustrating for captain Bill Lawry who lost his cool on more than one occasion in the face of poor Australian performance, immense South African strength, and some unhappy umpiring.

On both tours I made there, I found the umpiring to be somewhat lacking in competence. In 1966 I had become embroiled in a row with the president of the South African Umpires Association because I had the temerity to criticise the umpires on the air. On that occasion I had noticed the new man Michael Procter bowling outside the return crease. A good foot outside. Procter could bowl a mean inswinger, and it was a considerable advantage to him to be able to widen his angle of delivery in that way. The president of the Umpires Association had come to complain about the mild protestations I was making about his umpires over the air. He confronted me in the commentary box during a Test, and I invited him to stay and see for himself. He did, he agreed I was right, and he apologised for bringing the matter up with me. He also said he would see to it the matter was mentioned. But nothing happened. Procter continued to bowl that way for much of the tour.

In 1969, the umpiring brought a lot of criticism from the Australians, who were cranky enough already from fatigue as well as from the hidings they were getting. For the first Test one of the umpires was Billy Wade, who was a former wicket-keeper and quite handy batsman in the South African side. He was a good bloke whom I got to know pretty well. He had been spoken of highly by a lot of my friends who had been on earlier tours to South Africa. I asked him after one day's play in that first Test, during which his decisions had brought considerable argument from the Australians, how he was enjoying it out there.

'I'm not' he replied, unhesitatingly and without reservation. 'I'm fifty-six years of age and this is my one Test match. But I'm too old for this operation. Why I took it on I'll never know. I could have made five or six mistakes out there today.' Then he made the mistake of asking me what I thought.

'Ten or twelve' I said. Poor old Billy was very forlorn about the whole thing, but he was right. He shouldn't have been out there. It wasn't his fault that he made mistakes, nor do I believe that any of the South African umpires who came under fire from the Australians would have been in any way influenced by any thought of national identity. But they were inexperienced, and they were not as carefully chosen as they might have been. They were simply not good enough.

In the second Test of that tour at Durban, as Australia battled in vain to stave off defeat, Doug Walters faced up to the South African spinner John Traicos, selected for his first Test. It was the second innings and Walters, on 74, was looking like he might become the first and only Australian of the tour to get a hundred. Traicos bowled a rank long hop as umpire Coetzee cried 'NO'. Walters read that to be a no-ball. He could have hit the thing anywhere, but on hearing the call he took an almighty swipe and was caught on the fence at deep mid-wicket. He was astonished to hear the South Africans celebrating and to see Coetzee's finger up.

'But you called no-ball' Ian Redpath protested from the bowler's end. Lawry said later the umpire told him he had got out the 'NO', but since he had not completed the call by yelling 'NO-BALL' the delivery was good. Understandably, the Australians felt badly rail-roaded.

Lawry remained on a fairly short fuse throughout the tour, and it didn't take a great deal to bring his frustration to the surface. In the first Test, as Billy Wade struggled to sort things out and more often than not got them wrong, Bill was very short. He snatched the ball from Wade very forcefully on one occasion, and left no doubt whatever that he was most unhappy about the way the fortunes of war were falling. It achieved nothing of course, save to make Bill feel a bit better, and it did not paint the Australian captain well, particularly as the cause was lost anyway.

Umpire Coetzee also was rebuffed by Lawry when he tried to present him with a gift at the end of a game. It was a traditional thing as far as Coetzee was concerned. He presented a plaque or something of that kind to Ali Bacher, and he had another one for Lawry. It was nothing more than a token momento of the occasion. Lawry wanted none of that. That sort of relationship with an umpire was not part of his upbringing in cricket. Coetzee was rather peeved, and Lawry conceded later he should perhaps have been a little more conciliatory and taken the gift. But the atmosphere wasn't conducive to happy niceties.

I felt for Bill Lawry on that tour. He was a very pugnacious Australian captain and an opening batsman of tremendous fighting qualities who gave everything for the cause. He couldn't get many runs, like the rest of the Australians he felt he shouldn't have been on a double tour anyway, and things were going wrong for him from every possible quarter. An occasional blow-up, in the circumstances, was highly forgiveable. The Australians left South Africa in 1970 with their tails between their legs. Nobody could argue the Springboks were now the absolute kings of world cricket. The shame was, they were never again given an opportunity to show it.

I have been back to South Africa once since, at the invitation of the Wanderers of Johannesburg. Dennis Compton and I were invited to speak to about 2000 people at a mammoth function there. The Wanderers Club is without question the finest sporting club I have ever seen. It has five full cricket fields, including the Test match ground to accommodate 35 000 people, two Rugby grounds, a full sized swimming pool, more than thirty tennis courts, a vast expanse of bowling greens, and an eighteen-hole golf course. The club house has a dining hall for 500 people, numerous other dining rooms and bars, plus a squash court and a gymnasium. It is absolutely superb.

As I mixed about that night, the air of despair that now pervades South African cricket was obvious. They have changed the system as much as they are able to try to re-establish themselves on the world scene but to no avail. There is little else they can do. The opulence of the Wanderers, the great hospitality of South African cricket, the superb talents that have been nurtured there in recent times . . . these are things the modern cricketers of Australia and England and the world's cricketing nations cannot know.

And more's the pity.

THE INNINGS BUILDERS

Through the history of Australian cricket batsmen have forged partnerships that have added their own dimension to the game's character. The successful teams have generally had two batsmen whose names seem to belong together, men whose talent and reliability have invariably laid the foundation for the artists who follow. They are men who know that the most splendid spire on the most gloriously fashioned cathedral is worthless if the foundations are not adequate.

One such pairing was that between Arthur Morris and Sid Barnes, who opened the batting for NSW and Australia through a highly successful period after World War II.

Barnes was an extraordinary chap. He flouted convention, often upsetting the heirarchy with his disdain for their sacred cows. He loved to clown around. The more he shocked people, the better he seemed to like it. But above all he loved batting. His *pièce de résistance* was his innings of 234 in nearly ten-and-three-quarter hours at the SCG in 1946, when he and Bradman added 405 for the fifth wicket and thoroughly demoralised England. Legend has it Barnes threw his wicket away at 234 rather than score more runs than the Don who made 234 also. More likely, for the first time in his life, he had simply had enough.

When Sid wanted to bat, he didn't care a fig for circumstances. Good wickets and bad wickets were much the same to him, and when he hit the ball, there was a modicum of punishment involved. It was as if he was trying to hurt it. I remember an innings before the war when he was batting with Stan McCabe. Barnes was at his powerhouse best, bludgeoning the ball to the fence. McCabe called his attention, and suggested he calm down a touch. No need to break the pickets, he said.

Save some energy, hit it hard enough to get to the fence, but tire out the fieldsmen rather than yourself and you'll last longer. Sid shrugged his shoulders and continued to crash the ball through the off side as if laying an axe into an old gum tree.

About that time we were involved in a charity match at Waverley Oval in Sydney. I captained one side, and Barnes was in the other. Sid was making a mark for himself in Test cricket and was very much the star of the day amongst a collection of big names. Everybody wanted to see him play, so we made an arrangement that we'd allow him to get his hundred.

'The only way you can get out is to be bowled,' I offered before the game, 'So you can turn it on for the crowd.' We clued up the umpires and away we went. There was probably little need to offer Barnes any help. He got himself a very nice hundred and everybody enjoyed it.

'OK Sid,' I said. 'Now you've got your hundred you had better let the crowd see some of these other fellows.'

'Nothing doing,' Barnes replied. 'I can get 200 here'.

That did not suit the atmosphere of the afternoon as the rest of us saw it, so I explained the situation to the umpire. 'If I get his pad will you give him out?' I asked. 'Ask me,' replied the ump. Three or four boundaries later I caught Sid on the pads, a good foot outside his stumps. Up went the finger and out went Sid, rather grudgingly at that.

It was that single-minded approach to occupancy of the batting crease that earned Barnes a Test average in nine innings against England of 70.5. When you consider that Morris had an aggregate of 696 in five Tests against England in 1948 alone, it become obvious just what sort of partnership they formed. Morris was more fluent and a more versatile stroke-player, but very hard to get out as well. He provided the polish of the partnership, and with Bradman to follow, England had a few dark years indeed.

It is significant that the great opening stands of Australian cricket have brought left-handers and right-handers together. It was the case with Warren Bardsley and Herbie Collins back in the 'twenties. So it was with Barnes and the left-handed Morris. And so it was with Bob Simpson and left-handed Bill Lawry in the 'sixties, when they formed what to me is the best batting partnership I have seen in Australian cricket.

Simpson and Lawry were together for seven years. They had a triple-century Test stand, a double-century stand, and many stands of 100 and 50. They were very consistent, very dogged and very conscious of their importance to the Australian team. And most of their best work was done through a period when bowlers like Freddie Trueman, Peter Pollock, Charlie Griffith and Wes Hall were at their peak. The best partnership they had was a stand of 382 at Barbados in 1965 in a series when Charlie Griffith, in particular, was terrorising the Australians. Simpson had 201 and Lawry 210 and they missed by only a few runs the world Test record.

I well remember the Australian batting that day on a pitch polished so lovingly that you could see the batsmen's reflections in it from the broadcasting box. It was a ritual in Bridgetown that a small band of local women would take to the pitch with polishing cloths as part of its final preparation. It didn't make any difference to the pace of the pitch, but it gave it mirror-like sheen, which unnerved more than one visiting batsman.

The champion West Indies batsman Everton Weekes recalled batting there in a minor match years ago when the morning polish of the pitch was assisted by a liberal sprinkling of candle grease. Weekes took strike to the opening bowler and the first ball hit the greased spot, flew high over his head and clear out of the ground for six byes. It was enough for Everton. He forfeited the game there and then.

Lawry and Simpson broke the back of many a bowling attack by their splendid running between wickets. They had marvellous powers of concentration and wonderful co-ordination, and the quick singles they took constantly had bowlers adjusting their line from the right-hander to the left-hander. They were very dour, very protective of their wickets, and very correct, technically. Simpson could get runs when he was batting badly, for he so disciplined himself as to leave very little room for error in his approach.

It was that quality that earned him 311—his first Test century as it turned out—when he led Australia against England at Old Trafford in 1964. Lawry had been run out for 106, and the opening stand was worth 201. Simpson batted for 762 minutes—the third longest innings in all first class cricket. Unfortunately for Australia, England replied in kind on a very slow pitch. Ted Dexter got 174, Ken Barrington 256, and the five days were eaten out with an innings each.

That match is memorable to me for the high dudgeon into which Freddie Trueman was pitched. He was dropped for the game, and never stopped complaining about it. It was a strange decision to leave him out, but as the days passed Fred became grateful enough not to have had to bowl on so slow a pitch, and in a match in which wickets were like hen's teeth.

The other pairing, if you can call it that, that provided so much for Australian cricket of recent times was that of the Chappell brothers, Ian and Greg. Three partnerships in which they featured stand out for me. First there was the Oval Test of 1972, when they became the first brothers in history to score a century each in the same innings. Ian had 118 and Greg 113 and they were crucial performances in the light of Australia's rise as a cricketing power through the 'seventies.

Then there was the first Test of the 1974 tour of New Zealand at Wellington, in which Ian had innings of 145 and 121, and Greg scored 247 not out and 133. That set all sorts of records, not least of them Greg's performance in scoring more runs in a Test match than any man before him. The pair of them put on a stand of 264 in the first innings, which was also a record. They were simply ruthless together.

The Chappell partnership I remember best, however, was that in the second innings of the first Test against the West Indies in Brisbane in 1975. It was Greg Chappell's first Test as captain, and he had already had a century in the first innings. Australia had lost 2-60 in the second innings when Greg joined Ian, and the pair carried the total unbeaten to 219 to win the game. I have discussed elsewhere the reasons for Ian allowing his brother to beat him to the century in that second innings. Ian took a back seat and let Greg start his captaincy career with two hundreds, when Ian could so easily have had the century himself. It was the ultimate gesture in supporting a team-mate.

Greg went on to captain Australia 48 times for 21 wins, 13 losses and 14 draws. He holds the record for the most catches in Tests (122) and most runs in a Test (380 against New Zealand). He started his career in Test cricket with a century, and ended it with an innings of 182 in his last match. In that final Test against Pakistan, he broke Colin Cowdrey's record for Test match catches, overhauled Sir Donald Bradman as the leading Australian run-getter in Tests and became the only Australian to top 7000 runs in Test cricket. He went out in style.

Style was very much Greg's forte. He hit the cricket ball beautifully, and he conducted himself more moderately, more quietly and more reservedly than his comparatively pugnacious elder brother. He was not, however, the captain Ian was. Greg didn't have the same capacity for leadership, the same initiative when it came to controlling a game. That is not to say he did not do an excellent job, as his captaincy record suggests. But Ian was something special.

Together, they gave a lustre to the game that even Ian's most rebellious behaviour could not tarnish. My old friend Vic Richardson would have been pleased.

THE HUGHES AFFAIR

Greg Chappell's singular accomplishment as a batsman might have been even better portrayed had he reached his peak at a less turbulent time in cricket. The effect of the World Series split, and the continual chopping and changing of the Australian captaincy between Chappell and Kim Hughes shattered continuity and eroded spirit. Chappell's problems with his health, an aftermath of glandular fever, and growing responsibilities in other fields forced him to withdraw from a couple of overseas tours, including the major tour of England in 1981. Kim Hughes took charge at such times. It meant a seemingly continual debate, almost season-by-season, as to who would be the Australian captain and a strain on the team and the men concerned that was unprecedented in the game. That would not have helped Greg Chappell. It was an absolute disaster for Kim Hughes.

Hughes had first been appointed when Chappell was involved in World Series in 1980. He led Australia when Chappell was unavailable at odd times for the next three years. He was the centre of an enormous debate on the rights and wrongs of it all when he finally took over permanently after Chappell relinquished the position in 1983. Kim battled all sorts of prejudice, coped with a great deal of difficulty within his team, and had to operate amidst seemingly endless controversy and doubt.

It was a disturbing period in the game. Many were unfair to Hughes, perhaps. Others tried hard to support him. But he could never command the role as it was meant to be commanded, and for the greater part of his time the Australian captaincy was shrouded in an unhappy atmosphere of doubt. It became simply too much for Kim.

He finally called it quits after the second Test of the 1984-85 series against the West Indies. The Australians had just taken their second big defeat in a row. Hughes, at the end of his normal post-match Press conference, announced he had something to add and delivered his resignation, reading from a prepared statement. He choked with emotion and couldn't finish. The team manager read it for him. It was a disappointing exit on a couple of counts.

For a start, there was no need for Hughes to read the statement himself and risk letting his emotions get the better of him. He could have done as Ian Botham had done in similar circumstances in England a few years before and have the manager read the whole thing for him. Better that than to go out in tears.

Secondly, he chose to blame the media for much of his predicament. Certainly he had a rough time from one or two sections of the Press, but generally speaking a lot of people had gone out of their way to encourage and support him, and he was wrong to apportion blame.

That aspect of his resignation still rankled with me next morning when I was wakened very early by the national ABC radio program AM, wanting my comments on the whole affair. I said how disappointed I was that Hughes had resigned in that way, and particularly that he had chosen to blame the media for his demise. 'He's a little boy who hasn't yet grown up' I said. In my mind I was comparing him with captains of previous generations. In cricketing parlance, he did measure up as a boy against some of the giants who had been Australian captain before him. Unfortunately that comment was taken by the Press and a good section of the listening public to be some sort of personal attack on Kim. Of course it wasn't. It was early in the morning, and given more time I would have chosen my words more carefully. For the fact is, I like Kim Hughes. I admire his straight-forwardness and his pleasant manner. And many of his difficulties as Australian captain clearly were not of his making.

It is a little ironic that Hughes finally found captaincy too much for him at a time when he had his best chance of making a go of it. He started the 1984-85 series against the West Indies without the stars of so many years before—Greg Chappell, Dennis Lillee and Rod Marsh. The team, of course, was the less for their absence. But at least it was all Kim's show. There was no suggestion of the under-current of resentment that had plagued him for much of his term at the helm. There is no question that, on the field, Marsh and Lillee gave everything they had for their country under Hughes—as much as they would have under any other captain. But there is also little doubt they resented his having the job. They did not really try to disguise that. And in that area, Hughes had to battle, since he knew he did not have the full support of his team. That made it extremely hard for him.

Hughes, of course, should not have had the captaincy in the first place. He had assumed the reins in 1979, taking over from the injured Graham Yallop during the split in which all the senior players were playing

World Series Cricket and thus were unavailable. Hughes did well in that period. He lifted a sub-standard Australian team whose morale had been very low through a drubbing by England, and squared a series with Pakistan. He then led them to the World Cup in England, and on a tour of India. In these circumstances, he did a good job. The team liked him and he was a candid straight-shooter who won almost universal favour with those who dealt with him.

It all started going wrong for Kim Hughes when the World Series split came to an end. Greg Chappell resumed captaincy of the Australian side, as was logical if the reconciliation was not to carry overtones of discrimination. Hughes was granted the vice-captaincy. Clearly, the Australian Cricket Board and its selectors would have felt a loyalty to Hughes. He had done a fair job for them in difficult circumstances, and was showing potential as a leader of some substance. There was also, perhaps, the underlying feeling that the World Series boys should not just come back and take over completely. Placing an 'establishment' man in a position of power went some way to placating the good number of cricket traditionalists who remained very hot under the collar about the whole World Series affair.

So Hughes became vice-captain of Australia and captain of Western Australia. To do so, selectors at both levels had to turn their backs on the long-serving champions Rod Marsh and Dennis Lillee, who were now available again. Logically, if the events of the previous two years could be forgotten, one of that pair had undeniable claims ahead of Hughes. Both refused to accept the vice-captaincy of Western Australia. And from that point there was no doubt of their resentment at Hughes' appointment.

I recall a match at the Sydney Cricket Ground when Western Australia were playing NSW. I bumped into Rod Marsh at the nets. 'Come into the room and have a beer, Mac,' he invited. I didn't get time to answer before the invitation was withdrawn. 'Sorry, I'm not captain any more' he said. 'I don't have any right to invite you in.' His tone left me in no doubt as to his feelings on the whole affair.

That atmosphere prevailed more or less for the next five years. Hughes, for his part, did little to improve it. He knew where he stood with Marsh and Lillee, but he really made little effort to smooth things over. He was determined to be his own man and do his own thing. He might have sought their help and advice. He might have taken more time to talk with them, to try to reach some sort of common ground that would have made life more comfortable for him. But there was an obstinate streak in Kim that prevented his doing so. Maybe he tried. I doubt it. Too often the confrontation was too obvious for any real effort to have been made to heal the wounds.

The real pity of it is that had the selection processes followed a more conservative course, and Marsh been given his rightful spot as captain of Western Australia and vice-captain of Australia, Hughes might eventually have taken over as a captain of very high stature. Certainly he was a magnificent player. But even his batting was eroded by difficulties in his captaincy. At the end of his captaincy term he was a shadow of the player he could have been.

I doubt you would see a much better innings than the one Hughes played in the Centenary Test at Lord's in 1980. He scored 117 and 84 to be man of the match, and his century was a marvellously flamboyant exhibition of attacking cricket. One shot he hit off paceman Chris Old, back over his head and high into the stands for six, ranks with the best I've seen. An innings of 213 against India at Adelaide in 1981 was another gem of glorious footwork and timing. To me, however, Hughes always seemed to bat better when he was free of the captaincy.

One factor that counted against him as a captain, and ultimately as a batsman, was his impulsiveness. There is an often-told story about senior members of the West Australian team trying to settle Hughes down when he first joined the senior ranks and whacked away at everything. You have to build your innings, they told him. 'Okay' Rod Marsh said. 'You've been batting for 240 minutes. How many are you?' Hughes' reply came quick as a flash. 'Eight hundred.'

Later in his career it became no joke. So often he would get to 30 or 40, and would be batting so well it seemed he could dominate the day. Then he would charge down the wicket and do something outrageous, as if he had some divine protection that suggested he could do anything he liked with impunity. More often than not he would get out, and a position of real promise would be wasted.

Before the second Test of the 1981 tour of England, when Hughes was captain, I remember mentioning the recall of John Emburey to the England side. 'You'll have to watch this fellow, Kim,' I said. 'He can't bowl' Hughes replied. 'I'll take the Mickey out of him.' 'Well, I think he can bowl a bit,' I argued. 'I'd be wary of him if I were you.'

Australia were in a little bother when Emburey entered the attack for the first time in that game, bowling his off-spinners with that high action of his that made him a more than useful bowler. Hughes was on 42 and with Allan Border was showing encouraging signs of rescuing the innings and building a solid position.

On came Emburey. First ball Hughes charged down the wicket. He totally misjudged the whole operation and hit a catch to Bob Willis at mid-off. Whatever possessed him to charge a new bowler like that I will never know. There was simply no need, except for that seemingly uncontrollable obsession Hughes had for establishing his authority. Unfortunately, that was not an isolated incident. So often, when he was thoroughly set and looking good, he would lose control in that way and lunge into strokes that were mindless and needless. As a batsman, a forgiving mind might see it as aggression and daring. As a captain, it was basic irresponsibility.

I did not consider Hughes to be a good captain. He made too many mistakes for that. The third Test in 1981 represented one of his greatest

Kim Hughes had that boyish look of anticipation as he took a peek at the press conference where Greg Chappell announced his retirement. It meant Kim was now at the helm, unchallenged.

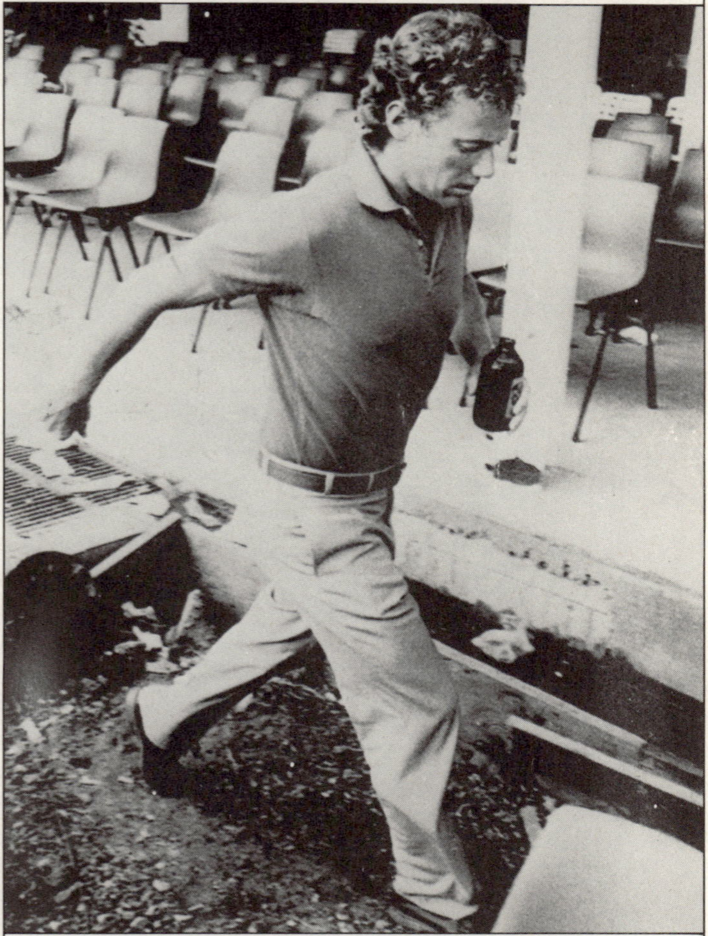

It was a less bouyant Kim who dashed out of another Press conference in Brisbane in late 1984, having just announced his resignation as Australian captain. He broke down as he made the announcement.

Hughes, on his day, was a fine player, with a great gift for attacking strokeplay. Captaincy probably robbed him of his full potential.

disasters. Australia won the first Test and were one up when they reached Headingley, Leeds, for the third. Hughes came to me before the game and asked if I would have a look at the pitch with him. We went down before breakfast on the first day of the game.

'Whatever you do,' I suggested, 'try not to bat last.' That Headingley pitch had been notorious through the years, and this one looked like it would play tricks towards the end as well.

In the event, Australia batted first and made 401. England managed only 174. That was an enormously handy lead. Despite our earlier discussion, and I believe against his own good judgment, Hughes then decided to force the follow-on. That meant Australia would have to bat last. From there the game got away from him hopelessly. Ian Botham hit a mighty 149 not out, and the No 9 man, Graham Dilley, hit a swashbuckling 56 that gave England a second innings total of 356. Hughes let Dilley, particularly, take the match right away from him. Lillee, Geoff Lawson and Terry Alderman were bowling half-volleys and the late order men were throwing the bat at them. He failed to use Ray Bright when spin seemed the obvious answer to attack players hitting with such abandon. Australia faced a target of only 130 in the second innings when the match really should have been over. They were out for 111.

It was a classic piece of poor judgment by Hughes and he knew it. So hopeless had England's position been after the first innings, the betting tents were quoting odds for an England win at 500-1. Two Australians took a piece of that, much to the consternation of officials at home.

By the fourth Test, the Australians were totally shellshocked. The reverse of Headingley had eaten at their spirit and when they needed just 150 in the final innings to win at Edgbaston, they couldn't do it. The series, simply, had been thrown away.

Hughes' career as a captain never really recovered from that tour. Perhaps he was the victim of his time. Some of those who thought he had no right to the job ahead of Marsh never let him forget it. They carped at him, and kept him totally on the defensive. He was never given the chance to settle himself and build his captaincy career free from the prejudice which had been built by the World Series split and all the hard words that had surrounded it. It must have been a never-ending battle for him to keep his head high when there were those within the team, and those outside the team, who would gladly have lopped it off. In the final analysis Hughes was not a good captain. But did he really have a chance to be? In the end the bold front he maintained publicly was hiding a very sensitive and very hurt inner man. The longer he fought the battle, the more he turned inside himself. He built a sort of protective wall around himself which ended up rejecting the bouquets as well as the brickbats. He seemed to be very alone.

It all spilled out that afternoon in Brisbane when the captain of Australia was reduced to tears in front of TV cameras which took his heartache and his humiliation to millions. It was a very sad day, for Kim Hughes and for cricket.

That could not have developed in the days when cricket was more a game and less a business; when it went without saying that the Australian cricket team was the showcase for the highest standards of sport and sportsmanship. In those days the Australian captain's position was unarguable. He was supreme and unchallengeable. Not that there was any need to challenge him. The more leisurely program by which the game operated meant captains could be very thoroughly tested before they took the job. Failure was almost impossible. But there was a code that demanded they be given total loyalty, come what may. The pressures that fell upon Kim Hughes could not have fallen upon a Woodfull or a Bradman.

Much has changed in modern cricket. I noted in the fourth Test of the West Indies campaign in Australia in 1985, when Allan Border had replaced Kim Hughes as captain, an occasion when the Australian fast bowler Geoff Lawson ignored the umpire's effort to return his sweater and hat at the end of an over. It was a petty protest about something or other.

Border chased Lawson all the way to fine leg to return the hat and sweater. That sort of thing, to me, demeans the game and the captaincy. I can imagine how Vic Richardson might have handled that. If a bowler of his day did that sort of thing, he would have stood him up. Perhaps he would have told him to keep going to the dressing room. To Vic, and to captains of his ilk, the dignity of cricket was very important. Embarrassing an umpire was not on. There was a strong and natural discipline that ensured sound and uniform standards in the way the game was played, and the way its players conducted themselves.

There is much about modern cricket that is superb, its athleticism, the positive aggression and ultimate competitiveness that the international game now embrace. Even the surge of one-day cricket, which annoys a lot of the traditionalists, has its place in a high-powered world in which speed and dynamism play such a large part.

But the one thing cricket is losing to an extent is the one thing it cannot afford to lose. It is losing some of its dignity. Kim Hughes might not have suffered the traumas that captaincy held for him had he lived through a more dignified age.

A LIFE OF CRICKET

Cricket is a game that encourages reflection, and as I look back over my time in cricket I have a nice feeling. There has been so much pleasure, so much joy, so much friendship. The first Test I saw as a young schoolboy went for seven days. It was the first in which eight-ball overs were used, and I saw every one of them. It was also the first Test in which the great English opening partnership of Hobbs and Sutcliffe faced up to Australia's bowlers. They had a century stand in each innings. It was the debut Test for Vic Richardson and Bill Ponsford, and Ponsford duly obliged with the first of many centuries for his country. And it was the match in which Johnny Taylor and Arthur Mailey put on their record last wicket stand of 127. I watched it all, engrossed.

I was no less engrossed sixty-one years later when I broadcast my last Test match on that same Sydney Cricket Ground. That was a match in which Clive Lloyd's West Indians, having led Australia 4-0 in the series, stumbled to spin at the final hurdle. It was significant for me for a couple of reasons. Firstly, at the end of my career, I had the pleasure of watching what I rate as one of the three finest sides I ever saw. Lloyd's team was that good. Secondly the match gave hope that spin bowling, and all its attendant craft, might not be a lost art after all. Much in cricket has changed over all those years, yet much remains the same!

My memories of those two games and all the games in between are rich and full of warmth. I was privileged to cross paths with every man who played in that 1924 Test, having played with or against all but one member of the Australian team. As I thumb through their names, pictures of great days run into my mind.

I remember the day I bowled to Warren Bardsley in one of my early

Sydney club games. The wicket was slightly damp, and the ball lifted on him and flew to slip for a catch. Bardsley stood there rubbing his arm. 'Cut it out Warren,' chipped in my captain, Reg Rowe, 'You've had enough'. Off he went, with some parting advice for me that if I was going to bowl to him again, I had better keep the ball up.

I remember too, the day I ran into the great Johnny Taylor at Trumper Park, Paddington. Reg Bettington was bowling his slow spin, and Taylor got hold of one off the back foot. He slammed it hard, the ball hit Bettington flush on the forehead, and rebounded to me at mid-on. Bettington didn't flinch. He had every right to be dead, but he merely appealed and the great Taylor was out, caught off the bowler's forehead.

Then there was the great Hunter 'Stork' Hendry, who came to play with us at Paddington and was a great help to us all. I batted with him at Manly Oval one day on a damp wicket. Manly had a left arm bowler who was pitching them in short, and I pulled a few through the on side for four. Stork collared me and told me to ease up. Just hit a couple per over he said, and play and miss at the rest. I did as I was told, and each time I missed Stork would let out a shriek and say 'well bowled, lad'. We picked up 50-odd runs before the Manly captain realised how Stork was keeping the left-armer in the attack, and plundering him.

And will I ever forget the day I first met the mighty Jack Gregory, the absolute hero of my schoolboy days? Gregory had just ended his illustrious career in the Australian side when I came up against him. To me his pace had always been frightening, and it was certainly no less so that day at Trumper Park. In his first over he caught one of our fellows in the face and broke his jaw, then bowled the next batsman so comprehensively he snapped a stump in two. Enter McGilvray, shaking! I can still see the sight of Gregory coming at me, every muscle and blood vessel in his neck straining and glowering at me. Through the first over I faced I could not lay a bat on him.

Eight balls, eight shots, eight air swings.

I had been getting runs at the time and eventually I snicked enough of Gregory's deliveries and picked up sufficient runs from the other end to get to 99. Gregory then offered me some gentle encouragement.

'Don't worry lad, you'll get it this over' he said. There was a comforting smile on his face and I thought to myself that the great man was going to give me a run and my first century. There followed the fastest over of the day. It was brutal stuff, and though I survived the over, I was out a few balls later for 99. After the game Gregory came into the dressing room looking for me.

'You thought I'd give you that one, didn't you?' he said. I nodded. 'Well,' he said, 'when you get your first hundred son, you'll earn it. Don't expect gifts from anybody.' A hard lesson but a good one.

I remember, too, my first Shield game, when I almost had Ponsford's wicket, then finished up with only one in the innings while Bill O'Reilly took the other nine. And my first Shield innings, when I batted with Bradman and stuck it out for a couple of hours as he built an innings of 187.

There were my days as NSW captain, when men like Oldfield and McCabe graced the team. I recall the courage of Bill O'Reilly when NSW played the MCC in 1936-37 and he announced on the last day he could not bowl. By the final hour England still had five wickets standing and O'Reilly with that determined manner of his, came to me and demanded the 'cherry'. He cleaned them up with a few minutes to spare and we won a memorable victory. In the dressing room later I asked why he did not want to bowl. As he pulled off his socks they were soaked in blood, and the nail off his big toe was stuck to one of them.

'Is that all?' I said. I took flight and Bill gave chase, and I have never been more grateful for my speed.

My early days in broadcasting too, are rich memories, embellished with names like Charles Moses and the immortal pairing of Vic Richardson and Arthur Gilligan. In those days I would listen to tapes of my broadcasts and practise improvements anywhere I happened to be. I did that in my car quite often, and I'm sure I seemed quite mad when I stopped beside a tram, oblivious to all around me, describing phantom matches to a bemused audience.

There were so many great days and so many great players. It is impossible to pick the greatest. Each era has had its champions, each era has had its particular strengths and its particular weaknesses. For all the change in the game there is as much quality in the play of today as there ever was. The game, for a start, is so much more athletic. The fielding standard that is commonplace now was the preserve of only the elite forty years ago.

If there is a disturbing trend to today's cricket it is the changing standard in attitude. To those of my time, the game demanded a dignity from all who involved themselves in it. Cricket became a byword for all that was proper, and for the ultimate in fair play. There was no need for a written code of behaviour as exists now. Nobody needed to know in black and white whether they could abuse an umpire or not, or whether they could swear at their opponents. Those things were never contemplated, and certainly would have been harshly dealt with by the captains of the time had they occurred. The petulance and abrasiveness of today is a pity, for it does a marvellous game no credit.

Significantly, there is rarely that sort of thing in the very good teams. What a delight it was in my last season of broadcasting in Australia to tour with Clive Lloyd's West Indies team. Lloyd was one of the great skippers of my time, tactically very astute, calm and in command of himself and his team at all times. And what a team he had! Men like Michael Holding, Gordon Greenidge and Viv Richards would all stand tall in any company. The cricket they produced in the 'eighties was as pretty near complete as any I have seen since Herbie Collins and Arthur Gilligan did battle in 1924.

Throughout my time in cricket I have tried to remember some important lessons which I suppose have formed the basis of my philosophy on the game. The great M A Noble impressed on me early in the piece that, even if I was not to be a good cricketer, I should always try to look like one in dress and manner. 'Those that hurt cricket will themselves be hurt,' he said. And how right he was. Those that live on in legend are always the gentlemen of the game.

And I remember the words of my father as I left on my first trip with the NSW side. 'You may be on the threshold of a new phase in your life,' he said. 'Try to make the game the better for your being in it.' He also had some pretty sound advice when I became NSW captain. 'You are getting up near the top, my son,' he said. 'But watch the splinters as you come down.'

Cricket has provided wonderful opportunities for me. With my late wife, Gwen, who supported me so well, I lived it constantly, and I loved it.

The game, indeed, is not the same. Change of one kind or another is natural and inevitable, but the game will endure, to be enjoyed by all who respect it.